A HISTORY OF
BAGSHOT AND WINDLESHAM

Pie Man's trip to Bagshot Camp — the occasion was the great military camp held at Wickham Bushes north of Bagshot in 1792.

A History of
BAGSHOT
and WINDLESHAM

by

MARIE DE G. EEDLE

PHILLIMORE

1977

Published by
Phillimore & Co. Ltd.
London and Chichester
Head Office: Shopwyke Hall
Chichester, Sussex, England

© Marie de G. Eedle, 1977

ISBN 0 85033 276 1

Text set in 11 pt. Baskerville
Printed by Unwin Brothers Limited
at the Gresham Press,
Old Woking, Surrey, England

Contents

Illustrations

The Pie Man's trip to Bagshot Camp   *frontispiece*

(Between pages 86 and 87)

LIST OF FIGURES

The author and publishers wish to thank the following for permission to reproduce illustrations:

Ordnance Survey: figs. 9-12 (1934 6in. maps). Crown copyright reserved.

British Library Board: figs. 9-12, plates I (above), II, IV, V, VI, IX, X, XI, XII, frontispiece and dust jacket.

Greater London Record Office (London): plate VII.

Mrs. A. M. Batten: plate XIV.

Surrey Heath Borough Council: plate XXV.

Mrs. G. Taylor: plate XXVI.

Mrs. J. K. Evans: plate XXVII.

ACKNOWLEDGMENTS

I should like to thank the archivists and staff of the Surrey Record Office, Guildford Muniment Room, Greater London Record Office (London and Middlesex sections), Hampshire Record Office, House of Lords Record Office, Methodist Archives Centre, Minet Library, and the curator of Camberley Museum for advice and assistance in finding material.

I am grateful for facilities granted for research on numerous occasions, to members and officials of the former Bagshot Rural District Council (in particular to Mr. O. V. H. Farrant) and the former Chertsey Urban District Council, to the Rev. N. E. Barlow (Rector of Windlesham), the Dean and Canons of St. George's Chapel Windsor Castle, the Church Commissioners and the Surrey Archaeological Society. I am indebted to the Master and Fellows of St. John's College (Cambridge) for permission to carry out research and to quote from college documents, and to Mr. N. C. Buck in the college library for his help.

The late Mr. A. S. Fromow was kind enough to allow me to photograph the old farmhouses at Astagehill and South Farm, and to supply answers to my questions on the history of the Nurseries. The following have generously helped with advice and information and the loan of material:
Rev. G. Armstrong, Mr. R. G. M. Baker, Mrs. J. Banks, Mr. J. C. Batley, Mrs. A. M. Batten, Mr. C. E. Beasley, Miss A. Bynum, Mr. J. T. Caller, Rev. O. F. E. Charleton, Rev. A. H. Currey, Mr. R. Davis, Mrs. J. K. Evans, Mr. D. J. Glanfield, Mr. D. Graham, Miss J. Harding, Mr. R. Hargrave, Mr. H. Hawkes, Mrs. V. Houghton, Mr. Jillings, Mr. W. H. Liddell, Mr. B. F. J. Pardoe, Mr. G. H. Pinckney, Mr. G. C. B. Poulter, Miss H. F. Rendle, Mr. and Mrs. L. Soan, Mrs. G. Taylor, Trust Houses Forte, Miss M. C. Wardle, Mr. and Mrs. T. Woodham.

Transcripts of Crown-copyright records in the Public Record Office appear by permission of the Controller of H.M.S.O.

M. de G. E.

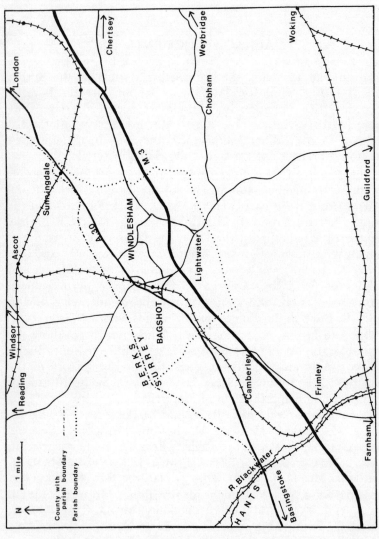

Fig. 1. The parish of Windlesham and surrounding area today (1974).

Introduction

'. . . to the scholar, who seeks for no response, but only to listen, the barriers of time are open; the fragments that come drifting through them are warm with life.'

(Freya Stark in *Alexander's Path*)

WILLIAM COBBETT (in 1822) called the Bagshot country on the borders of Surrey and Berkshire 'as bleak, as barren, and as villanous a heath as ever man set his eyes on'. Bagshot Heath was much more extensive in earlier times, but a walk north from Bagshot in the direction of Surrey Hill on the county boundary still gives some idea of the desolate nature of the country, which has not been improved by the more recent activities of the army. One of the main roads to Exeter and Land's End (A30), which is now accompanied to just beyond Basingstoke by a new motorway (M3), runs across the heath through the parish of Windlesham. This road, which used to be known as 'the great western road', was notorious in the 17th and 18th centuries as the haunt of highwaymen. Among those who operated in the district were William Davis (the 'Golden Farmer'), Claude Duval from Normandy, who is said to have had a cottage in the Lightwater area, and Captain Snow, after whom Snow's Ride at Windlesham is supposedly named. The heath has only been really tamed in the last 150 years by the erection of houses: Cobbett was already complaining of the number of houses built hereabouts by the 'Stock-Jobbing crew', and from the later 19th century building was intensified, with the result that the area today is largely residential.

Earlier writers tended to sum up the district and its history in the words 'heath and highwaymen', while later guidebooks emphasise the presence of the military, but as it is hoped to show in this book, there is a great deal more of interest to be said about the history of Bagshot and Windlesham. In contrast to the heath, on the eastern side of the parish where it is bordered by Chobham, the country is softer. There are still some farms on this side, which is surprisingly rural in aspect and is described by Ian Nairn (*Buildings of Surrey*, 1962) as 'almost the first true countryside on this bearing coming out of London'. The other main features of the parish are the two large nurseries for trees and shrubs: one of 200 acres, belonging to W. Fromow and Sons (at which during the 80 years of its existence have been produced and sold over two and a half million trees), and the other of 100 acres belonging to John Waterer, Sons and Crips, the history of which goes back to the late 18th century. Before mechanisation these firms of course employed far more labour than they do today.

Because of the contrasting nature of the two parts of the ancient parish of Windlesham, the separate communities at Bagshot and Windlesham developed very different characters. John Cree, the parish historian of the early 20th century, addressing a Hospital Sunday Parade on 3 October 1903, remarked that 'he sometimes thought that Windlesham and Bagshot were husband and wife but which was the husband and which the wife he should not like to say'. Laughter followed this remark, probably a favourite speculation of Mr. Cree, which some of the audience may have heard before. At the time he spoke, new development was already going on in other areas within the parish, at Sunningdale and particularly at Lightwater, which in its early days was sometimes referred to as 'new Bagshot'. All the places still retain their separate entities, but it is not possible to deal intelligibly with any one settlement on its own. Over a considerable period, the parish was not only the ecclesiastical area, but the unit for local government administration, and most of the existing records relate to the whole parish.

Bagshot today has still the appearance of an urban village. Ian Nairn describes it as 'demure, almost a backwater', and has not a good word to say for the existing buildings, which he finds nondescript, if not, like Bagshot Park (1877), positively ugly. But 'Queen Anne House' and 'Laird House', both 18th century, though plain, are pleasing, and 'The Cedars' (which he does not mention) has an attractive shell porch. The *Three Mariners* is the only old inn building still in use, but opposite, inside No. 77 High Street, is concealed some of the framework of the old timber inn called the *Bell*, where a wooden gallery of a similar type to that of the *George* Inn at Southwark, has recently come to light.

Windlesham continues to develop as a residential district, its houses being widely scattered. A recent magazine article describing a journey through north-west Surrey found only this to say on arrival at the *Sun* corner: 'Look out for the sharp right-hander as we go on to Bagshot!' The church, on top of the hill, was transformed 100 years ago by the construction of a new nave, chancel, and north aisle. It retains, however, the 17th century nave and chancel as a south aisle, and also the rather nice 17th-century south porch: from this side it must look, apart from the added height of the tower, much the same as it did then. Next to the church is 'The Cedars' (mainly early 18th century), and other 18th-century houses are 'Windlesham House' north of the church, and 'Windlesham Park' on the Chobham border. Down Pound Lane are 'Pound Meadow' and 'Pound Cottage', both 17th century, the latter described by Nairn as 'in beautiful condition, without being at all dolled up'.

Although the parish has not a great deal to show in the way of well-preserved historic buildings, most of the features on John Rocque's map of over 200 years ago are still recognisable on the ground today, and even older medieval landmarks are not yet entirely obliterated. Some of the bridleways, footpaths, and green baulk ways across the old common fields remain. Jane's Lane, which has been newly signposted and is 10 feet to 12 feet wide, though somewhat overgrown, ran round the southern edge of the common field called Church Field. The old 'church path' starts from near Bagshot Park, and if you stand on the footbridge over the railway—itself a nice piece of Victorian ironwork—which carries the path, you will see Windlesham church straight ahead on the hill about a mile away, though the path twists before it emerges near the *Half Moon*. A new bridge over the M3 carries what may be an even older path (now partially diverted), which came from a crossing over the Bourn Brook across Eastersh common field, making for the church and Hatton Hill beyond. A branch path along the Bourn Brook, which could be followed right to Bagshot, has been severed by the motorway, but happily the bridleway called Scutley Lane, winding down past Twelve Oaks and Manor Farm (two very old farms) to the site of Hook Mill, has been preserved.

The story told in this book is divided into five parts. Part One not only deals with the early history to the end of medieval times, but sets out the framework and the more permanent features over the whole period covered by the book. It discusses boundaries, manors, parish church, royal park, and other subjects which would not gain from being split up into chronological sections. Owing to a multiplicity of manors, the manorial history is in any case rather complex, and so it is best got out of the way early! It may be found helpful to refer back to this section occasionally in the course of reading the book.

Part Two covers the development of the settlements at Bagshot and Windlesham between 1500 and 1800. Bagshot, owing to its position on the main road, became a community of innkeepers and tradesmen, while Windlesham remained largely agricultural. There is not enough information however, about these comparatively small settlements, to identify the stages in development over this long period of time, for the only 'parish records' before 1800 are the registers of baptisms, burials, and marriages (and even these do not start until just before 1700), and some church rates and accounts.

From the beginning of the 19th century the documentation from all sources is so much greater that it is possible to identify several periods of change. The first of these, to about mid-century, which is dealt with in Part Three, is a particularly interesting period, during which there was a surprisingly large increase in the population of the parish, followed by a temporary decrease. A time of prosperity and a subsequent depression were attributed by contemporary writers to the rise of the coaching trade and its later disappearance with the coming of the railways (1838). The enclosure of the waste (1814) was, however, another event of economic importance during the early part of the century.

Part Four describes a period of renewed development and prosperity in the old centres from the late 1850s up to almost the end of the 19th century. Growth is probably due in part to an improvement in the general economic climate, but also to the opening of railway stations at Sunningdale and Bagshot.

In the final part, we deal with another period of expansion and large increase in population, when the first considerable development took place in the Lightwater and Sunningdale areas. The year 1895 is an appropriate starting date for this period, for not only can the beginning of our expansion already be seen by the mid-1890s, but a change took place in the system of local government in the country as a whole following on the Local Government Act 1894. The story is taken up to the 1930s, just before the Second World War, and covers the formation in 1933 of Bagshot Rural District, comprising the ancient parishes of Windlesham, Chobham and Bisley. It has not been possible to treat in great detail the more recent history of particular houses and their owners, or of churches, schools and other institutions. A separate study could well be made of the development for building of the Sunningdale and Chobham estates of St. John's College, Cambridge. The unprinted census returns (enumerators' books) for the years 1841, 1851, 1861 and 1871—the last-named only recently available—would be a good subject for group research.

Under the Local Government Act 1972, Bagshot Rural District Council disappeared, in common with all existing districts, on 31 March 1974, and its area was joined with that of Frimley and Camberley to form the new district of Surrey Heath. It seems an appropriate time to examine and record the past, and this history of Bagshot and Windlesham, which is based largely on primary sources, is offered as a contribution. I hope it will be of interest to people living in the parish of Windlesham and in other parts of the area of Surrey Heath, and also—as their studies have been to me—to the many people elsewhere engaged in the fascinating pursuit of local history.

PART ONE—THE PARISH

1 The Framework

The Area in Early Times

IN PREHISTORIC TIMES a great deal of what is loosely called
'the Bagshot country' seems to have been marsh and forest.
Much of the area is now covered by heath, together with the
bracken, gorse, and Scots pine which tend to invade it, but the
heath may represent the degeneration, under pasturing and
burning, of dry oak or birch wood. Digging in the large peat
beds east of the Chobham Ridges has revealed the former
existence of a vast forest of small oaks. The soil, though easily
worked, is sandy and rather acid, and early settlement may
have been fairly limited, though a certain number of neolithic
flints have been found. In the parish of Chobham there are
three or four bowl-shaped barrows on West End Common, and
while ground was being laid out for golf links in 1901, a bowl
barrow about 75 feet in diameter and five feet high was
excavated on high ground at Ridgemount Road (Sunningdale) on the boundary between Windlesham and Chobham.
A Late Bronze Age cremation cemetery was found in the south-
west side of this barrow, with 25 burials in 23 cinerary urns
in separate stone settings; it is not certain whether this was a
primary or secondary burial.[1] On the western boundary of
Windlesham, an old road known as the Mault Way runs up from
the downs near Crondall (Hampshire) along the Chobham
Ridges. Its name is said to come from the Celtic word for
sheep (*Mollt*), because of the huge flocks which are supposed
to have passed along it. To the north-west of Windlesham in
the parish of Easthampstead (Berkshire) is Caesar's Camp, a
univallate Iron Age hill fort of over 15 acres.[2] Half a mile south
of the fort is the Romano-British settlement site of Wickham

Bushes; here an excavation in 1878 found traces of wattled sheds and timber buildings with red-tiled roofs, associated with Roman pottery and coins dating to the second to fourth centuries A.D.[3]

Roman Roads

The Roman road from London to the important Roman town of Silchester (Margary No. 4a) runs along the northern edge of the parish of Windlesham from a point a little west of Scotswood as far as Bagshot Park. The road, known locally as 'The Devil's Highway', is followed over this section by the Berkshire–Surrey county boundary, this being also the parish boundary (see Fig. 2). Near Earlywood, and also north of 'Erlwood House', traces of the agger or bank can be seen, mainly on the south side of the boundary within the parish. The road transfers to the north side just before reaching the Bagshot to Bracknell road at Duke's Hill, where road improvements recently revealed a section of it with evidence of considerable wear.[4] Here a distinct change of direction occurs, after which the road points almost due west by Rapley Farm, where Roman pottery was found in a field in 1783.[5] In a paper read to the inaugural meeting of the Surrey Archaeological Society in 1854, the outline of the road was said to 'present a remarkable appearance' where it ran through the nursery garden of Henry Hammond (north of Lavershot Hall), a substratum of gravel having been removed for the purpose of repairing the roads.[6] (Two acres near here were allocated to the highway surveyors for gravel in 1814.)

Excavations for the M3 motorway (1972) disclosed a possible section of a Roman road at a point south of Windlesham church (SU 932631). Both side ditches of the motorway showed a band of pebbles 12 inches below the surface, 18 inches thick and approximately 30 feet wide, aligning with the church and with gravel fords to the south. It is thought that this could be a continuation of the Farley Heath branch road from Stane Street (Margary No. 151), and it was possibly an early military road used during the advance north and west.[7] A footpath runs more or less on the same line from near Broadway Bridge across the old common fields (Eastersh, Northersh and Woodcote) to Hatton Hill (see Fig. 2).

Saxon Settlements

The names of the settlements at Windlesham and at Bagshot, a mile or two away, are of Saxon origin. Generally speaking, Saxon settlement in the Bagshot country is thought to have been late. The termination *ham* (homestead or settlement) does, however, suggest an early phase, and settlement at Chobham, Windlesham's eastern neighbour, appears to be relatively early. The name of Windlesham occurs as 'Windesham' in 1178 and as 'Wyndlesham' or 'Windlesham' in 1225. It may derive from a combination of *Winel* (O.E. personal name) with *ham*. The village is, however, on the Bourn or Windle brook, and while the latter name may be just a back formation from the village name, it is possible that the brook was actually called *windol* (O.E. denoting a winding brook) and gave its name to the settlement.[8] There could be a confusion between *ham*, homestead, and *hamm*, water meadow, if the village name is in fact derived from the brook.

The name of Bagshot occurs in 1165 as 'Bachesheta' or 'Bagsheta', in 1204 as 'Bacsete', and in 1253 as 'Baggeshete'. The second element is *sceat* (O.E. meaning angle, corner or strip of land) and the first element could be the personal name *Bacga*. In place-names having the first element 'bag', however, the second element is usually a word for a natural and not an inhabited place, and it is possible that there may have also been a word *bacga* which denoted some small wild animal such as a badger or fox.[9] References in early Norman times to a wood called Bagshot, near Winkfield (Berkshire), suggest that it was extensive,[10] and the settlement may have been quite a small clearing taking its name from the surrounding wood.

Boundaries of the Parish

The parish of Windlesham (5,700 acres) measures five miles north-east to south-west, and three miles north-west to south-east. On the north-west is the county of Berkshire. Most parish boundaries were defined by about the 10th century A.D., but as all the country round about was forest and sparsely inhabited, the county and parish boundary here may have remained a little vague. The perambulation of Windsor Forest made for Henry III in 1226 seems to have more or less followed the county boundary, fixing it as the forest limit, but it is not certain whether this boundary was known already and followed deliberately, or whether a line taken for other reasons connected with ownership of land or natural features was then adopted as the county boundary. The perambulation ran from Bredeford (Blackwater) to Bagsete (Bagshot) by the King's highway, and on from Bagsete to Bromhull (Broomhall).[11] The present main road from Blackwater to Broomhall runs a little south of the county boundary, but we do not of course know the route taken in medieval times. The Roman road runs for a mile or two with the boundary near Bagshot; its course is lost between there and the Thames, but Ogilby (in 1675) marks the line of a road from Egham Hill towards Egham Wick 'to Bagshot a different way', and this could be a continuation of the Roman road still in use at that date.[12]

The Edward III version of the forest boundary varies a little from the earlier one, but is more detailed:

> From Bredeford along the road from Frimley to Wishmere [north-
> west point of parish]
> By Ralph's Cross to Gonericheford formerly called Batechesford
> Through the middle of la Shete to Horton
> From Horton by la Lee towards the Watercourse.[13]

The cross may have been erected by the Ralph who held land in Bagshot in the time of Henry II.[14] Gonericheford (O.E. *ric*, stream or ditch) or Batechesford must be a ford over the Bourn brook on the way through Bagshot, while la Shete may be meant for Bagshot. A 15th-century grant from the Prioress of Broomhall however mentions 'le Gutter called la Thete';[15] this gutter (? la Shete) could be the stream shown on Rocque's map of Surrey (1768–70) running down from Hatton (?Horton) Hill to the Bourn brook. In order that the water could run away through the gutter, a ditch at the entrance to 'Donyfeld' must be cleaned out, 'Donyfeld' being reached from the 'high road' by 'Dellam Lane'. This is probably the road now called School Road, which was earlier known as Windlesham Road; the will of Thomas Edshaw (1604) refers to 'grounds on the further side of Dellams lane and abutting upon Incry stone',[16] and a meadow just south of School Road is shown in the Tithe Award as Inkery Mead. It is conceivable that 'Incry stone', which occurs in 1690 as 'Ingre or Ingram stone',[17] was an ancient boundary stone, though the name probably just means 'water meadow'. It is possible that a boundary route could have

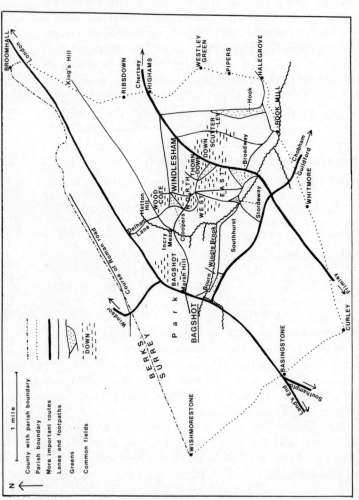

Fig. 2. The parish of Windlesham at the end of the medieval period. A reconstruction based on contemporary records, and on Norden's plan of Bagshot Park 1607, and Rocque's map of Surrey 1768-70. Boundary points are derived from the description of the perambulation of Godley Hundred in Chertsey Abbey Cartularies. Distribution of common fields is based on the Enclosure Award of 1814. The names Hatton (Haddon) Hill, King's Hill, Woodcote, Scutterley and Incry have not been found until post-medieval times.

run from Bagshot Park over Marsh or March Hill (probably
O.E. *mersc,* bog, but could be *mearc,* boundary) by the old path
which led to Windlesham church (see Fig. 2). From Inkery
Mead another path goes on north towards Hatton Hill, and
on Rocque's map the same line is carried on by a road over
King's Hill. There are some grounds for thinking that the
Saxon way from the Thames to Windlesham and Bagshot lay
through Stroude Green (near Callowhill) and King's Hill.[18]

On the east and south the parish of Windlesham is bounded
by Chobham and on the west by Frimley and Camberley. The
parish was included in Woking Hundred in the Lay Subsidy of
1332, and was surrounded on three sides by Godley Hundred,
held by the Abbot of Chertsey. Although as the power of
Chertsey Abbey grew its possessions in this direction were
extended, Windlesham was never included. A perambulation
of the bounds of Godley Hundred made in 1446 thus went all
round the boundaries of Windlesham except for the county
border.[19] The perambulation reached the north-west corner
of the parish at Wishmorestone, a boundary stone between
Berkshire and Surrey (see Fig. 2). It proceeded south to the
Besauntstone or Basingstone, which stood near the present
Jolly Farmer. From there the procession went to the stone
above 'Curle', presumably a boundary stone on Curley Hill,
and then turned east to 'Haukmer' (probably modern Hang-
moor) and through Whitmore (near Lightwater Pond) to
'Pillewell hill'. It then proceeded to the Blakestrode (Black
Stroud Lane) and so to Hoke or Hook Mill, which takes its
name from O.E. *hoc,* bend in a river. From the mill the procession continued by the water (the Bourn or Windle brook)
between the Prior's mead and the Hook mead, and along
Moris atte Hale's lane till it reached the Halegrove at the
south-east corner of the parish (O.E. *halh,* nook of land on a
parish boundary). Here the perambulation turned north through
Halegrove to Piperesgate (modern Piper's Farm) and 'Westriche-
grene' (Westley Green), and thence to Highams, Ribsdown
and out on to the London road near 'Bromehalepondehede'
at Broomhall in the north-east angle of the parish.

The churchwardens' accounts record sums of money
expended on 24 May 1773 for beer at the *Golden Farmer*
and the *Half Moon* (at Windlesham) when 'going the bounds'
of the parish. On the north-east, over the open heath between

Ribsdown and Broomhall, the boundary was disputed at the time of the enclosure (1814). Windlesham claimed a line further east over Longdown Hill, while Chobham set a line nearer Ribsdown. The Commissioners fixed the boundary between the two lines, but rather in favour of Chobham. On 15 August 1878, the whole distance of the boundaries, 'estimated at 22 miles', was walked by at least some of those taking part in a peram- bulation. The names of nine men and 18 boys (probably the choirboys at St. Anne's chapel as the list is headed by the vicar of Bagshot) are recorded. The names and ages of the boys were as follows:

> Walter Houlton, Robert Lee, Guy Cave, Thomas Parrack (11 years);
> Thomas Hammond, Edwin Nash, Henry Houlton, James Cotton (12 years);
> Albert Lee, Ernest White, Richard Jenkins, William Higgs, Mark Brudewell, Thomas Simmonds, Albert Spooner (13 years);
> Edward Bullen, Thomas Nash (14 years);
> Harry Lee (15 years).

Many of these are old Bagshot surnames and some are still represented today. It was reported that at some points the boundaries were not well defined and that boundary stones would help, but there is no record that any were erected.[20]

Windsor Forest

In medieval times the parish was much affected by its proximity to Windsor and by the royal forest. The nearness to Windsor and the presence of a royal hunting lodge at Bagshot may have acted as a deterrent to the involvement of any of the greater nobility with the area. Royal forests did not of course consist entirely of wooded and waste land, but were rather areas—which might include villages—subject to a special law, whose object was the preservation of the King's hunting. William the Conqueror had designated Windsor as forest, but Henry II went further, afforesting in Surrey the royal manors of Guildford, Woking, Brookwood and part of Stoke, and finally affirming the whole county to be forest. (Or so at least it was stated subsequently, though it could be sug- gested that only royal demesne was actually meant.) Bagshot, which was royal demesne, was certainly included in the forest, and the rest of the parish may well have been also. Richard I agreed for a sum of money to disafforest all the county of

Surrey east of the river Wey and south of the Guildford downs. This left the parish of Windlesham, together with 15 other neighbouring parishes in Surrey, subject to a bailiff and forest law as the Bailiwick of Surrey or Bagshot. Richard's agreement was not in fact honoured and the county later had to pay again for the same privileges. In 1226 Henry III agreed to the disafforestation of all afforested tracts, but royal demesne was specifically excluded.[21] When the Prioress of Broomhall was granted (in 1228) 50 acres of heath of the King's demesne 'in Laverset upon the water of Bagset', it was to be 'assarted and cultivated and held quit of regard and view of the king's foresters'.[22] In 1283 a licence was given to the nunnery to enclose 100 acres of land, which the nuns had brought into cultivation within the forest, with a small dyke and hedge, but this must be sufficiently low for the entry and exit of deer.[23] Edward I tried to re-afforest the county, but in 1327 Edward III finally granted a charter excluding all Surrey from forest jurisdiction.

It seems that even after this forest charter, north-west Surrey, having once been afforested and then disafforested, remained a 'purlieu' of the forest, the King still having rights in connection with the deer. Arguments in fact continued as to whether the Bailiwick of Bagshot was inside or outside the forest. Forest eyres, dealing with major offences against vert and venison, were held for Surrey at Bagshot or Guildford in later medieval times.[21] In 1379–80 a new tower or lodge of stone and lime for the King's foresters was built near Bagshot on the part of the forest known as Blackdown or Collingridge.[24] The site of this lodge may have been on Black Hill on Chobham Ridges south-west of the village, which is the highest point hereabouts (417 feet), in which case it was not precisely where Bagshot Park Lodge stood by Tudor times. The 14th-century lodge was probably similar to the 15th-century foresters' lodge still standing at Thetford in Norfolk.

The Bailiwick was still reputed part of the forest in Elizabethan times, as Loseley MSS. contain records of swainmote or attachment courts (at which presentments were made for minor offences) being held at Bagshot between 1570 and 1573. John Attfield, for instance, was presented for enclosing a piece of land containing two acres without a warrant.[25] Charles I took the unpopular step of trying to revive the forest pleas.

An extract from a swainmote roll refers to Sir Anthony Thomas having cut down and sold 20 oaks on a piece of land called Inholmes near Valley Wood (on the Chobham boundary) within the perambulation of Windlesham and the Bailiwick and Forest of Windsor, without view of forester.[26] In 1642 however, an Inquiry was held, whose decision meant in effect that no portion of Surrey was forest.[21]

In spite of this decision it was necessary for the Gentlemen of Surrey to petition in 1665 for the withdrawal of the red deer from the Bailiwick and to reiterate that the King's Council had declared that Surrey was not part of the forest. The petition was drawn up by Robert Field, vicar of Chobham, and Jonathan Polewhele, rector of Windlesham: the signatories included Sir James Zouch (manor of Bagshot), Sir William More (Loseley Park near Guildford), and John Attfield, church-warden of Windlesham. The compaint made was that the deer caused much damage to crops, farmers having to watch their corn all night—or pay 6d. a night to a man to watch it for them —from March to September. Especially hard was the case of the poor daily labourer in his cottage who, having sown a bushel of corn, 'after he hath been at hard labour all day, must watch that small quantity of corne all night, or els the deere will devour that as well as all his garden fruits'. The petition ended by asking the King to make an enclosed park;[27] we do not know whether any immediate result was achieved, but in 1683 the fences of Bagshot Park were renewed when Charles II decided that the park should be a nursery for the red deer.

The Manors

The manorial history of the parish is somewhat complex. In the enclosure award of 1814 only two manors were recognised as having claims on the waste: the manor of Windlesham held by St. John's College, Cambridge, and the manor of Windlesham (*alias* Fosters) held by the Earl of Onslow. The parish was then divided rather arbitrarily between them on a line giving north and east to St. John's College, south and west to Onslow. At least seven manors and sub-manors were, however, concerned with land in the parish at one time or another. The other five manors were Broomhall (also held by St. John's College), Bagshot, Freemantle, the manor of the Dean and

Canons of Windsor (which also bore the name of Windlesham), and the manor of Walton Leigh (Walton-on-Thames), to which a few pieces of land belonged. The royal manor of Bagshot became merged with the manor of Fosters, which appears to have absorbed also the other manors or sub-manors which arose during the later Middle Ages. A claim was even made about 1805 (presumably on behalf of the manor of Fosters) in opposition to the claim of St. John's College to hold a manor of Windlesham, but the title of the College was found to be clear.[28]

Unfortunately the surviving manorial records are very patchy and seldom contemporary with one another, so that it is impossible to distinguish all the holdings. Some account—even if imperfect—must, however, be given, not only because the manors are part of the history of the parish, but because they do help to provide a framework for other information.

Manor of Windlesham (St. John's College)

According to Manning and Bray, the manor of Windlesham was among those granted to the Church at Westminster by Edward the Confessor,[29] but it has not been possible to trace any evidence for this. The manor is not mentioned in Domesday and it has been suggested that the land was of so little value that it was exempt from taxation.[30] From at least the early 14th century the manor was held by the small convent of Broomhall or Bromhall, which had been established by 1200 just over the Berkshire border at the north-eastern corner of the parish.[23] Manor court rolls in existence include the first court held at Windlesham by Gunnhilda de Bokham, who was elected Prioress in 1327.[31] These rolls and various grants of similar date refer to land in the five common fields Estersh, Westersh, Northersh (the earlier name of Church Field), Down and Thorndown,[32] and most of the tenants can be recognised from the list of taxpayers in the Lay Subsidy of 1332 (see Chapter 2).

The Prioress of Broomhall (Joan Rawlyns) made a voluntary surrender of the property of her house in 1522 and the manor of Windlesham was granted to St. John's College, Cambridge.[33] An inquisition into the Priory property stated the value of the manor to be £3 6s. 8d.[34] Surviving 16th-century

court rolls for Windlesham include three courts of Joan
Rawlyns (1512-14), and a court of which the first portion is
missing, but which seems to be the first one held at Windlesham
by St. John's College in 1523.[28] The most important holdings
in a rent roll of 1588, which lists 21 free and copyhold
tenures,[28] were the following:

(1) 'Delham lands', of which Edward Quinby and William
Milton each held a moiety. In the Tithe Award Delham
Field (No. 228) was near Cooper's Green. Quinby also
held 'Donyfeld', which may be connected with Dunny
Grove (Tithe Award No. 209): the grant which gave
permission for carrying to Donyfeld from the high road
by Delham Lane shows that it was in the same area.

(2) 'Verbrokes' (O.E. *wer*, weir) and 'Wulwicks', held by
John Wise. In the Tithe Award Nos. 212 and 213 north
of Inkery Mead were called Willicks.

(3) 'Ullons alias Ully's' held by Henry Lee—later Ulliams
or Rectory Farm.

After a further rent roll of 1606 there is a gap in the records
until a court roll of 1666, due in part no doubt to the unsettled
times of the Civil Wars. In 1805 R. and J. Dyneley of Grays Inn
reported to the College as follows:

> some of the Rolls are so ancient as to be scarcely legible, and as we
> cannot see any reasonable ground for the College's title . . . being
> disputed with any prospect of success, we did not think it right to
> put the College to the expense of our fully investigating the very
> old Rolls, as it would take up a great deal of time and we have
> therefore confined our minute examination of them to those sub-
> sequently to the year 1666 . . . would have been better had the
> courts been held more frequently, the tenants would then have
> attended as a matter of course, without even a murmur, and the
> Free Rents as well as the Copyholds would all have been preserved
> whereas we are apprehensive that it will now be difficult to procure
> the attendance of a sufficient number of free tenants to form a
> homage, and many of the free rents are totally lost to the college.[28]

A comparison of the rent rolls of 1606,[35] 1749,[36] and 1828[28]
show all too clearly missing tenants and diminishing rents! After
this a court book was kept rather more regularly.[37]

Under the customs of the manor of Windlesham as set out
in 1749, freehold tenants paid two years quit rent as relief on
death or alienation and one-third of two years quit rent for
heriot. In addition there was 2s. 6d. for court fees and 4d.

for the crier who proclaimed vacant holdings to be claimed by the heirs. Copyhold tenants held their land at the will of the lord; it was heriotable, i.e., 'best live cattle on every death.'[36] For instance, when John Chipps died about 1528, the heriot was a bay-coloured horse called 'le bald mare', presumably because of white marking on its face.[28]

Manor of Broomhall

The Priory of Broomhall (and St. John's College later) also held the manor of Broomhall, which was mainly in Berkshire, but included some land in Surrey. The Enclosure Act of 1812 stated that part of the Manor of Broomhall extended into the parish of Windlesham and that St. John's College, as lords of Broomhall, should receive one-sixteenth part in value of the commonable land lying in this manor. The Award does not actually mention Broomhall, but the land belonging to the manor must be that in the north-eastern corner of the parish near Broomhall Farm. A rental of 1606 for the manor of Broomhall included a house and 15 acres called Newbridge, which were then said to be in Sunninghill.[35] There is an undated, but probably mid-19th-century map of the College land in this area, covering Broomhall Farm and nearly 80 acres in Sunninghill, together with some 50 acres in Windlesham.[38] It shows (in Windlesham) a Newbridge Field with adjacent bridge, and this is probably part of the same holding, by then absorbed into Broomhall Farm. (There seems to have been some doubt as to the correct parish at this point where two counties and several parishes meet: the map, which was originally entitled 'Broomhall in Sunninghill and Windlesham', has been amended to 'Broomhall in Windlesham'.) It is possible that the land here is connected with the grant to the Priory in 1228 of 50 acres 'in Laverset, upon the water of Bagset'.[22] The name Lavershot is found in the mid-19th century on the Surrey–Berkshire borders in Lavershot Farm and Lavershot Nursery. A stream flows not far away and the name comes from O.E. *laefer,* rush or reed, with 'shot' as in Bagshot, a strip of land often on a boundary.

Manor of Fosters *(*alias *Windlesham)*

The origin of Fosters, the other manor recognised in the Enclosure Award, is obscure. No explanation has been found for the name, presumably a surname deriving ultimately from Foresters, and there does not seem to be any connection with the manor of Imworths *alias* Fosters in Egham. Although there are considerable later records of Fosters, no manorial documents survive from before the 17th century. The manor is mentioned in 1557, when Alan Fryday released one-seventh of it to John Taylor.[14] One of two farms belonging to a John Taylor in the early 19th century was Harrishaws, which had been in the family for some time; it is possible that Fosters originated in land which at the dissolution of the monasteries was part of the possessions of the late Priory of Newark, for these included a parcel of arable called Harrishawes.[39] In 1603 George Evelyn at his death was in possession of three-fifths of the manor, which passed under the terms of a settlement to George, second son of his second son John.[14] The Evelyn family held the whole manor in 1636, when they sold it to James Lynch, the quit rents being 57s. 8d.[40] There is a record of one court which Lynch held for the manor;[41] after his death in 1648 it passed through various hands until in 1717 it was bought by John Walter.[14] It was sold by his son Abel in 1752 to a trustee of the Onslow property,[14] and was held by the Earl of Onslow at the time of the enclosure.

The land of the manor was scattered (particularly after it had absorbed other manors), but the holdings included the farms of Southhurst (South Farm), Astagehill, and most of Broadways, as well as Harrishaws. In 1714 there were 53 tenures listed in a rent roll, and 40 small leaseholds were granted between 1715 and 1720.[42]

Manor of Bagshot

The manor of Bagshot was royal demesne in early times and was apparently included in Windsor Forest. In 1211 Hoppeschort and Michael Belet both held land in Bagshot by sergeanty, the service being that of providing the King with a leash of hounds.[43] In 1254 Geoffrey de Baggesate *alias* de Bagessete died holding the manor of Bagesset' of Sir William de Windsor in chief, by service of half a knight's fee and half a mark (6s. 8d.) yearly.[44] In 1331 the manor of Bagshot was held by the Earl of Kent by castle guard to Windsor Castle. It was said to consist at this time of a ruinous messuage, 80 acres of arable,

eight acres of pasture and 20 acres of wood.[29] Early in the 16th
century the manor was back in Crown hands, and in the middle
of the century it included as well as Bagshot Lodge and Park,
five free tenants, three of whom held inns in Bagshot.[45] In 1609
the free holdings were much the same, but there were in addition 20 tenants at will, 13 of whom held cottages newly built
on the waste or land lately enclosed from the waste. The manor
probably covered much of the village and the old common
fields. Tenants of the manor had common pasture 'in the great
waste called Bagshot Heath'.[46]

In 1621 the manor—with the exception of Bagshot Park—was
granted to Sir Edmund Zouch. It was then described as 'the
Manor of Bagshot, with Court Leet and all that our waste and
lands called Bagshot Heath . . . within the said manor containing by estimation 1,000 acres; which with the . . . Bailliwick
of Surrey or Bagshot Bailliwick within the Forest of Windsor
and without, the Manor, Park and Perquisites of the Court of
the manor are valued at £6 0s. 9d. per annum, and were late
parcel of the possessions of the Castle and Honor of Windsor'.[47]
Bagshot manor, like the manor of Fosters, was acquired by
John Walter (1715). In 1748 Abel Walter obtained permission
to convert his lease for 1,000 years into fee simple[48] and sold
the manor to the Onslow estate. At some stage it seems to have
become merged with the manor of Fosters, and it is not mentioned at the time of the enclosure.

Manor of Freemantle

The manor of Freemantle is a particularly interesting one,
because it was connected with the parish church at Windlesham and with the early chapel at Bagshot. It apparently
originated in land held by Richard Freemantle in the time of
Edward II. This passed in 1443 to William Skern (a Kingston
family) and Robert Hewlett or Hulot, when Richard Freemantle
(grandson of the first Richard) quitclaimed to them the manor
and advowson of Windlesham.[49] In 1467 Edmund Skern, heir
to Robert Skern, released to Robert Hulot all his right in the
manor of Freemantle in Bagshot and Windlesham, with the
advowson of the church.[50] Robert Hewlett apparently now held
the whole manor, though subject to the dower rights of Agnes
Curteis, former wife of Robert Skern. Part of the manor went

to endow the chantry which was set up in the chapel at Bagshot (see Chapter 2). The subsequent history of the moieties of the manor is extremely involved and the pieces of the puzzle which are available do not fit. No court rolls can be traced today, though according to a rather obscure paragraph in Manning and Bray[51] a Guildford solicitor named Niblett was apparently then in possession of manorial documents which showed that early in the 16th century the number of tenures was twenty-five. (Mr. Niblett afterwards went bankrupt and ceased to practise.) As to the lands of the manor, these can only be guessed at, mainly by eliminating the lands of other manors. They seem to have included Hall Grove, Freemantle Farm, part of Twelve Oaks, part of Woodlands (now Windlesham Park), and part of Bagshot village.

In 1509 a moiety of the manor with the advowson of the church passed from Sir George Maners and his wife Ann to Ralph Lathom. It was described as 'a messuage, a mill, 80 acres land, 20 acres meadow, 40 acres pasture, 40 acres wood and a rent of 12s. 3¾d., two iron spurs and two autumn day-works in Wyndelesham, Bagshot and Chobham', in all 180 acres.[52] Henry Quynby or Quinby was one of the 'plaintiffs' in the case, and it seems to have been the same moiety which was transferred in 1514 by Henry Quynby, clothier of Farnham, together with other lands in the parish, to the use of William Lewtye or Lowthe (a London goldsmith) for 21 years, in repayment of a sum of £180 borrowed from him for the purchase of the moiety. Accounts drawn up of the rents and profits of all the lands made over by Quinby to Lewtye between 1514 and 1536 refer to repairs carried out to 'Hogmyll' (by which must be meant Hook Mill), and to timber sold out of Skern Grove, Dedryge Grove, Mill Grove, Hatch Croft and Hall Grove.[53] The names Skern Grove, Dedryge Grove and Mill Grove suggest a connection with Twelve Oaks Farm. In 1680 a Release by Doctor Thomas Doughty and his wife of this farm included Skerne Grove Coppice, Rye Grove Close, Mill Lands Coppice, and what was obviously Hook Mill.[54] Hatch Croft on the Chobham boundary (Tithe Award Nos. 52 and 53, 14 acres) was held by Henry Quinby of the Prioress of Broomhall in 1512, and the reference in the accounts to Hall Grove is probably to the Hale Grove near Hatch Croft, and not to Hall Grove in Bagshot.

John Quinby, son of Henry, presented to the living in 1536 and 1554,[55] and it is not clear whether it was Quinby's moiety which passed from George Molyneux *alias* Brewer to John Cooke in 1549, being then described as '2 messuages, 100 acres land, 40 acres meadow, 40 acres pasture, 20 acres wood and 500 acres of heath and furze in Wyndlesham and Bagshott'.[56] This description is however very similar (though not precisely the same) to that of the manor of Freemantle which was released by William and Cristofer Molyneux *alias* Bruer to John Attfield in 1561, consisting of '2 messuages, 2 orchards, 2 gardens, 100 acres land, 20 acres meadow, 40 acres pasture, 10 acres wood, 13 shillings rent'.[57] Neither of these transactions mentions the advowson of the church, but John Attfield presented to the living in 1588.[55]

Meanwhile in 1560 a part of the manor had been granted, after the dissolution of chantries, by Queen Elizabeth to Thomas Reve and George Evelyn under the title of a moiety of the manor of Freemantle in Windlesham lately belonging to Hewlett's chantry in Bagshot chapel.[58] This moiety was sold as part of the Evelyn estate to James Lynch in 1636. According to Manning and Bray, Sir John Evelyn transferred to James Lynch various manors and lands '. . . and a moiety of the manor of Freemantle, and the Mansion-house and land let at 60 *1* a year and two fat capons; farms in Bagshot and Chobham . . .'.[40] If the reference to a mansion house does apply to the manor of Freemantle—and this is not absolutely certain—the only house which could be meant seems to be Hall Grove (see Chapter 4). When James Lynch died in 1648 he held the manor of Fosters as well as half the manor of Freemantle in Bagshot,[59] and some at least of the Freemantle holdings (for example 'Ryeland and Rye Grove' and Hook Mill, held by Doctor Doughty) seem to have become merged with Fosters.

By the late 17th century, the manor of Freemantle had become even further fragmented. In 1660 a Court Baron held for the manor was attended by 'Robert Field, Clerk, and Daniel Mower, fermer of the heirs of James Lynch'.[51] In 1683 Daniel Mower was lord of the manor of Fosters, which he must have inherited from James Lynch together presumably with part of the manor of Freemantle. Thomas Mower, yeoman, left a fourth share of the manor of Freemantle in his will in 1689.[60] Robert Field (vicar of Woking 1637–65, and of of Chobham 1665–80) may have been the uncle of the James Attfield (or Field) who was said in 1683 to have held at his death 'a moiety of Hall Grove', his heir being John Attfield. In 1694 a Court was held in the name of James Field, lord of one moiety of the manor, and of John Hart and Edward Greentree, lords of the other moiety. In 1705 a Court was held in the names of Hart and Greentree, and of the representatives of James Field, deceased.[51] The part of the manor then held by descendants of James Field seems to have consisted only of a farmhouse and 55 acres of land (called Ryegrove *alias* Freemantles in Fosters court rolls) which was transferred, with half the manor of Freemantle, to Leonard Child by Francis Bartholomew and Henry Wapshott in 1718.[61] (The two men had respectively married Jane and Anna, daughters of James Field.) This small portion must surely have been only part of an original moiety. In 1812 Richard Dare, then owner of Free-mantle Farm, claimed to hold a moiety of the manor of Freemantle, but his claim was disregarded.[62] Meanwhile, the rest of Hall Grove, whether or not it formed part of the original Attfield or Field moiety, had been disposed of to a Mr. Montague, and by him to a Mr. Ragette.[51] (The latter was in fact Charles Rackett, husband of Alexander Pope's half-sister—see Chapter 4.)

Manor of Windlesham (Dean and Canons of St. George's Chapel, Windsor)

The catalogue of St. George's Chapel archives includes the manor of Windlesham among the constituent properties of St. Anthony's Hospital in London,[63] which was granted to Windsor Chapel in 1475.[64] This is however doubtful: Canons of the College of Windsor in fact held lands in Windlesham from 1463, and it seems likely that two separate gifts of lands were later amalgamated and designated a manor.[65] In 1505 Roger Banister appears on a rent roll of the College estates as collector of 33s. 4d. per annum, being rents for lease of certain lands and tenements in Windlesham.[66] In 1535 lands in Windlesham were leased by the Dean and Canons to Thomas Bone of Windlesham for 20 years at a rent of 33s. 4d., and similarly to William Spenser for 31 years in 1542. The tenant could employ the lands to arable or pasture, except for certain groves and copses which were called 'Martens', 'Orcharde', 'Pippis', 'Thrugez', and 'Throsshys', the woods and underwoods of which the Dean and Canons could fell and carry away.[67] Orchard Grove seems to have been a wood of three or four acres off Hook Mill Lane, sometimes called White's Lane in the 17th century. The other names may have been attached to parts of the 16- to 17-acre Great Grove or Manorfarm Wood at Manor Farm, which was the nucleus of the manor.

Frith's Register of College Revenues, made in 1620, contains an entry of a lease to John Attwood for 60 years in 1550. Here the land is referred to as 'the Manor of Windlesham' but the rent is the same as in the previous leases and the same restrictions are made about the same copses. The tenant was to 'build a new house in 3 years next and after to repair'.[68] One early court roll survives, probably dating to Edward VI.[69] A lease to William Hanley of Windsor, Walter Harward and William Harward the younger dated 1567 refers to the manor of Windlesham 'now in the tenure of Nicholas Attwood by lease of 8 Oct. 1550 to John Attwood'. It was now stated that the tenants were to keep courts as farmers and to deliver court rolls at every fifth one.[70] There is one isolated record of a court held in 1639.[71]

The Parliamentary Survey made in 1649, when the lands of Deans and Chapters were confiscated, refers to the 'great and mannor house of Windlesham alias Grove Lands'; there were 88 acres of land in demesne and some pieces of land let to copyholders for lives.[72] The Commissioners sold all the manor to Edward Harward to Windlesham for £163 19s. 3d.[73] After the Restoration, however, the Dean and Canons evidently recovered the manor and they leased it to Walter Harward the elder and Walter Harward the younger (of Roke, near Odiham, Hants.) in 1661 for 21 years at forty shillings. The proviso was entered that 'they will save and keep harmless and indemnify the Dean and Canons from all manner of charge and composition which hath been made from the late usurped power or any trustee'.[74]

The manor was leased on subsequent occasions to members of the Harward family, and then to various other tenants from 1689 onwards. It is probable that the Chitty family, who had a long connection with Manor Farm, were already the farmers,

an Edward Chitty being witness to a lease of 1668. During the
time the manor was leased to Mrs. Jane Brown of Basingstoke
in the early 18th century, a terrier set out 69½ acres of land.
Another terrier made out about the same time for Widow
Chittie, tenant of Mrs. Brown's lands, mentions that in addition
there were four or five pieces of land let out to copyhold
tenants.[71] From 1752 onwards there is a series of leases to
members of the Chitty family[75] and John Chitty's terriers of
1760 and 1781 enumerated 120¼ acres.[71] The copyhold land,
which was scattered over the parish (Linges or Hay plat near the
church, Hopgarden off Hook Green, Dale Brooks running down
to Lightwater Pond), had by this time become absorbed into
the main holding, although the leases still stipulated that the
lessee should hold manor courts. From 1831 to 1866 there
is a series of leases to the Fyler family, first to James Chamness
Fyler, and then to his son, Rev. James Fyler, who became
rector of Windlesham in 1861.[76] In 1867 the manor became
vested in the Ecclesiastical Commissioners, and it was purchased
from them by Rev. James Fyler on 31 July 1873 for £4,255.[77]

The manor seems to have been a sub-manor, for the Dean
and Canons were shown as free tenants in court rolls of St.
John's College. In 1531 they held 'mertons crofte alias mertons
lands', and in the 1588 rent roll 'Martins house'.[28] The 1606
rent roll gives 'le Grove lands 5s.' as well as 'Martens house
5s', but this could be a mistake as this roll contains several
doubtful entries.[35] There is no trace at all of the holding in
St. John's College rent roll of 1749,[36] but meanwhile the Dean
and Canons appear in a manor of Fosters rent roll of 1694
paying the same rent of 5s. for unspecified lands of which later
tenants are the Chitty family.[78]

2 The Main Features

The Parish Church

THE CHURCH OF ST. JOHN the Baptist at Windlesham stands on a spur of higher ground towards the centre of the parish, with open views to the south and west. In early times the church would have been surrounded by the common field known as Northersh or Church Field. John Aubrey, in his account of the church, says that it was about half a mile or more from the road, but we do not know from which direction he came.[1] Rocque's map of 1768-70 shows, on the line of approach from the *Half Moon,* only a narrow though well-defined way between cultivated fields, the final stage of the path which ran to the church from Bagshot across Bagshot common fields and the meadows below Hall Grove.

A comprehensive book on the church, using most of the printed sources available for its history, was published in 1927 by John Cree, whose work was described in a review in *Surrey Archaeological Collections* as a 'valuable addition' to the monographs on Surrey churches.[2] Considerable use of John Cree's book has been made in the account of the church which follows.

The date of foundation of the church at Windlesham is unknown; there may have been a Saxon church, but we have no evidence for it. The advowson is first mentioned in 1230, when it was stated that it had been granted by Hoppeschort (who held land in the parish) to Sherborne Priory in the time of Henry II (1154-89), in which case the church must have been in existence by 1189.[3] The parish was (until this century) in the Diocese of Winchester, Archdeaconry of Surrey, and Deanery of Stoke, near Guildford. The church is included in a list of Surrey churches (*c.* 1270) in the register of John de Pontissara, Bishop of Winchester.[4] The record of a suit of 1226, when the right of Sherborne was disputed by Newark Priory, near Guildford, describes the church as 'Chapelle',[5] and one may imagine at this time quite a small chapel. In 1230 Newark

was successful in obtaining the advowson, and in 1262 the
living was appropriated to Newark and held by them until
1447.[6] It would seem that the Priory appointed a 'vicar', for
a lawsuit of *c.* 1399 refers to 'Richard, that was the parish
priest of Windlesham'.[7] In the mid-15th century the living
passed into private hands, the church becoming attached to
the manor of Freemantle, the holders of which acquired the
right of presentation, Peter Warner being presented in 1447
by William Skerne and Robert Hewlot (Hewlett).[8]

The medieval church consisted of the tower and of a nave
and chancel, now the south aisle and chancel aisle of the
present church. Some portions of the walls of this church
still stand, though hidden in a later casing of brick. A part of
the original wall near the tower doorway was exposed when
the doorway was replaced in 1898. The rector at the time
(Rev. J. M. Freshfield), writing in the parish magazine,
described the wall as built of chalk and lumps of the ironstone
conglomerate found locally in the peaty soil, which were
arranged in a chequered pattern, similar to that in the low
wall of the south aisle (late 12th century) of the church of
St. Lawrence at Chobham.[9] The tower of St. Lawrence,
which was built about 1450, is faced with heathstone,[10] and
heathstone is also found in the south aisle wall making a
chequered pattern with ironstone conglomerate, together
with some lumps of chalk. Heathstone or sarsen—a kind of
sandstone found locally in the Barton (Upper Bagshot) sands
of the heath—was earlier used occasionally for building, for
example at Windsor Castle in the 12th century. It is therefore
possible that heathstone was also used at the church at Windlesham. At least one of the two two-light windows in the
present south aisle is late-13th-century Decorated, and there
is a three-light square-headed Perpendicular window in the
centre of the south wall of this aisle. Aubrey appears to have
visited the old church before it was burnt down in 1676. He
says that on two beams was written—

> William Whitehill was maker of this Werke: Pray ye for all the
> werkemen of this precious Werke of this . . . of Windlesham.
> Amen. Quod R. Marmion.

The date of the church was then given, but 'being a very dark
Day', Aubrey could not read it.[1]

It must have been on a subsequent occasion that Aubrey saw the plaque on the west wall stating that the church had been burnt by lightning. In 1679 the inhabitants of Windlesham petitioned the Bishop of Winchester as follows:

> that upon the 20th day of June 1676 the Steeple and part of the Body of the Church of Windlesham aforesaid was Burnt downe by lightning, the Bells melted, and many of the Seates burnt, and spoiled, and that the remaineing part of the said Church is soe miserably shaken and cracked, That at a meeting of the Inhabitants of the said parish July 28th 1679 called on purpose by the Churchwardens to consult and advise what was to be done to the Church, It was agreed by those that were there present and whose hands are sett to the Agreement that the said parish Church should be all pulled downe and rebuilt . . .

The petition asked the Bishop to arrange for such persons as he thought fit to inspect the state of the church, and an inspection was carried out on 28 May 1680 by Anthony Thomas of Chobham, White Tichborne of Frimley (a well-known family at Frimley Park in the 16th and 17th centuries), and Andrew Lamont, rector of Bisley. They reported that in their judgement the church was so ruinous that it could not be repaired

> but must of necessity be wholly taken downe until good foundation be found, and then to be wholly new built to the same extent of the old foundation being but competent roome for the number of the Assembly of the Parishoners. Except the Tower which may be reduced into a lesser compass. We also certify that we find one halfe of the Timber roofe of the Church wholy burnt and consumed and that there remaines the other halfe of the said roofe fit to serve to be laid on againe when the Walls are rebuilt. And further that the East end Wall of the Church (to which the Chancell adjoyns) cannot be taken downe without some prejudice to the contiguous ends of the Walls of the said Chancell.[11]

A Faculty was duly issued by the Bishop for the church to be rebuilt to the same length, breadth and height, and the plaque was put up by the then Churchwardens, John Attfield and Richard Cotterell, after the work had been carried out. The portions of the walls which were left were cased in the new brickwork, the tower being also given a facing of bricks. There is a picture of the 1680 church in Cracklow's views of Surrey churches.[12] The tower was certainly shorter then than it was after 1838, when several feet were added to the brickwork.[13]

Possibly the original tower had also been higher and it was prudently 'reduced into a lesser compass', for fear that lightning should strike twice in the same place!

It is interesting that the report recommended that the church should be built to the same size 'being but competent roome' for the assembly of parishioners. In 1676 (the same year as the fire) the number of communicants was returned as 253,[14] and when the church was enlarged in 1838 it was stated that the original number of sittings was two hundred and fifty-seven.

Although the church is dedicated to St. John the Baptist, in earlier times the dedication was to 'All Hallows' or 'All Saints'. In 1456 Peter Warner was referred to in a deed as Rector of All Saints, Windlesham,[15] and in 1488 William Riall was instituted to the parish church 'omnium sanctorum' at Windlesham.[16] John Rosyer (1515) and Thomas Elyet (1534) left directions in their wills for their bodies to be buried in the churchyard of 'All Hallows'.[17] [18] It would seem that a likely time for the church to be re-dedicated was when it was rebuilt in 1680, but no record of this has been traced. Aubrey said that there were no monuments in the church. This was presumably because of the recent fire; particulars of mural tablets placed in the church (including a number set up after the 1874 rebuilding) are given by John Cree.[19]

In 1838 the parish church was enlarged by the building of a rather curious north transept jutting out at right-angles to the body of the church, with a gallery at its north end. A gallery was also built in the tower. The total cost of the alterations and additions made at this time was nearly £1,500. The subscription list was headed by the Duchess of Gloucester, then living at Bagshot Park, for whom a large pew was provided near the pulpit. It was contributed to by all the local gentry, and there were grants from two church building societies.[20] A steel engraving of this church, viewed from the west, is reproduced in Brayley's *History of Surrey*; the architect was R. Ebbels. Another architect, Ewan Christian, who was responsible for the rebuilding of the church in 1874, then expressed the view regarding the north transept that 'nothing could probably have been devised more utterly devoid either of external beauty or of internal convenience'.[21]

The north transept was removed in 1874. A new nave, chancel and north aisle were built in polychrome brick, the

nave and chancel of the ,17th century being retained as an
aisle on the south side. The galleries were removed and open
benches were substituted for the pews. These alterations, which
amounted almost to a rebuilding, cost nearly £3,000.[22] The
church was lighted by candles up to 1887, when oil lamps
were installed as a memorial for Queen Victoria's Golden
Jubilee. In 1907 the cost of gas lighting was raised by subscription.[23]

In 1712, at the visitation of Archdeacon Gibson, the communion plate consisted of a silver chalice, a pewter patten
and a pewter flagon. New communion plate was presented
by the Duchess of Gloucester in 1841.[24] The church fittings
and the stained glass, which are modern, are described in detail
by John Cree, who also provides a corrected list of rectors.[25]

The district churches of St. Alban, Sunningdale (1902)
and All Saints, Lightwater (1903) are described in Chapter 10.

Parsonage and Glebe

The original glebe lands of the church cannot be traced,
and the sites of early parsonage houses are unknown. At the
Taxation of Pope Nicholas (1291), the value of the church was
£8,[26] and the Priory of Newark paid 16s. annually to the King
as their due tenth.[6] In the Valor Ecclesiasticus of 1534 the
living consisted of greater and lesser tithes, parsonage and
garden, meadow, pasture, wood and heath, the annual value
being £10 16s. 6d. The living had by this time passed from
the Priory into private hands and was thus safe from confiscation by Henry VIII. The Valor refers separately to temporal
possessions of Newark Priory in Windlesham which consisted
of rents of 38s. 8d. per annum.[27] A survey of ex-monastic
lands made in the time of Edward VI includes a parcel of
the possessions lately belonging to Newark Priory, the rents
of which amounted to 37s. 11d.; Agnes Street held a 44-year
lease dated 1533 of a messuage in Windlesham 'anciently
called the old parsonage' at a rent of 30s.[28] These are probably the temporal holdings in the Valor, and the reference
to the 'old parsonage' suggests that there had been a parsonage on Priory land and that some time after the living passed
to the manor of Freemantle a new parsonage had been built
elsewhere.

During the second half of the 16th century, the parsonage may not have been in use. Two rectors, John Hill and John Wollward or Woolward, also held livings elsewhere and were probably not resident in Windlesham.[29] The glebe may have disappeared at this time, and a reference in the will of John Attfield (Wollward's patron) in 1628 to 'copyhold in Windlesham sometime Wollwards which I took' could have some connection.[30] A meadow called Church Meadow in the Tithe Award (No. 297) was presumably once glebe meadow. In reply to a visitation question asking whether he held a terrier of the glebe, the Rev. Edward Cooper replied in 1764 that he had no glebe.[31]

It is possible that the church or parish lands, which appear in a terrier of 1662 with no explanation as to their origin, could be part of the old glebe. The terrier states that the income from the lease of these parish lands (which are also dealt with in leases dated 1663, 1684 and 1695) 'formerly went to the use of the church'.[32] The lands consisted at this time only of the following:

½ acre in Hither Common Field in Bagshot, adjoining to Marsh hill hedge.
a butt of arable in Church Field common field.
1 acre arable, ½ acre arable, and a butt of arable in Eastearsh common field.

It is interesting to note that these are all strips in the common fields, apparently set aside for the endowment of the church. These pieces of land were included in the claim for land belonging to the parish poor made out by the overseers before the enclosure (1812).[33] In 1824 the church lands were described as Ben's Platt (three roods near the church) and three acres of land at the north end of Bagshot Green;[34] the latter was subsequently sold and the proceeds invested, the income being applied to the repairs of the church.[35] At some time the charity became known as 'Polewhele's charity', a list of charities on a tablet in the church stating that Jonathan Polewhele (rector 1635-69) gave the rents of some lands on his death in 1669, though this does not fit in with the date of the first lease (1662).

In the 1664 Hearth Tax returns the rector (Polewhele) lived in a house with four hearths.[36] In 1764 Rev. Edward Cooper reported at the visitation inquiry that his parsonage house and premises were in proper repair, and that he resided upon his parsonage.[31] A valuation of property in the parish for the poor rate made in 1808 included a parsonage house owned by the rector, but occupied by another person, the annual value of which was only £5 5s. 0d.[37] The Enclosure Act of 1812 stated that there was no glebe and that the parsonage was 'small, inconvenient, ancient and in a ruinous state and totally unfit for residence of the incumbent'. The last two rectors (Edward Cooper and Thomas Snell) had in recent years been granted dispensations to reside elsewhere.[38] It is probable that this house was on the west side of Rectory Lane where land in Westridge (Westersh) common field was allotted to the rector at the enclosure, as the word 'Rectory' appears here on Bryant's map of Surrey (1823). There are two illustrations which may be of the house in question. The earlier, entitled the 'Parsonage', is by W. Porden, perhaps dating to not long after 1800. In the other, a water-colour by John Hassell (undated, but probably early 1820s), the house, which is called the 'Vicarage', seems to have been somewhat improved.[39] Meanwhile the house called 'The Cedars' (next to the church) which was owned by Brigadier Thomas Panton in the 1720s, had been acquired by the Rev. Edward Cooper at some stage, and used as his rectory. It was purchased by Rev. Thomas Snell about 1831 on the death of Mrs. Cooper. In 1840 a new rectory was built on the land formerly common field referred to above, the existing parsonage house presumably being pulled down. The rectory was designed by the architect who rebuilt the church in 1838 (R. Ebbels) to harmonise with it.[40]

The First Chapel at Bagshot

Bagshot was a chapelry of Windlesham and did not become a separate ecclesiastical parish until 1874. The date of the first chapel is uncertain. The first positive reference which has been traced is in 1480 when a gild was licensed in St. Mary's chapel at Bagshot,[41] and it is possible, though this is only conjecture, that the chapel, in which a chantry was founded, was built by one of the lords of the manor of Freemantle. A number of chantry chapels were in fact built to serve as chapels of ease at some distance from mother churches, because the lord of the manor would find the erection of a free chapel under the guise of a chantry foundation less difficult than sub-dividing the parish. The chapel is not mentioned in Bishop Pontissara's list of churches,[4] nor in the taxation of Pope Nicholas,[26] although other chapels in Surrey are referred to in both documents. In 1464 Bishop Waynflete of Winchester certified that from 1262 Newark Priory had held 'Capella de Wyndelsham'.[6] (Manning and Bray repeat this correctly under Windlesham, but in the section on Newark Priory incorrectly as 'Windlesham cum capella'.[42]) 'Capella' must here refer to the church itself, which was called 'chapelle' in 1226; in Henry Woodlock's register a list for collection of crown dues in 1305 shows 'chapel of Windlesham 8d.'.[43]

In 1547 it was stated that the chantry in the chapel of Our Lady at Bagshot had been endowed with half the manor of Freemantle.[44] The chapel and chantry then had lands to the value of £6 a year. A chantry, which was literally a mass celebrated at an altar for the well-being of a benefactor during his lifetime and for the repose of his soul after death, was usually endowed by a wealthy family, but gilds were also formed by humbler men to support chantries. A licence was required for the foundation because alienation into the hands of the church of the property which was to furnish the endowment might deprive the Crown of services and death dues. In 1480 a licence was granted for John Ingilby (prior of the house of Jesus of Bethleem, Shene), Robert Houghlot, Richard Newbrigge (clerk), Richard Merchall, John Marten, Robert Rutter, and John Tynmarden to found a fraternity or gild perpetual of themselves and other persons. They were to elect for themselves a guardian 'of the gild of St. Mary in Bagshote'. The gild was permitted to acquire lands and rents, not held in chief, to the value of £10 yearly, to find a chaplain to celebrate divine service in the chapel, and to do other works of piety according to the ordinance of the founders.[41] Robert Houghlot, or Hewlett, was by this time lord of the manor of Freemantle. The Rutters and Tymberdens (probably the same as   Tynmarden) were local families. By his will of 1515, John Rosyer, an innkeeper in Bagshot, left to the chapel a Torch price 3s. 4d., the lands of Fynshamstede, a mark (13s. 4d) to the finding of the priest, and 6s. 8d. to the reparations of the chapel.[17]

The chapel of Bagshot is not mentioned in the Valor Ecclesiasticus of 1534, nor is it in a Valor of 1536 in the registers of Bishops Gardiner and Poynet. However, in John Cooke's copy of the 1536 Valor (made at the end of Bishop Fox's register, but inaccurate and incomplete) was entered: 'Chapel of Bagshot. Chris. Fawkoner, chaplain. Value £6 1s. 5½d.'[45] In the list of stipendiary priests (1541) there is an entry under Bagshot that John Butte was the chaplain, and that he was paid by Mr. (blank) Bruer there.[46] The Bruers or Brewers were connected with the manor of Freemantle. An Agnes Brewer, late wife of Harry Quinby, was receiving an annual payment of dowry out of Quinby's moiety of Freemantle between 1519 and 1536. (There was also a link between the Brewer family and the Molyneux family, who appear twice in transfers of a moiety of the manor of Freemantle, for an Alice Brewer *alias* Molyneux is mentioned in 1547). Accounts in connection with Quinby's moiety of the manor include an entry for quit rents of 3s. a year paid to the guardians of the chapel of Bagshot between Christmas 1514 and September 1536.[47]

In the Particulars for Sale of Chantries (1547) it was said that Bagshot chapel was three miles distant from the parish church and that parishioners dwelling near used to resort to it, but that there was no incumbent at the time.[48] The chapel may have fallen into decay after the confiscation of the chantry endowment; it does, however, seem possible that after the appointment of a separate chaplain ceased, it became the practice to include the chapel at Bagshot in the care of the incumbent of the living. Manning and Bray state (early 19th century) that presentations to the living were formerly made 'cum capella de Bagshot', but that this was now no longer done.[49] No early presentation deeds can be traced, however, and records of institutions to the living made in the Bishops' registers of 15th, 16th, and 17th centuries do not refer at all to the chapel at Bagshot. Ecclesiastical visitations—inspections of the parishes in their area made by bishop or archdeacon— from 16th to the early 18th century are equally silent, with one exception. In visitation records of 1664, during the incumbency of Jonathan Polewhele, Windlesham entries refer to 'capella de Badshott [*sic*]', and there are separate entries for Bagshot with the same churchwardens as Windlesham.[50] It is not possible to say whether this means that the chapel was actually still in existence at the time. The earliest surviving presentation deed, that of Samuel Piggott in January 1718, does not contain the phrase 'cum capella',[51] but by this time the chapel had certainly disappeared. Its memory continued, however, for in the middle of the 18th century some of the parishioners recalled having heard that it had stood in the centre of the village on the side of a road to Chobham, a small distance from the main road through Bagshot, but they 'did not remember any remains of it'.[49] This could fit in with the chapel having been still there a hundred years or so before, and seems to suggest that it was just down the Guildford road, somewhere near what became the *King's Arms* inn. Aubrey said, in fact, that the inn itself had previously been 'a chauntry for the Freemantles',[1] and Manning and Bray point out that the east end of the back part of the inn appeared to be old.[52]

The new chapel built in Chapel Lane, Bagshot, in 1821, is described in Chapter 5, and St. Anne's church (1884) in Chapter 8.

Bagshot Lodge and Park

In 1331 the Earl of Kent, who then held the manor of Bagshot, was said to have 'one ruinous messuage' there.[53] Parks were often enclosed within a forest in order to prevent the deer from straying. The first reference found to a royal park at Bagshot is in 1486, when the office of keeper of Bagshot Park was granted to William Michell;[54] there are many subsequent references to the granting of the post. In the mid-16th century there was a 'badly ruined' mansion, with a park two miles in circuit. It was let to Edward Tyle, who paid no rent because the mansion and park remained in the King's hands for his access.[55] The early Stuart kings, James I and Charles I, were very fond of hunting and were often in residence at their hunting lodge at Bagshot. In 1607 John Norden described the park as 415 acres in extent and two and seven-eighths miles in circuit, a small part of it being in Berkshire. There were, he said, about 17 roe deer which 'lie covertlie and hardlie are discovered'.[56]

A survey of Bagshot Lodge, which had recently been enlarged and repaired by the keeper, Sir William Harmon, was made in

1610 by Simon Basyll, Surveyor-General of Works. He found that the total cost of materials and workmen's wages came to £861, while Sir William Harmon's account was for £1,042; the difference was attributed to such items as working during the winter in order to get the job done sooner, carriage of materials, casting (clearing out) of the moat, and making the foundation of brickwork under it for the new offices. In his report, to which was attached a plan of the ground floor, Simon Basyll said that the main building had previously consisted of the north, east and west sides of a square, but certain rooms 'of great proportion' being required, the buildings had been taken down and rebuilt together with a new range on the south. The existing square building, of timber, was 70 feet by 78 feet, and was built round a courtyard with hall, parlour, kitchen and five lodgings or offices on the ground floor. On the floor above there was a dining chamber over the hall, a withdrawing chamber over the parlour, and six more lodgings, while there were other rooms in the garret. Besides this square main building, there was a range of new buildings 60 feet by 18 feet, having one storey of brick for kitchens and a half storey of timber over it for offices and lodgings. There was a stable 30 feet long by 16 feet wide with two 'returns' 20 feet square. A manuscript of contemporary date preserved at the British Library throws some interesting light on the disposition and use of the rooms. The hall served as a guardchamber, and next to it was a parlour and lobby near the foot of the stairs for the captain of the guard. The King's three private rooms were on the first floor above the hall, parlour and an adjacent lodging, while the 'Robes Groomes' and pages of the bedchamber slept in the great gallery, and the gentlemen ushers, grooms and pages of the privy chamber in the other galleries. The King had a private buttery, kitchen and larder, and there was a great buttery and an out kitchen for the lords in attendance. Other service rooms included a 'silver scullery' and a 'ewrye' (or yeuerye) for wine ewers.[57]

In 1631-2 an extension to the Lodge was built by Inigo Jones, then Surveyor of the Royal Works. It seems to have been a self-contained building, all of timber, painted stone-colour. The accounts suggest a miniature Palladian villa with four columns prefacing a loggia as at the Queen's House, Greenwich.[58] There is no mention of such a building in the

Parliamentary Survey of 1650; presumably it was destroyed
during the Civil War, as being of timber it would easily be burnt
down. Sir William Waller's troops were quartered at the Lodge
for a time, inflicting 'irreparable losses' on the keeper.[59] When
Charles I was being brought from Hurst Castle to Windsor
in December 1648, he arranged to dine at the Lodge with Sir
James Livingstone, Viscount Newburgh. It was planned that
he should escape by means of the fastest horse in the stable,
but the animal went lame at the crucial moment.[60] A rather
curious episode occurred during the Commonwealth when
Lt.-Col. Sam Barry and Capt. Peck, having resigned their com-
missions when the King was seized, were 'obliged' to purchase
Bagshot Park for £4,000 in lieu of arrears of pay. After the
Restoration John Barry (brother) claimed some sort of com-
pensation, saying that having bought it from them for £2,000,
he had spent another £2,000 on it.[61]

According to the 1650 Survey, Bagshot Park was 449 acres
in extent; there were no deer, they having all been destroyed
in the Civil War. There were 1,257 trees, mostly old decayed
pollards, in addition to the 704 trees which had been cut down
or earmarked for the use of the Navy. The Lodge was described
as a building of brick and timber. The accommodation below
stairs consisted of hall, two parlours, withdrawing room,
buttery, kitchen, two beer cellars, two wine cellars, pantry,
three larders, pastry room, laundry room, and four other rooms.
Above stairs was 'a fair dining room wainscoted', 'three fair bed
chambers', a withdrawing room and 16 other chambers, with
four garret rooms over them.[62] There seem to be more rooms
than in 1610, and possibly the court had been filled in. In the
Hearth Tax of 1664, the Earl of Newburgh at Bagshot Park
Lodge had to pay for 22 hearths.[63] The adjoining brick and
timber building contained in 1650 bakehouses, washhouse,
milk house and bolting room, the last-named used for sifting
meal for bread from the rest which would go for pig food.
There were two stables for 20 horses, with grooms' quarters
adjoining, and a coachhouse. The Surrey surveyors valued the
Lodge with its outhouses, stables, etc., at £10 a year. They
thought it would be of more value if continued in use as a
dwelling house than the materials would be if it were pulled
down: the house was large and useful, the air 'good and whole-
some'.[62]

The park was disparked during the Commonwealth period. In 1665 the overseers and inhabitants of Windlesham petitioned the justices against the refusal to pay poor rates of certain farmers and tenants to whom 'certain lands and tenements called Bagshot Park for several years past disparked and plowed up' had been let.[64] It may be that this area was never enclosed again, although the park was restored, as the southern boundary of the park seems to take a sharper turn away from the village on later maps than it does on Norden's map of 1607.

In 1682 a Royal Warrant was issued for the constitution of Col. James Graham, Privy Purse to Charles II, as ranger and keeper, the King having decided that the park should be a nursery for red deer and other game. Not long afterwards Graham was allowed up to £1,200 to be spent 'in and about the building and repairing of our house called Bagshot Lodge, and the impaling of our said park'.[65] After the death of Charles II, James Graham petitioned James II to the effect that the house being 'very ruinous' he had in fact spent very much more money on it. On enquiry into the matter, the royal auditors found that he had expended £3,758 9s. 7d., and still owed £247 0s. 4½d. for materials delivered and work done. No details are given of the actual work carried out to the house on this occasion.[66] John Evelyn visited Bagshot Lodge on two occasions soon after the work had been completed. On 15 September 1685 he records that the house was 'very commodious, & well furnished', with a park full of red deer about it, while on 22 October he describes it as 'new repaired, and capacious of a good family'.[67]

From the beginning of the 18th century, Bagshot Park Lodge may perhaps be regarded as the 'big house' of the neighbourhood rather than a royal seat. It was granted by the Crown from time to time to members of the nobility. Queen Anne let it to the Earl of Arran with the office of ranger in 1706, for 99 years terminable on three lives. In 1766 George III leased it to George, Earl of Albemarle, for the lives of the Earl and his brothers, Augustus and William Keppel.[68] In 1772 it came to Admiral Augustus Keppel (well-known commander of the French wars), and paintings of the house at this time show a building of Georgian appearance with sash windows. It was probably at this period that two wings were added to the original square structure, which was either rebuilt or re-fronted entirely in brick, with a hipped roof.[69] In 1783 it was said that 'This most delightful habitation . . . has cost at least £50,000 for improvements since it has been in the Albemarle family'.[70]

The more direct connection with royalty was renewed by the allocation of the house to the Prince of Wales, but he was not very interested in it. In 1798 the Duke of Gloucester was made ranger of the Bagshot Walk and after their marriage in 1816 he and the Duchess lived at Bagshot Lodge. Many improvements were carried out in the then rather neglected house and grounds under the supervision of Lt.-Col. Edmund Currey, who was appointed Secretary and Controller of the Duke's household. The Duchess found that 'barring our own rooms there is not another place in the house fit to be seen', the Duke's gentlemen having to be lodged in the garrets. The house was enlarged after a plan by Nash and defective drains were also tackled, although in 1848 the family of Prince Albert's equerry (then living in part of the house) still blamed an attack of fever on drains 'in a most imperfect state'! The grounds were cleared and a flower garden laid out.[71] The 'American garden' and the head gardener, Mr. Toward, who was later given the management of the gardens and grounds at Osborne House (Isle of Wight) by the Prince Consort, became well known. The Duke of Gloucester died in 1834, but the Duchess continued to live at Bagshot Park until the mid-1840s. The Duke and Duchess were patrons of the parish, heading the subscription lists for worthy causes. In 1853 the removal of the Duchess was said to have been 'a great loss to the neighbourhood; in her the poor found a constant friend'.[72] The Prince Consort, who was in charge of the Bagshot Park estate in the late 1840s and early 1850s, was probably responsible for modernising the farm, later known as Bagshot Park Farm.[73]

The house was subsequently occupied by Sir James Clark, physician to Queen Victoria, who lived there for several years from the early 1860s. Over the period 1875–99 a new house on a different part of the estate was built for Arthur, Duke of Connaught, third son of Queen Victoria. A full description of this (the present) house, which is of brick and stone in Tudor style, is given in a short booklet recently published.[74] The old house was demolished in 1878. The Duke of Connaught was in residence at Bagshot Park from time to time until his death in 1942 at the age of ninety-two. The Duke, who was interested and expert in horticulture, spent much time and care on the grounds,[75] which were frequently opened to the villagers.

The Medieval Villages

Having outlined the framework of the parish and described some of its main features, we must now go back to consider the medieval settlements which were in existence for three or four hundred years. As we have already seen, there is practically no information about the parish before the late 12th century. From the absence of mention in Domesday it seems probable that the number of inhabitants was then small, owing partly to the rather poor land. The parish lies in part on the Barton (formerly called the Upper Bagshot) Beds, but is in the main on the Bracklesham (Middle Bagshot) Beds, with extensive peaty alluvium in the beds of the Bourn or Windle brook and its tributaries. The dry and acid Barton sands have no water-holding capacity, but in the sand of the Bracklesham Beds there are upper and lower bands of clay. The soil produced by these beds is reasonably fertile, though surface drifting of the finer deposits tends to result in ground being covered to some depth by sand not really in place, and the clayey series sometimes give rise to peaty swamps. The manure needed to bind the light soil together would have been scarce in medieval times; the use of chalk or lime to counteract acidity may not have been common before the 18th century.

The fact that from the time of Henry II much of the area was technically within Windsor Forest would also have tended to keep the population down. Because it was hunted over periodically, and there were harsh penalties for poaching and trespass, the forest had the effect of hindering farming and impeding colonisation of new land. It did not, however, entirely stop peasants from making assarts or clearances, provided they were prepared to pay the fine due under forest laws. The extension of cultivation that took place in most parishes during the two centuries after Domesday, as a result of the general growth of population, doubtless led to the better parts of the land of Windlesham being exploited by the peak of the medieval

period about 1300. Indications that cultivation had reached
the limits of the parish on the Chobham side to the east and
south are given by names of taxpayers in the 1332 Lay Subsidy,
such as John 'le pipere' (probably connected with what became
Pipers Farm) and William 'ate Strode' (compare Black Strode
in the Tithe Award, near modern Black Stroud Lane) from
O.E. *strod,* marshy land overgrown with brushwood. Cultivation probably also extended to the Guildford road on the south-
west, where the Bracklesham Beds are overlain by the Barton
Beds: here William 'de Suthurst' (Southhurst or South Farm)
would be found.[76]

There were only 36 taxpayers in the 1332 subsidy (which
was levied on movable goods or personal property, not on
real estate), and the total paid between them was £3 10s. 11d.
Medieval Windlesham certainly had far fewer taxpayers than
some of the other villages in north-west Surrey, but the average
amount paid was similar. Eight of the 36 taxpayers contributed
50 per cent. of the total, and 11 of them paid the lowest
amount (8d.), so wealth was quite unequal.[76] Some poor people
would have been exempt because the value of their possessions
did not exceed a certain minimum. The proportion of such
people varied from place to place, so that one cannot be certain
about even the relative size of village populations. A very rough
guess would place the population of the parish about this time
at between 200 and 300, probably nearer the lower figure.

The houses of the villagers fringed the large open common
fields, and substantial traces of this pattern at Windlesham can
still be found on Rocque's map of 1768-70. At the time of the
enclosure (1814) the common fields in the village were named
Eastridge, Westridge, Church, Down, Thorndown, Ashington,
Woodcote, and Scutterley. The three original fields of the
settlement were Estersh (Eastersh), Westersh, and Northersh,
the latter being the earlier name of Church Field. The ending
'ersh' comes from O.E. *ersc,* ploughed field. These names,
together with Down and Thorndown, all occur in the documents of Broomhall Priory.[77] A winding lane (known as Jane's
Lane in the 19th century) ran between Church Field and
Westersh, and another (later Rectory or Try's Lane) between
Westersh and Eastersh. These lanes were not specified as access
roads at the enclosure and have gone out of normal use. More
common fields would have been brought into cultivation as

demand for land increased: Woodcote, for instance, would indicate a further clearing of wood. Scutterley has not been found earlier than 1649, when it appears as 'Shutterley' in the Parliamentary Survey of the lands of the Dean and Canons of Windsor. It may come from M.E. *shute,* that which shoots forth, and could denote an angle of cultivated land projecting into woodland, which would be in keeping with its situation. The M3 motorway has recently severed the common fields, thus obscuring some of the last traces of the medieval landscape.

Owing to the low yields of grain per acre in medieval times, to maintain a population of a couple of hundred people would have required the cultivation of some 200 or 300 acres of arable, though of course this may not all have been in open common fields. An approximate reconstruction of the medieval common fields of Windlesham village can be made, based on the disposition of the 150 acres remaining in common fields at the time of the enclosure, as indicated by names of areas in the Award (see Fig. 2). The distribution of these remaining portions suggests that the fields were once considerably larger, possibly even up to as much as twice the extent. Another 90 acres, making, say, 240 acres of former common field, can readily be suggested. Some 50 acres which had already been enclosed before 1814 are indicated by the names borne by certain areas in the Tithe Award, for example, six acres called 'Scutterley Field' and three acres called 'Thorndown Field'. A further 40 acres, and maybe more, could well from their situation have been part of the common fields. 'New Close', for instance, which is mentioned in the terrier of 1662[32] and is still called New Close in the Tithe Award, looks as if it had once been part of Eastersh common field. Another example of land presumably enclosed by agreement is provided by the holding of the Dean and Canons of Windsor of '7 acres of land intermixed in the Downe Field' in 1649, which by 1781 seem to have become '2 closes Down 5 acres' and '3 pieces in common field Down 1¾ acres'.[78]

At Bagshot, the common fields may have disappeared at an early date with the development of trading activities on the great west road offering alternative employment. The Surrey Musters of 1596 (lists of fighting men available) include only one husbandman and two labourers at Bagshot, the other men being in trade.[79] Only six acres or so of common field north of the village remained at the enclosure: the area was called Bagshot Field, and an adjacent area of some eight acres with the same name was one of the ancient enclosures in the Tithe Award. Church terriers of 1662 and 1695 refer to land in a common field called the 'Hither Common Field' adjoining Marsh Hill Hedge,[32] south of Bagshot Field. The 1609 rental of Bagshot manor mentions other common fields called 'Hull-field' (possibly Hilly Field, Tithe Award No. 236) 'Wellmin-parke' and 'Watergate'. It seems possible from the lie of the land that the common fields may have originally extended—before Bagshot Park was enclosed—over the higher ground on both sides of the present main road. As we have already seen, there may well have been another road north of the present one from the direction of Egham, and in 1607 Norden marks an area opposite Bagshot Field (but apparently then within the park) as ploughed land, so this land must have been suitable for cultivation.[56] The original settlement may have lain more to the north of the Bourn brook: all this part of Bagshot is on the more profitable Bracklesham Beds.

Beyond the common fields, some separate enclosures almost certainly already existed in medieval times and further land was doubtless enclosed as the population grew, particularly from Tudor times onward. William 'de Suthurst' was perhaps already farming what became known as Southhurst Farm. Adam 'ate Rydebrok' may be connected with Redbrook, near Broadway Green, probably the nucleus of Broadway Farm. The common fields and the other arable were all on comparatively high ground on the Bracklesham Beds. Lower down on both sides of the Bourn brook in between Windlesham and Bagshot, there was a large band of meadow, which may in very early times have been common meadow. All the low-lying area here below the 150 foot contour line was valuable as it was already enclosed before 1814. In earlier times the Bourn brook (one of the tributaries of the Bourn, which flows into the Thames near Weybridge) must have been a much more important stream. Hoke (Hook) Mill is mentioned in a court roll of about the same date as the Lay Subsidy, in which Henry 'ate Mulle' is listed. A footpath runs across Down Field on the shortest line to the mill from the settlement at Windlesham. The subsidy also lists Godfrey the smith and John the cooper, the latter presumably to be connected with Coopers

Green. Among other places which can be identified are Marsh or March Hill, north of Bagshot Green (William and John 'ate Merssh'), and Dunny Grove, from the Tithe Award (William and Gilbert 'ate Donye').

One of the highest payers in the 1332 subsidy was Stephen the shepherd, a pointer perhaps to the importance of sheep-rearing in the parish at this date. The sheep population of England underwent a remarkable increase during the later Middle Ages and about 1500 there may have been as many as three sheep to every human being. In several wills of this date sheep are left as legacies to relatives and to the church at Windlesham. For instance, in 1487 Robert Burdon left the following:

> To the light of St. Mary the Virgin in the church of Windlesham one sheep. To the light of St. Nicholas there one lamb. To the light of St. Katherine of Waverley one sheep. To Henry my son a heifer aged 3 years, and 6 sheep. To John my son one sheep with a lamb. To Philip my son one sheep with a lamb.[80]

The 1332 subsidy comes at what was probably the peak of medieval population. In the late summer of 1348 the bubonic plague known as the Black Death reached England, and it is thought that successive outbreaks of the plague may have reduced the population of the country by about one-third. Its local effect cannot be assessed, although we do know that Juliana le Pope and William le Bastard, who held two messuages and 11 acres of land in the parish, died without heirs 'in the first pestilence'.[81] We find few records connected with the parish in the 15th century, a century which has in general left less documentation than the centuries immediately before and after. Records, both official and private, increased under Tudor administrations.

3 Twin Occupations

OVER THE THREE HUNDRED YEARS from 1500 to 1800 there were two main factors in the economic life of the parish: agriculture, and trading on the great west road, the latter becoming more important as time went on. As we have already seen, the settlements at Windlesham and Bagshot were quite distinct. Already by the Tudor period they have established very different characters.

Agriculture and Land Use

Windlesham remained agricultural: the Surrey Musters list of 1596 includes six husbandmen and seven labourers in the 19 names.[1] Owing to the patchiness of surviving records we know very little about the transition from the peasant economy of medieval times to the profit-farming of the 16th and 17th century yeoman farmer. By the first Land Tax returns (1780), most of the older yeoman families had disappeared in their turn, being replaced by new owner-occupiers or by absentee landlords and tenant farmers. The fact that several of the farmhouses were built or enlarged in brick in the late 17th or early 18th centuries (see Chapter 4) suggests that this period was quite a prosperous one locally, though the main improvements in farming methods may not have come until later in the 18th century.

There is not a great deal of information on land use before the late 18th century. At the time of the enclosure of the waste (1814), about 2,000 acres (rather more than a third of the parish) was in use and under cultivation in arable, meadow and woodland (see Fig. 3). All of this, with the exception of 156 acres, was then in enclosed fields, and if as suggested in Chapter 2, the common fields were once much more extensive, the actual process by which enclosure was carried out is no longer recorded. The rest of the parish (about 3,700 acres) was heathy waste on which sheep and cattle grazed, part of the larger area of Bagshot Heath. In 1791 it was said that a few years before 'the whole tract of country round Bagshot for near twenty miles very much resembled one of the deserts of Westphalia'.[2]

In Tudor times a considerable area, particularly on the southeast of the parish, must have been covered by groves and coppice woods, which were grown for hoops, poles, charcoal, etc. There were at least 20 acres of copse in the manor of the Dean and Canons of Windsor, and 40 acres of wood, including several groves and copses, in one moiety of the manor of Freemantle. The main arable crops were probably rye, barley and oats. Until about 1700 much more rye than wheat was used for making bread, the bread of ordinary people being made from flour obtained by mixing wheat with rye. Robert Goghe left an acre of the best rye in Down Field at harvest time to his son Anthony in 1570.[3] Thomas Edshaw in 1604 left to his son John an acre of rye in Eastersh common field, to his son William half an acre of rye, and another acre and a half to be divided between his son Henry and his daughter.[4] Hops were grown in places where they would not be found in later times, and in the earlier 17th century there was a two-acre field called 'Hopgarden' off Hook Green.[5] Some wheat may have been grown on Manor Farm for the Dean and Canons of Windsor from the later 17th century, the leases specifying that four bushels of wheat 'or as much money as the best wheat is worth in New Windsor', were to be delivered to them.[6] During the 18th century there was increasing use by farmers of alternate husbandry (involving the laying down of parts of the arable in temporary leys and sowing it with clover and grasses) and of marling and manuring. Up to about the middle of the century the soil of Windlesham was generally thought too poor to bear wheat. 'When the first experiment was made, it was visited as a wonder. Improved Husbandry has taught them better. They fetch Free Chalk from a pit on the Downs between Guildford and Farnham . . . lay it on Clover Seeds, next year plough it in . . .'.[7]

When the Basingstoke Canal was opened in 1794, great hopes were entertained of the benefits which this, the first 'agricultural' canal, would bring in the promotion of cultivation of the barren lands through which it passed, for the chalk required for marling would cost very much less to transport by canal than it did by road. It has recently been concluded, however, that the benefits of the Basingstoke Canal were 'useful, but not substantial . . . agriculture did not, as might have been expected, develop along the line of the canal'.[8] The canal certainly does not seem to have had much effect on the development of the parish of Windlesham, from which it is about three miles distant at Pirbright. A project was started in 1801 to build a branch of the canal from Pirbright to Bagshot, the proposed plan being for a four and a half mile extension running from Chilton Moor to Bagshot Green.[9] The main idea was to capture the 4,000 or so tons of coal, corn, groceries and other goods which went up the Thames to Staines and were then distributed by road waggon to Bagshot and other places in the neighbourhood; additional traffic, including vast quantities of chalk, was estimated at 10,000 to 12,000 tons annually. The Duke of Gloucester and six other gentlemen subscribed £800, but the scheme failed for lack of finance.[10]

The 1801 crop returns of land sown since the last year's harvest with wheat, rye and other grain show 763 acres of arable land in the parish, split up as follows: wheat, 230; barley, 124; oats, 191; potatoes, 22; peas, 62; beans, 43; turnips, 88; rye, 3.[11] (Carrots are not mentioned, though in 1813 Stevenson refers to these being grown to a considerable extent in Bagshot, a sandy loam being preferred.) It is thought that the arable reported in the crop returns, which were made by the clergy, was often under-estimated owing to farmers being wary over tithes. Moreover, no attention was paid to bare fallow or to rotation grasses. The 763 acres of arable shown in 1801 may be roughly compared with the 883 acres in the Tithe Award of 1843. This covered all the 'old enclosures' (except Bagshot Park), which were still titheable, but not the 156 acres in common fields, now freed of tithe, which would have been included in the 1801 total. The Award also showed 686 acres of meadow or pasture and 215 acres of woodland; some change of use may of course have occurred between 1801 and 1843.

The use of the drill to sow seeds in widely-spaced rows (which could be kept free from weeds by regular hoeing) was by this time very general on the light soils of north-west Surrey.

The extent to which turnips, which were particularly useful on light soils for a flexible arable rotation, were cultivated is sometimes taken as an indication of the degree of agricultural improvement: the percentage of the recorded arable occupied by turnips was twice as high in some other Surrey parishes (in 1801) as it was at Windlesham.

Sheep continued to be mentioned frequently in legacies in Tudor times: the will of Thomas Edsawe (1555) left 30 sheep, 10 to his eldest son and five each to his other four children, and Nicholas Attfield (1587) left 36 sheep in his will.[12] In the late 17th century, Aubrey said 'The sweet but little Mutton hereabout is taken notice of by Travellers'.[13] The *Universal Directory* of 1791, which it was hoped would be consulted overseas as well as at home, still extolled the virtues of Bagshot mutton in glowing terms:

> The sheep bred upon it [the Heath] are small, but remarkably fine flavoured, and when well fatted, and in proper order is allowed to be the sweetest mutton in the world; which induces many people who pass through the town, to stop their carriages, on purpose to carry home some . . .[2]

The truth of the matter is, however, more likely to be expressed in the following contemporary statement by James and Malcolm:

> We saw only a few starved animals unworthy the name of sheep. From what circumstance the title of Bagshot mutton has derived its name, is perhaps now very difficult to be discovered: certain it is that no animal can live upon these wastes in their present state.[14]

So far as cattle were concerned, Stevenson says that there were few in Surrey, but the suckling of calves for the London market was carried on 'in the retired and more distant parts about Chobham and Bagshot'.[15]

With regard to the timber available, James and Malcolm were unable to find out (about 1794) whether the numbers of young birch and Scotch fir growing on the heath 'to all appearance in a state of nature' had been sown by anyone. They suggested that if timber were grown on the hills it would in a few years 'make that part now waste of as much value as any inclosed land' in neighbouring districts.[16] By the early 1800s, planting of softwoods had certainly taken place.[7]

The later 18th century saw the introduction into the parish
of a new branch of cultivation: nursery gardening. The enormous growth in the population in the second half of the
century, together with the rising prosperity of the middle class,
had greatly increased the general demand for ornamental and
fruit trees, shrubs and plants. Nurseries, hitherto more or less
confined to the London area, were now appearing further out.
The sandy Bagshot soil was very suitable, and indeed James
and Malcolm (themselves nurserymen) said it was 'so much
in request by every nurseryman that he can scarce grow a plant
that is a native of America . . . without having equal to four-
fifths of this species of soil'.[17] John Taylor of Bagshot had
already by 1791 converted part of the peat moor at 'Townsend',
the western end of the village, into a nursery-ground. Manning
and Bray describe it as extensive, adding the comment that
'he sells all his plants when young, for the bottom is a gravel
and will not allow them to stand long'.[7] Richard Dare of
Freemantle Farm had also turned some land over to nursery
work, and Edward Hammond of Windlesham was described
in a court roll of 1813 as a nurseryman.

The Farms

No early estate maps have been traced for the parish. The
first map on a reasonably large scale is Rocque's map of
Surrey, 1768-70 (two inches to the mile), which agrees very
substantially with the enclosure map of 1814 (13 and one-
third inches to the mile) if the new enclosures are removed,
but from neither of these maps can we get the names of farms
or their fields. The names of the old enclosures are given in
the Tithe Award of 1843, which is accompanied by a map on
the scale of 26 and two-thirds inches to the mile. In the meantime names of some of the minor physical features such as
fields, copses and lanes have been preserved from as far back
as the 14th century in court rolls and deeds, and some of these
names have already been mentioned in connection with the
manor records and the medieval villages. Many minor names
were not important enough to be recorded early, but they
become much more common by the 16th century, when field
names are found frequently in wills, leases and rent rolls connected with the parish. Many of them are obviously related

to such things as location, size, shape, appearance, function, characteristic feature or nature of the soil. For instance, Great and Little Kettle (Tithe Award Nos. 131, 132) are the names of fields next to Lightwater brooks. This is probably the same as 'le Ketele' found in the mid-16th century, and derives from O.E. *cetel*, a kettle, which in names connected with water may mean a bubbling stream. Another name still used in the Award is Jolly Robin (No. 306, an acre of meadow near Broadway Bridge), which is recorded in 1523 in a court roll, and may refer either to a person or to the bird. About 1400 surnames became settled and hereditary, and people then began to give their names to places, so that a considerable proportion of minor names are found to refer to people holding the land, though it is not always possible to distinguish a surname from some other type of name. Field names can, of course, help in tracing holdings and amalgamations of land, but records often skip intervening owners' names, and 'late so and so' can mean any time in the past! A large number of names in the Tithe Award are probably of fairly recent origin, dating to 18th-century enclosures. Roundabouts, for example, which is applied to seven acres of arable near Hatton Hill, usually refers to a field surrounded by a wood or with trees in the middle.

The earliest point at which we can obtain any proper idea of the size and location of the farms is at the beginning of the 19th century. A valuation of property for the poor rate (1808) lists the farmhouses, their owners, and occupiers, and in 1812 landowners presented their claims in connection with the enclosure of the waste. Sometimes the farms and their fields are described in some detail.[18] Stevenson suggests that in general the size of farms in the western part of Surrey around Bagshot at this period was 150 to 200 acres,[19] but of the 12 farms within the parish of Windlesham, four were between 100 and 150 acres, four between 50 and 100 acres, and the remaining four about 50 acres or less.[18] Most of the farms were owned by landlords from elsewhere. Astagehill, Broadways, Manor, Twelve Oaks, Ulliams, and the farm owned by Edward Hatch, were all farmed by tenant farmers, the family names of only two of the farmers being encountered before the 18th century. Three owner-farmers were descendants of older farming families: John Taylor of Harrishaws and Stawdway, James Lane of Highfields, and Rev. Henry Hammond of

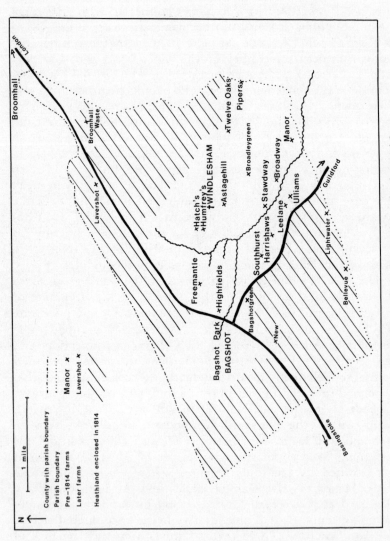

Fig. 3.   Approximate location of farms in the parish.

Southhurst. Richard Dare of Freemantle Farm, Henry Rogers of Home Farm, and Thomas Humfrey had acquired their land in the 18th century. Farming units are not of course necessarily contained within one parish and farms in Chobham had land over the border in Windlesham and vice versa. For example, Piper's Farm was owned by William Beauchamp of Russell's Farm, Chobham. Manor Farm included one meadow in Chobham, while part of Broomhall Farm, Berkshire, was in the parish of Windlesham. The proprietors of all the farms owned between them a little less than two-thirds of the land of the parish, excluding the large area of waste.

The farms are given below alphabetically by name of farm or (where not known) by name of owner. (For location see Fig. 3.)

Astagehill. This seems to have consisted of land which was held of Fosters by John Strangeways in 1694.[20] (The 1596 Musters include a Jasper Stranguish, husbandman; the surname derives from Strangeways, Manchester, a branch of the northern family being prominent in Dorset by the 15th century.) At the time of the enclosure William Try claimed 26 acres of land and 19 acres in the common fields. The first part of the name Astagehill derives from Eastersh or Eastage common field.

Broadway. In 1637 the chief free tenant of the manor of Fosters was John Attfield 'of Broadwaies'.[21] With this holding were incorporated two parcels of land held of St. John's College.[22] One parcel, which belonged previously to the Stroude or Strode family, was probably near Stawdway Green. The other parcel was called 'White's': the lane from near the farm to Hook Mill was earlier known as 'White's Lane',[5] and a field off the lane was named White Field in the Tithe Award. The Godfrey family were the farmers in 1812, when the owner (Hufsey Fleet) claimed a house and 133 acres. The disposition of the land was not given, but Fleet was allocated 12 acres in Eastersh common field and nearly 12 acres in Down common field.

Broomhall. Some of the land of the manor of Broomhall was in Windlesham. At the time of enclosure 106 acres were already enclosed on both sides of the main road, although about half of this (on the south-east) may only have been taken in from the waste in the later 18th century as it is not shown on Rocque's map of 1768-70.

Freemantle. This was now owned by Richard Dare and used at least in part as a nursery. It consisted of about 50 acres held of the manor of Fosters by James Attfield in 1683.[20]

Harrishaws. The name appears as 'Harry Shaws' in 1536 in the will of William Chotter (Chuter).[23] Among the late possessions of the Priory of Newark *c.* 1547 was a parcel of arable called Harrishawes, for which Alan Lee paid 5s. a year.[24] The holding seems to reappear in 1683 as part of the manor of Fosters; the tenant was George Taylor, and it remained in the Taylor family thereafter.[20] At the enclosure it consisted of 21½ acres (of which four and a half were in the common fields) owned by John Taylor and William Ellis.

Farm owned by Edward Hatch. This was near Coopers Green. The land, which was held partly of the manor of Fosters[20] and partly of St. John's College,[22] [25] came to Hatch through Richard Sorrell, son-in-law of a John Wise in 1700. It seems likely that this is the farm of John Wise, an important yeoman of the late 16th century, and it may be connected also with Richard Wisdom, whose will of 1550 mentions a house called 'Copers' and some of the same fields (see Chapter 4). In 1812 the farm consisted of 80 acres of land with 12 acres in the common fields: the farmer, William Perrin, then had a farmhouse in Church Road.

Highfields and New Farm. The enclosure claim made by James Lane covered 101 acres in several different parts of the parish. The nucleus of Highfields (later Hillhouse Farm) seems to have been in land north-east of Bagshot village in what may once have been common field. New Plantation or New Farm at the west end of Bagshot dates back to Daniel Mower and the second half of the 17th century. Both these parcels of land were held of Fosters.[20] Lane also owned 17 acres of arable not far from the *King's Arms.* This was then known as Surridges and could be the same as 'Southwich', arable land earlier held of the manor of Bagshot.

Home Farm (later Leelane). The claim of Henry Rogers details 34 acres at Home Farm itself, 12 at Hook Green, and 10¾ in the common fields. The earlier history of the farm is obscure, but the land at Hook Green was certainly held of Fosters and was acquired by Henry Rogers by 1749.[26]

Farm of Thomas Humfrey. This was next to Hatch's farm. The land seems in the main to have belonged to the Hart family previously (see Chapter 4), some of it being held of Fosters. In 1749 John Hart the younger held of St. John's College 35 acres of arable and five acres called Inkery Mead[25] and Humfrey's land in 1812 included a five-acre meadow of this name. In 1690 John Hart, yeoman, was presented at Quarter Sessions for obstructing a water-course to a place called 'Ingre alias Ingram Stone', which had always been in common use:[27] this is probably the ditch through Inkery Mead mentioned in Chapter One. Humfrey also owned Delham Field, which suggests that this area is part of 'Delham lands', an important holding in St. John's manor of Windlesham in the 16th century. Humfrey's farm consisted of 79 acres of which 17 acres were in six common fields, and the Humfreys were also the millers at Hook Mill:

Manor Farm. The history of this 125-acre farm, with which the Chitty family were associated for nearly 200 years, has been largely dealt with under the manor of the Dean and Canons of Windsor. The claim is missing from those made at the enclosure, but the Dean and Canons received eight acres in Thorndown common field.

Piper's Farm. A house and 16 acres of land on the Chobham border which was held of Fosters in 1694 was known as 'Pipers'.[20] (The name is probably connected with John Pyper who held land near here of St. John's College about 1400.[28]) In the later 18th century William Beauchamp of Chobham acquired the land, and in 1801 he purchased Halegrove or Russell's Farm, part of which was in Windlesham.[29] The enclosure claim concerned 33 acres.

Southhurst. In 1683 the land which became known as Southhurst Farm was held of the manor of Fosters by John Hamond.[20] It was still owned by the Hamond or Hammond family at the time of the enclosure, when the Rev. Henry Hammond (perpetual curate of Horsell) claimed 92 acres of arable, meadow and pasture. None of this seems to have been in the common fields.

Stawdway. This farm near the Bourn brook was owned by John Taylor and was probably run in conjunction with

Harrishaws which was just south of the brook. The land was held by George Taylor of St. John's College at the beginning of the 18th century.[25] There were 18¾ acres at the enclosure, of which 9¾ were in the common fields. The name occurs both as Stawdway and Strawdway, while in 14th-century deeds of Broomhall Priory it is found as Stordeway or Fordeway, so that it is not clear whether it comes from O.E. *strod,* marshy land, or is connected with a ford nearby over the brook. The farmhouse appears on later 19th-century maps as Old House Farm.

Twelve Oaks. The farm is first referred to by this name in 1547, when land called '12 okes alias preyplace' was held of St. John's College: in 1512 this land seems to have been called 'Ryelands alias Merlecrofte'.[22] The land was acquired by Doctor Thomas Doughty,[25] who also acquired Hook Mill and 'Ryeland and Rye Grove', held of the manor of Fosters.[20] He apparently amalgamated the properties before 1680.[30] The farm subsequently passed through the Sorrell and Hatch families, but at the time of the enclosure it was owned by the Rev. James Pears (of Pirbright), and was farmed by Thomas Fladgate. It then consisted of 107 acres and seven acres in Scutterley common field.

Ulliams (later Rectory Farm). The land was held of St. John's College and the name first occurs in 1523 when it belonged to John Chipps; it appears as Ully's, Ullons, or Ullows, and passed from the Chipps family to Henry Lee by 1588.[22] The holding is last entered in St. John's records in a rent roll of 1749.[25] Stephen Yates owned it at the enclosure, when the farmer was Henry Street and the total acreage 85 acres, including 10 acres in the common fields. Not long afterwards the farm was purchased by the rector, Rev. Thomas Snell, and re-named.

The Great West Road

Norden's map of Bagshot Park (1607)[31] includes a detailed picture of the compact village of Bagshot, situated on the great west road, with the road to Windsor branching off by the Park. The Bourn brook, flowing out of Bagshot Park, crossed the high street at the site of the later bridge, where it was joined by another stream which had crossed the street further to the west before running across the Guildford road. There were perhaps some 30 buildings in the village, including a number of inns and some shops. The gild founded at Bagshot in late medieval times suggests the existence there of a separate community of a social as well as a religious nature. In complete contrast to Windlesham, the importance of Bagshot must have lain in its positon on the road, and the contribution made to the communications network by its inns, which provided accommodation for travellers and stabling for their horses. How early did the road through the village become a major route?

It is likely that in earlier medieval times when Winchester was still very important, the main route through Bagshot was in fact one linking Windsor with Winchester, through Farnham. The Gough map of the mid-14th century tends to corroborate this. It is generally accepted that places which were shown on it though not on one of the marked roads, would normally be on important unmarked roads. The map thus showed Bagshot as a probable link between Windsor Castle and Farnham, but as it omitted Staines did not connect Bagshot and London. At this date the great west road from London to Exeter and Lands' End was routed to Salisbury through Kingston, Guildford, Farnham and Winchester. The route through Staines, Basingstoke and Andover to Salisbury did not become the main western route until perhaps early Tudor times. In 1571 Bagshot was shown in a French Guide de Chemins as a stage on this road from London to Exeter via Basingstoke.[32] The London end of the main road as far as Bagshot was also the route of the London, Farnham and Southampton road which Ogilby indicates (in 1675) leaving the Exeter road just beyond Bagshot at the Frimley border.

From the late 16th century, traffic on the roads increased, mainly owing to the development of London, and of foreign trade. Southampton was now a major importing centre, and goods landed there were conveyed to London by cart and waggon. Post horses were supplied to travellers at regular intervals, and in 1658 a stagecoach from London took two days to Salisbury and four to Exeter. The great increase in travelling by well-to-do people encouraged the activities of highwaymen on the notorious Bagshot Heath, which was

then very much more extensive. The popular association of
the area with such events is illustrated by the fact that John
Gay in the *Beggar's Opera* gave one of Macheath's gang the
name of 'Robin of Bagshot', while in Farquhar's *Beaux Strate-
gem* there is a highwayman called 'Bagshot'. The highwayman
William Davis, who was known as 'The Golden Farmer' (apparently because he paid all his debts in gold), leased a farmhouse
near the Basingstone in the middle of the 17th century. He
was executed and hanged in chains opposite his house in 1690.
His exact connection with the *Golden Farmer* inn, which stood
on the Windlesham side of the parish boundary, is not known,
but a full account of the legends surrounding him has been
given by Mr. Geo. C. B. Poulter.[33]

We have the occasional traveller's description of the great
west road and the heath which it crossed. Celia Fiennes, in
the course of her journeys at the end of the 17th century,
twice mentions passing through Bagshot on the way between
Basingstoke and London. She describes the road from Hart-
fordbridge to Bagshot and on from Bagshot to Egham as 'a
heavy sandy way', whereas that from Bagshot to Windsor (on
another occasion) over the forest was 'most Clay deep way,
the worse by reason of the raines and full of Sloughs'.[34]
Daniel Defoe, taking the coach road over Bagshot Heath in
the 1720s, compares the desolate area to a sandy Arabian
desert, '. . . a vast tract of land . . . which is not only poor, but
even quite sterile, given up to barrenness, horrid and frightful
to look on . . . nor are there any villages worth remembering,
and but few houses, or people for many miles far and wide
. . .'.[35] On the other hand, we have a contemporary comment
on the traffic in the locality by Magdalen Rackett (half-sister
of Alexander Pope), who was then living at Hall Grove. Visiting
Pope at Chiswick in 1718, she says '. . . Chiswick is a very lonely
place in comparison of Hallgrove; where, & whereabouts, there
are kept above 20 coaches, besides Stages on the Heath which
are without number'.[36]

Road Repairs: the Turnpike Trust

The increase in travel must have led to great strain being
placed on the exiguous repair facilities and to many complaints
over the state of the road. By the Highway Act of 1555 the

primary responsibility for roads, including the main highways where these ran through, had been laid upon the parish. On four (later six) days in the year every person holding land to a certain value, or keeping horses or plough, had to send a cart and two men to work on the roads; other inhabitants had to labour themselves, or send a substitute. An unpaid surveyor of highways was appointed as one of the parish officials. His main job was to view the roads three times a year and to organise the repairs. (Gravel from local deposits would be used: in the 19th century there were gravel pits at Ribsden and at High Curley and Black Hill on the Chobham Ridges.) Naturally many parishioners tried to avoid the work, and people were frequently presented at Quarter Sessions for not sending any labourers on the appointed days: in 1664 Richard Thare, Richard Slaughter, and John Butler (all yeomen of Windlesham) were presented, as was Widow Goffe.[37] The parish surveyor was doubtless unpopular as he attempted to get some work out of unwilling conscripts. A case came up at Quarter Sessions in 1665, in which it was deposed that on 15 October 1664 four labourers 'assembled riotously at Windlesham with swords, guns, staves etc. and made assault on John Newbery, one of the surveyors of the highways there'.[38] Parishes themselves were indicted and fined for failure to repair the roads; the fine would be applied to hiring labour to do the work, and this method was often used by the J.P.s. On more than one occasion the parish of Windlesham was presented at Quarter Sessions in connection with the main road. In 1681, for instance, it was reported that 'a common highway in Windlesham leading from Bagshot to Egham is out of repair; the Inhabitants of Windlesham are liable'.[39] One can readily imagine the problems of a small parish with only some 150 adult males which found itself responsible for five miles of an increasingly busy road.

It was to find a remedy for such problems that turnpike trusts and tolls were introduced. The earliest turnpikes were for the most part on the great routes from London to major provisional cities. A section of the great north road was the first to be turnpiked in 1663, and most main roads had been turnpiked for nearly the whole of their length by the mid-18th century. The great west road via Salisbury to Exeter was the last to be taken in hand: although the first Act was passed

in 1728, up to 1753 it was only turnpiked for some 40 miles
between Hounslow and Basingstoke.[40] A letter to the *Gentleman's Magazine* in 1754 complained that the road was a great
tract of 'terra incognita' with few turnpikes 'except, which is
certainly the wisest way, people go round by Bath or Wells'.[41]
(The whole 125 miles to Bath was already turnpiked.) Several
Acts had in fact already been passed in 1753 setting up trusts
for various sections of the road from Lopcombe Corner (a few
miles east of Salisbury) to Axminster and Exeter via Sherborne
and Yeovil.[42] Not long afterwards the alternative route from
Salisbury via Dorchester was turnpiked, and also the two roads
from Basingstoke to Lopcombe Corner via Andover or Stock-
bridge. Two further Acts had filled the remaining gaps in the
route by 1762.[43]

Under the Act of 1728 the Bedfont and Bagshot Turnpike
Trust had charge of the road from the Hounslow Powder Mills
to the Basingstone, an old stone which stood on the parish
boundary near the present *Jolly Farmer* inn. The preamble
to the Act referred to the road, 'part of the great road leading
to several trading towns in the West part of this kingdom',
having become 'very ruinous and bad'. The western parts,
'they being the most ruinous', were to be repaired first and
the first meeting of the trust was to be held at the *King's Arms*
inn at Bagshot.[40] The tolls laid down by the Act were as
follows:

Coach, chaise etc. ..	Drawn by 6 or more horses ..	9d.
	Drawn by 4 horses	6d.
	Drawn by less than 4 horses ..	3d.
Waggon, etc.	Drawn by 5 or more horses ..	9d.
	Drawn by 4 horses	6d.
	Drawn by 3 horses	3d.
	Drawn by less than 3 horses ..	2d.
Mule, horse	Not drawing	1d.
Drove of Oxen, Cows etc. ..	.. .. per score	10d.
Drove of Calves, Hogs, Sheep	.. .. per score	5d.

Repair work was immediately started on Bagshot Lane,
near Bagshot Park, which was to be 'well mended with Heath
Sand and Gravel laid round'. This was followed by Hallgrove
Hill and Shrubs Hill. In September 1733 Bagshot High Street
was viewed and the trust surveyor was ordered to make a
tumbling bay out of the watercourse into the street in order

to take off the overflowing waters in a flood. In 1743 16 milestones were set up along the road. (The first regular use of
milestones since Roman times was in 1727 when they were
set up on the old road to Cambridge between Trumpington
and Barkway; milestones were made compulsory by the general
turnpike Act of 1766.) The stones were ordered from Stephen
Hart of Chertsey, mason, for the sum of £2 10s. 0d. each. They
were of Portland stone, six feet high and one and a half feet
square: one example still standing in quite good condition is
the milestone nearly opposite the *Cricketers,* which indicates
26 miles from Hyde Park Corner.[44]

In 1763, for better organisation of repairs and taking of tolls,
the road from Hounslow to the Basingstone was divided into
two districts each having their own trustees. The western
section covered seven and a half miles from the 20th milestone
on Egham Hill to the Basingstone.[45] There was no tollgate on
this stretch and the minute book of the western trustees records
the decision taken at their first meeting on 20 May 1763 to
erect a tollgate at the east end of Bagshot. A temporary gate
was put up, and by early 1764 a permanent gate together with
turnpike house had been built at the eastern end of the pale
of Bagshot Park. Two gatekeepers were engaged and also a
supernumerary to attend when either of the regulars was unable
to be there. Fifty thousand tickets of different sorts were
ordered for issue to travellers. Up to 1787 the trustees continued to appoint their own gatekeepers, but there was more
than one instance when a gatekeeper was suspected of pocket-
ing some of the takings and was dismissed. It was decided to
let the Bagshot tolls at auction to the highest bidder for three
years from September 1787. The tolls, which were put up at
£471 (the net produce for the previous year), were leased for
£500 a year, though a deduction had afterwards to be made
for the cost of collecting the tolls which it was found had not
been allowed for. The tolls were put up to auction again in
1790, 1793, and 1796, at the amount specified in the current
letting.[46] Traffic was meanwhile increasing and there were
regular stagecoach services stopping at Bagshot.[47] The Poole
and Exeter mails, which left the G.P.O. at 8 p.m., travelling
through the night, reached the *King's Arms*, Bagshot (the post-
office), just before midnight:[48] mail coaches were usually
exempt from tolls. In 1796 the Bagshot Gate tolls put up at

£497 fetched £575; in 1799 it was thought prudent to let them for one year only, but this did not work out so well. In 1800 it was decided that it would be more advantageous to take the tolls direct again rather than to let them. This decision was probably influenced by the fact that a weighing machine had just been purchased by the trust, and the amount which would be produced by charges for overweight loads was unknown. In order to set up the machine it was necessary to move the tollgate to a more convenient spot 'between the old and new gateways of Bagshot Park' (probably near the *Cricketers*), and a new tollhouse was also built.[46]

The western trustees carried out quite a number of improvements and repairs in the village of Bagshot during the later 18th century. In 1768 a 'new' bridge was built over the Bourn brook by Edward Brown, bricklayer of Chertsey. We do not know the date of any previous bridge: though it might be expected that there would be a bridge replacing the ford by the 17th century, none is shown on any map, not even Rocque's map of 1768-70. In less than 10 years this bridge had broken down, and in August 1777 John Brown of Chertsey promised to rebuild it by 31 October of that year. He also gave a bond undertaking to maintain the bridge, which cost £232, against damage from floods for seven years. Details of how the foundations for the piers and side walls, and the arches and parapet walls, were to be constructed were entered in the minute book. There is no indication of the overall measurements of the bridge so presumably these were the same as those of the previous one, the materials of which were re-used.[46] A water-colour of Bagshot Bridge by John Hassell (1824) shows a not unattractive bridge with three brick arches as on early 20th-century postcards.[49]

In 1770 it was ordered that two brick arches be built across the road by 'The Cedars', evidently to channel the stream which crossed the road there, it having been reported two years previously that the road was 'much damaged by the rapidity of the waters'. Between 1770 and 1772 Bagshot Street was paved for 393 yards (approximately its length from Bagshot Bridge to 'The Cedars') with local heathstone. In 1792 orders were given for several improvements. The watercourse below the *King's Arms,* which presumably still ran across the Guildford road, was to be turned in such a way as to flow into the ancient watercourse running to Bagshot Green. On the south-eastern side of the High Street by the *Red Lion*, the open watercourse was to be arched over or filled up, and the road was to be widened on the opposite side by setting back some paling. Footpaths were then to be made on both sides to guard foot passengers, and paved with heathstone.[46] Footways of any sort were still fairly uncommon at this date: in London the new footpaths made by the Westminster Paving Commissioners in the 1760s and 1770s greatly excited the admiration of foreigners. Carl Moritz remarked in 1782 that 'one may there walk in perfect safety in no more danger from the prodigious crowd of carts and coaches than if one was in one's own room . . .'.[50]

Inns and Trade

The earliest references to inns occur in the 15th century. In 1417 a man was accused of stealing from 'one John Hostiller of Bagshote 8d. and a pair of knives worth 6d.'.[51] In 1486 the farm of a messuage called 'le Crowne', on demesne land of Bagshot manor, was granted by Henry VII to William Michell.[52] The *Crown* presumably stood near Crown Gate, which is shown on Norden's map at the south-west corner of Bagshot Park, where the second stream crossed the street. In Norden's time, there was a large building on the site of the 18th-century house, 'The Cedars', and this may have been the *Crown*. Together with the lands which went with it (Crown Meadow, six acres; Long Pyx, six acres; and Southwich, nine acres), the *Crown* was granted on many subsequent occasions with the office of keeper of the park.

By the mid-16th century there were at least four inns in Bagshot: the *Crown*, the *Bush*, the *Saracen's Head*, and the *Bell*.[53] In the list for the 1596 Musters, there were four innkeepers with 10 servants between them.[1] The *Bush* (innkeeper, Thomas Baker), owned 16 acres of pasture called 'le frith' (O.E. *fyrhoe*, woodland) off Thrift (modern Swift) Lane in 1609,[54] and there were still four acres called Bushey Thrift in the Tithe Award. A meadow named Edmonds Mead also belonged to the inn in 1609, and we may have a very early reference to the *Bush* in a deed of 1316–17 which refers to 'Pokenhale next the path of Bousses Mede'.[55] 'Pokenhale' may

be the same as Pucknells (Tithe Award No. 268), and Bousses
or Bushes Mead—which was probably Edmonds Mead—may
then be equated with Inner Meadow (Tithe Award No. 261).
Even before inn-signs developed, a bush or branch of evergreen
tied to the pole was used to indicate a tavern, that is an alehouse selling wine as well as ale. Taverns were under the control
of the Wine Commissioners, not the J.P.s, and in the 16th
century at least their numbers were restricted. The *Bush* was
certainly a tavern, for Thomas Baker, the landlord, was licensed
to sell wine in the town of Bagshot.[56]

The *Saracen's Head* (innkeeper, George Faroll), which was
to the west of the block in which the *Three Mariners* now
stands, was re-named the *Red Lyon* by 1603, when it was
mentioned by Faroll in his will.[57] Nearly opposite was the
Bell (innkeeper, Robert Brabant), which formed part of the
endowment of the John Stephen Chantry set up in the chapel
at Frimley.[58] In 1549 the inn was described as 'le Bell in
Bagshot with its shops . . .'.[59] The *Bell*, a timbered inn which
may date to the 15th century, is now hidden inside brick-
fronted cottages and shops at Nos. 75, 77 and 79 High Street.
It was a continuous jetty house of which as far as can be ascer-
tained five and a half bays remain. Running the length of the
back of the building was a gallery, framed as an open balcony,
part of which still exists. One of the bays has a higher ceiling
than the others, and this is thought to have been an entrance
for coaches.[60]

There were also a number of alehouses by the end of the
16th century: three 'vitlers' were named in the 1596 Musters,
and Robert Eliot left a house called the *Blackboye* (later the
Fighting Cocks) to his wife in 1596.[61] A water-colour of the
old *Cricketers* inn, now hanging in a bar at the hotel, has the
words 'Est. in 1605' painted on the end of the building, though
no other evidence has been found for this early date.

The only inns in Bagshot to be listed by John Taylor in his
'Catalogue of Taverns about London 1636' were the *Bush*
and the *Red Lyon*.[62] The *Crown*, which was included in royal
demesne lands in the rental of Bagshot manor of 1609,[63]
was not mentioned in the Parliamentary Survey of Bagshot
Park in 1650; its disappearance may be connected with the
Civil War. The *Bush*, too, disappears some time in the second
half of the 17th century, although it was still there in 1653

when the owner, Scipio Le Squire, claimed rights of pasture and turbary on Bagshot Heath. Some impression of the trade then enjoyed by the inn, owing to its situation, is conveyed by the reference made to expending turf and heath 'to brewe, bake, burne, and make fires to boile and roste there'. The owner goes on to claim the right to enjoy the springs of water rising at the west end of Bagshot south of the great highway or western road, which had always passed freely into the fishponds belonging to the inn in the grove next to the house 'and so from thence into the kitchin and brewehouse there in pipes of lead'.[64]

Meanwhile there was a new and important inn, the *King's Arms,* which a century later (1772) was insured against fire to the value of £1,530 in timber and £250 in brick. It was then described as two-storeyed, with part over a gateway.[65] The origin of the inn is not altogether clear. John Aubrey described it as 'a very fine inn, anciently a chauntry for the Freemantles'.[13] An inn with this name was mentioned, according to an obscure passage in Manning and Bray, in a court roll of the manor of Freemantle in 1660. The implication seems to be that the inn was what had been in 1509 a messuage held by the feofees of the chapel at Bagshot, which had lately belonged to William atte Mersh.[66] It is possible that this messuage was part of the endowment of the chantry, perhaps a 'chantry house' for the priest, and not the chapel itself.

There was some sort of connection between the *Bush* and the *King's Arms.* After the dissolution of chantries, Alice Molyneux (*alias* Brewer, a family connected with the manor of Freemantle) held of the manor of Bagshot a cottage called 'Marshes', and also the *Bush* inn.[53] The name 'Bush Grove' was given in deeds to fields between the *King's Arms* and 'The Cedars'.[67] Lands originally belonging to the *Bush* became the property of the *King's Arms,* but the two inns do not seem to have been one and the same, as the lands were still called 'the bush lands' in, for example, church rates of 1725. It is possible that the *King's Arms* and the *Bush* stood side by side for a little while. Two large buildings in the Hearth Tax of 1664, having 20 and 18 hearths respectively, may reasonably be identified with two inns.[68] One of them, which was occupied by John Kinsington or Kensington, an innkeeper who had been named as a suspected person (royalist) in 1655,[69] could

be the *King's Arms,* with which Kensington was later connected. The other building could be the *Bush*: it was occupied
by William Mower and an innkeeper of this name had had a
'sudden and lamentable fire' in his barn 'to the value of above
£300 to his utter ruin' only a few years earlier.[70] In 1669
William Mower issued a token coin, a halfpenny with a tree
on the reverse side.[71] Many token coins were issued for small
denominations by village traders about this time, owing to the
lack of copper coinage. They sometimes showed inn-signs,
but we cannot tell whether this one indicates the continued
existence of the *Bush*, or simply signifies 'a tavern'.

Trade continued to increase and between the late 17th
century and mid-18th century two more inns were opened:
the *Golden Farmer,* at the western parish boundary, and the
White Hart, by the Bourn brook. The first reference which
has been found to the *White Hart* by name is in 1763, when
the inn is mentioned in turnpike trust records. One account
of the duel fought on Bagshot Heath in 1763 by John Wilkes,
publisher of the *North Briton,* and Lord Talbot, steward of
the Royal Household, after Wilkes had ridiculed Talbot in his
paper, says that the two men dined together afterwards at
the *White Hart.*[72] There are two drawings of what seems to
be one and the same inn, a building in Georgian style, with
a bay window on the first floor and a hart depicted over a
columned entrance portico. One of them is entitled 'The
White Hart, Bagshot', while the other is dated 'Dec. 15 1787':
both are probably by Thomas Rowlandson.[73] Meanwhile,
the 16th-century *Red Lyon* (which is referred to in a deed
of 1782 as the 'new Red Lion') seems to have been rebuilt
or enlarged. In 1762 when the *Red Lyon* was insured for
£1,250 against fire (by Thomas Harris, junr., merchant of
London), it was described in the policy as a two-storeyed
building, half brick, half timber, with bow windows and
having a yard surrounded by stables with lofts and lodging
rooms over.[74]

The later 18th century saw the opening of two more inns.
In 1758 John Willimot, citizen and wheelwright, took out a
policy for £300 on a brick building 'being the first 4 houses
south west from the Brook & opposite the Rose & Crown &
in the possession of Wheatley, Bristow, Lacey & Hughes'.[75]
This must be the building which not long after became the

Three Mariners inn. The road through Bagshot was a convenient route for sailors travelling between Plymouth or Portsmouth and London, and the tradition is that the inn was opened by three brothers who had served in the navy. The building was occupied by William Middleton in 1780, and when Sarah Middleton, victualler, died in 1788, her will referred to the house in which she lived 'called the Three Mariners'.[67] The *Rose and Crown* opposite the *Three Mariners* was, of course the *Bell,* which must have been re-named by 1725, when Edward Greentree paid church rates on an inn of this name. By the 1780s the building had been sub-divided and was no longer in use as an inn. Round about this time an inn named the *Chequers* was erected by Richard Jenkins on Jenkins Hill at the west end of the village. Bagshot is first found in a commercial directory in 1791, when it was described as 'a very pleasant little town . . . remarkable for the neatness of its inns, and the good accommodations they afford to travellers'.[2]

It is hardly surprising that the small industries in the village in the late 18th century were associated with the requirements of travellers. There was more than one brewing business: the principal brewery occupied a brick and timber building in Brewhouse (now Park) Lane, and there was also a brewery at the *King's Arms.*[67] There was a tan yard by the brook near Bagshot Bridge. Water was essential for soaking the hides, and there may have been a tannery at the ford in medieval times, where travellers would get the leather harness for their horses and their own sandals and water bottles mended. Tanners are recorded from Tudor times: by his will proved in 1596 Robert Eliot, tanner, left the use of his tan vats to William Rawnce.[61] The lists of freeholders include as tanners Henry Vickrey in 1764 and Joseph Child in 1773. From 1801 Habbakuk Robinson is shown in land tax records as owner and occupier of the tan yard, but the extent of the business cannot be assessed.

4 The People of the Parish

WE HAVE SEEN SOMETHING of how the parish developed up to the end of the 18th century, its economic life based on the twin factors of agriculture and trading on the main road. What do we know about the people of the parish during this period?

Population

Firstly, what about the actual size of the population? The only information available before the first census of 1801 is to be found in taxation returns, ecclesiastical returns and parish registers, with church rate books also contributing some impression of the growth of the community. There was probably little if any net increase in the population between the mid-14th century (prior to the Black Death) and the mid-16th century. It has already been suggested that the population may have been between 200 and 300 at the peak of the medieval period. In 1547, when the particulars for the sale of chantries were taken, the number of 'houselinge' people (communicants) in the parish of Windlesham was said to be one hundred and forty seven.[1] In a return made by the Bishop of Winchester in 1603, the number of communicants was 218; there was one recusant (papist), but no other non-communicants.[2] The return made in the Compton census of 1676 gives 253 conformists, no papists, but two nonconformists.[3] We may disregard the small numbers who were not communicants of the Church of England. The three figures for communicants are roughly comparable, though the age limit for children may have varied in the different returns. If a ratio of 2·8 communicants per household (the average found for Leicestershire in a comparison between communicants in 1676 and Hearth Tax households in 1670[4]) is applied, we can arrive at some sort of estimate of the number of households in the parish at the three dates:

1547   147 communicants, 52 households
1603   218 communicants, 78 households
1676   253 communicants, 90 households

These estimates suggest something like a 50 per cent. increase in the population between 1547 and 1603. Over this period the country as a whole was in fact experiencing a population boom. In medieval times Bagshot had probably been smaller than Windlesham. By 1800 the population of Bagshot had certainly overtaken that of Windlesham, and it could be that it was in the later 16th century that Bagshot caught up, as a result of the increase in trade and travel. In the lists of men (aged between 16 and 60) for Surrey Musters in 1596, Bagshot men are slightly more in number than the men of Windlesham.[5] The erection of at least 10 new cottages on the waste of Bagshot manor sometime just before 1609 may well be an indication of this expansion.[6] During the first three-quarters of the 17th century, on the other hand, the increase in the parish population was very much smaller. As it happens, the number of households estimated above for 1676 is the same as the total number of occupiers (chargeable and not chargeable) in the 1664 Hearth Tax returns for Bagshot and Windlesham.[7] Although there was no doubt some evasion in connection with the number of hearths per household, it seems likely that the number of households is reasonably accurate. Opinion varies as to the factor for multiplication in order to assess total population, but one of four and a half to five persons to a household would give a population of some four hundred to four hundred and fifty.

Between the later 17th century and the end of the 18th century the population increased by round about two and a half times, for in the first census (1801) it was one thousand and sixty. This is in line with the general increase in the population of the country which accompanied the Industrial Revolution of the 18th century. The granting of 99-year leases for 33 houses and cottages by the lord of the manors of Fosters and Bagshot between 1715 and 1720 may be a sign of an increase in the parish population just before this.[8] Church rates show a noticeable increase in the number of people rated between 1725 (81 rated) and 1765 (110 rated).[9] These figures are roughly comparable with the figure of 59 in the Hearth Tax of 1664, when there were a further 31 households (that is one-third of the total of 90) who were too poor to pay any rates, but it is impossible to say whether this proportion would apply at the later dates. The only estimate of actual population which we have for the parish during the 18th century is one made by the rector in 1788. In answer to a visitation inquiry which asked the number of souls he supposed there to be in the parish, he gave a round figure of seven hundred.[10] This is likely to be an under-estimate: the natural increase (taken from parish registers) between 1788 and 1800 was only 147, which, since the population was 1,060 in 1801, would leave a very large number (213) to be accounted for by under-registration and/or immigration.

Parish registers do not start until 1677, the earlier ones having been lost in the fire. To what extent can they be used to estimate the rate of increase in the population at different periods during the 18th century? One book of baptisms which covers the period from 1677 to 1689, and two books of baptisms and burials (and marriages) covering 1695 to 1783 have been printed.[11] There is a gap between 1697 and 1717 and all the entries between 1695 and 1749 were badly kept. The date order of both baptisms and burials before 1728 is so erratic that it is often not clear which year is meant. Most of the entries between 1743 and 1749 are stated to be copies. The third book from 1749 is pretty well complete, and there are further books (at the parish church) which run from 1783 to 1810. So far as under-registration is concerned, although dissenters did increase significantly in the country as a whole from the last decade of the 18th century, there is no evidence of any substantial body of dissenters in the parish. The distance of Bagshot from the parish church may have led to some under-registration, which for obvious reasons would be more likely in the case of baptisms. There would almost certainly have been people from outside the parish settling in Bagshot in the later part of the century, when it was becoming steadily more important as a stop on the great west road.

Between 1721 and 1740 inclusive 228 baptisms and 236 burials were recorded, so that there was little if any natural increase. This period was one in which there tended to be little growth of population nationally owing to great mortality from epidemics. Above average numbers of deaths in Windlesham in

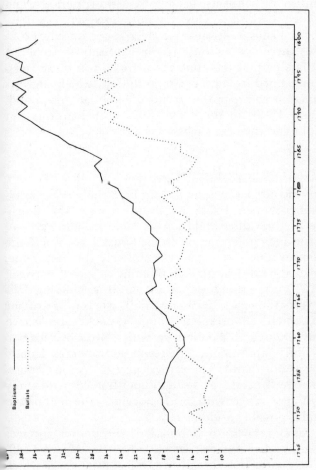

Fig. 4. Parish of Windlesham, population 1745-1800. Totals of baptisms and burials, smoothed out into five year running averages in order to show the trends more clearly. Both sets of figures include odd persons from outside the parish, but burials in 1800 of 15 soldiers and members of soldiers' families from regiments which must either have been stationed in Bagshot or in transit to and from Portsmouth have been excluded.

the years 1740, 1741 and 1742 suggest that the parish shared
in the effects of the very bad harvests general in those years.
Baptisms and burials between 1745 and 1800 are shown in
Fig. 4. From the middle 1750s an upturn in burials coincided
with a downturn in baptisms, leading to a short period when
burials exceeded baptisms. This did not, however, last long
and early in the 1760s baptisms rose clear above burials. From
the mid-1770s there was a steady rise in baptisms up to about
1790. In the last part of this time the increase was quite steep
and was accompanied by an increase in burials, which suggests
a rising population as emigration seems unlikely at this period.
From the early 1790s to the early 1800s both baptisms and
burials level out and then fall slightly.

Houses

From later medieval times, in areas where timber was available the timber-framed house began to replace the flimsy
constructions of the earlier Middle Ages, built from the ground
of either wattle-and-daub or mud. In the South East, where the
method of construction was almost exclusively the box-frame,
not the cruck, a great deal of such building occurred between
1400 and 1500. A second period of prolific building falls
roughly between the years 1570 and 1630, when many of the
substantial yeomen's houses had chimney-stacks and glazed
windows. Two houses at Windlesham which probably date to
the 16th century are 'Cooper's Green' and 'Astage House'
(formerly Astagehill Farm). The earliest part of 'Astage House'
appears from the outside to be a timber-framed two-storey
two-and-a-half bay range with brick nogging. The half-bay is
at the end and is possibly a smoke bay.[12]

With the rapid growth of population, the poorer cottages
also multiplied, and it was this which led to the Act of 1589,
whose purpose was to put an end to the inconveniences which
had resulted from the building of such cottages, 'which are
daylie more and more increased in manye parts of this realme'.
The Act provided that no one was to build or convert existing
buildings into cottages without setting apart at least four acres
of land to each, on which the occupier could grow crops for
the family. The land did not necessarily have to be adjacent to
the cottage, but might be in the common fields. This Act was

much evaded by the farmers, who begrudged the land, and there were frequent presentments at Quarter Sessions. In January 1668, for example, Thomas Sadler, late of Windlesham, yeoman, was presented because having built a cottage for habitation, he had not assigned to it or laid out four acres of land.[13] None of the poorer buildings will have survived from this period. The two 17th-century timber-framed 'cottages' still standing in Pound Lane, 'Pound Meadow' and 'Pound Cottage' (whose thatched roof comes down in hips to the ground floor ceiling), would have been the homes of lesser husbandmen or craftsmen, not mere labourers. The Act of 1589 excluded houses for tradesmen and craftsmen, who were obviously not so dependent on land for growing crops, and this probably explains the larger number of cottages built in areas which were not exclusively agricultural. Some of the 10 cottages which in 1609 had been 'lately built on the waste' of Bagshot manor on plots ranging from one perch to three-quarters of an acre, may have been for craftsmen. Of the 17 cottages listed altogether in the rental, 12 had two bays, four had one bay, and only one had three bays.[6] (A bay was the horizontal distance between one wallpost and the next—if could vary from four feet six inches to 16 feet.)

Some idea of the houses in the parish in the mid-17th century can be obtained from the Hearth Tax returns of 1664, though there is no precise relationship between number of hearths and number of rooms, and we have no inventories (often attached to wills, listing rooms and their contents) which might help. Bagshot Park Lodge (Earl of Newburgh) had 22 hearths, and there were seven other households which had between six and 20 hearths each. It seems probable that most of these were the larger inns (the *King's Arms* was probably the building with 20 hearths), but one may have been the house at Hall Grove. One-quarter of the houses in the parish had three, four, or five hearths. A number of these would be the houses of substantial farmers, with possibly six to nine rooms, as for example, hall, one or two parlours, kitchen and buttery, and two to four chambers above. Houses occupied by the two most important yeoman families (James Attfield and John Wise) had five hearths. Others may have belonged to larger tradesmen: a house occupied by a butcher (Humphrey Sutton) had three hearths. Another quarter of the households had two hearths; these were the homes of lesser husbandmen (with perhaps four to six rooms such as hall and/or kitchen, parlour, and one, two or three chambers above), or the premises of small shops or alehouses. One-third of the total had only one hearth, implying one, two or maybe three rooms, such as hall with lean-to, parlour/bedroom, with perhaps a chamber over the parlour; these were occupied by labourers or cottagers.

Some of the smaller dwellings may have been overcrowded. The Act of 1589 had prohibited the sub-letting of cottages: in 1662 it was presented at Quarter Sessions that William Edsore of Windlesham, husbandman, had 'kept Isaac Hart in his house there as a common subtenant . . . ever since April 1 1662 to the grave damage and depauperisation [*sic*] of the said parish'.[14] By the latter part of the 18th century, there was probably considerable overcrowding. There are several references in the rent rolls of the manor of Fosters to houses and cottages which, having been in single occupation in the early 1700s, a century later had been sub-divided into two or even three.

By 1700 brick was probably the predominant building material, as in most of the stoneless areas of the South East. The lower bands of the Bracklesham Beds consist of loam and clays well suited to brickmaking, and a number of pits were worked. (In the later 19th century soft red bricks made locally were known as Bagshot bricks.) In 1739 Thomas Finch, brickmaker, was granted the lease of a two-acre plot on Windlesham East Common by Abel Walter (lord of the manor of Bagshot) with permission to dig brick and tile earth. Documents relating to the purchase of the freehold by his son, John Finch (landlord of the *Cricketers*) in 1785 refer to brick and tile kilns.[15] Bricks and tiles were also made by the Gunner family at Ribsden (near the *Brickmakers' Arms*) off the Chertsey road.

There are indications that a number of the farmhouses were built or rebuilt in brick during the 18th century. A brick kitchen bay with side chimney was added at the back of Astagehill Farm, possibly before the end of the 17th century, as there are some darker bricks very similar to those used in the rebuilding of the church nearby (1680). The brick farmhouse in Church Road (Whitmore Farm) appears to date to the early 18th century, and may have been built for Richard

Sorrell. South Farm has the initials H.H. (for Henry Hammond) and the date 1736 carved on two flat bricks over the porch. The initials J.C. for John Chitty, and the date 1757, are to be seen on the older part of the building standing at Manor Farm Cottages; in 1869 the farmhouse was described as a small brick and tile building, with two sitting rooms, scullery and dairy on the ground floor and three rooms above.[16] When James Humfrey's farmhouse in Church Road was up for sale in 1889, it was said to be brick-built, with dining room, sitting room, kitchen, etc., and five bedrooms.[17]

Several attractive Georgian 'gentlemen's houses' were also built of brick. One of the first was the neat red brick house at the eastern end of Bagshot, now called the 'Queen Anne House'. In 1791 the directory refers to 'romantic villas and pleasant hunting seats which are dispersed more or less over every part of this prodigious waste [Bagshot Heath]'![18]

The Gentry

It was perhaps as a result of the improvement in road travel with the turnpiking of the main road in 1728 that more 'gentry' began to live in the parish. Up to the beginning of the 18th century, the only gentleman's house, apart from the Lodge in Bagshot Park, seems to have been the one at Hall Grove, which was apparently sold by the Attfield family to a Mr. Montague.[19] About 1700 it came into the possession of Charles Rackett ('Racout' in the 1701 list of freeholders), who had married Magdalen, half-sister of Alexander Pope, and they resided at Hall Grove until his death in 1728. From about 1700 to 1716 Pope was living with his parents at Binfield (Berkshire), some seven miles north of Bagshot, and there are several references in his correspondence to visits to Hall Grove, though he does not describe the house then standing. During some reconstruction work in 1957, half-timbering was found, which may have been part of this house.[20]

When Charles Rackett died, he seems to have left his family in some financial difficulty. The estate at Hall Grove was leased to a Mr. Butler, and Magdalen went to live with one of her sons. (A Mr. Butler, probably related to the Earl of Arran who was at this time residing at Bagshot Park, heads the list for church rates in Bagshot in 1725. In 1761 Mr. James

Butler was living at 'The Cedars' in Bagshot High Street.)
In 1731 the lands at Hall Grove were being let to a farmer,
while it was hoped that a certain Duke would lease the
house.[21] In January 1739 Pope told Michael Rackett (eldest
son of Charles) that although he had executed a deed to his
mother, the laws against papists

> render it Ineffectual to Secure that Estate from being taken
> possession of and Seized upon by Compares Executors for your
> Debt . . . the moment my Sister Dyes, they will inevitably Enter
> on the Estate, and Receive the Rents in your Stead till all the
> Debt be paid . . . The House will every year be worth less and
> less, (being in a Decaying State) and the Whole Land without it
> is let but at 55 *1* a year . . .

Pope advised Michael Rackett to join with his mother to sell
Hall Grove after her death to a protestant. Such a sale would
hold good in spite of the legislation against papists, and in
that way he might 'receive some hundreds of pounds soon'.
The estate was still unsold towards the end of 1739 and the
outcome is unknown.[22]

About 1769 Hall Grove was acquired by Ralph Leycester
of the Leycester family of Toft in Cheshire, and the house
now standing dates from this time. It originally had a mansard
roof, as pictured by W. Porden (before 1822) and H. Prosser
(in 1832).[23] The grounds, with plantations and lakes, were
presumably laid out by Leycester, who lived at Hall Grove until
about 1813, several children of Ralph and Charlotte Leycester
being christened in the parish church.

In the 1720s Brigadier Thomas Panton lived at the brick-
built house next to the church at Windlesham, now called
'The Cedars',[24] which was later bought by the rector, Rev.
Edward Cooper. According to the sale catalogue when the
house was put up for auction in 1969, it was built *c.* 1720
on Tudor foundations. The house still has the original painted
oak panelling in the dining room and a fine galleried oak divided
staircase.The house opposite the church, 'Birch Hall', is probably on the site of a 16th-century hunting lodge, but the main
part of the present house was built *c.* 1740. In the later 18th
century the property was acquired by a Mr. James Birch, who
added a wing at right-angles to the original five-bay brick block.[25]
'Woodlands' (now Windlesham Park) was built not long before
1796 for John Farhill of Chichester on 43 acres of land called

Woodlands, which he had bought in 1788.[26] In 1798 Woodlands was acquired by John Bradburne and it was to remain in this family until 1824, when it was sold to James Chamness Fyler of Monksgrove, Chertsey. There are two water-colours showing different views of this house in the early 19th century.[27] The late 18th century red brick house called 'Windlesham House' (in Kennel Lane) belonged to the Graham.family, who also owned at this time the old farmhouse at Coopers Green, now named Walnut Tree Farm. 'Hatton House' (later Hatton Hall), also an 18th-century house, was for some years the home of the Breton family.

Yeomen and Tradesmen

By the middle of the 16th century we can glean a little information about individual yeoman and husbandmen and their families. Most of this comes from wills: the will of Richard Wysdome (Wisdom), husbandman of Windlesham, made in 1550, is particularly informative.[28] He owned two houses, one of which called 'Copers' (presumably at Coopers Green) he bequeathed to his wife for her natural life, with all the land belonging to it, and all his other lands, except for various parcels of lands which he gave to his seven children. The other house, 'Somerfolds', went to his eldest son Richard. 'Somerfolds' was held (before the dissolution) of the Priory of Newark,[29] but its situation is not known. It is interesting to note that Richard Wisdom, who was perhaps typical of the husbandmen of earlier Tudor times, had 20 acres in the common fields. In the reign of Henry VII 20 acres had been considered 'a competent proportion of land' to provide for a family, which would 'of necessity enforce the dweller not to be a beggar or a cottager, but a man of some substance that might keep hinds and servants and set the plough on going'.[30] Each of Wisdom's four sons, Richard, John, Thomas, and Gregory, received five acres of land in the common fields, it being specified in the case of Richard that this was in 'fyve comen fyldes that is to saye in every fylde one aker'. Each son was also given a grove (Richard's grove was of two acres) and some meadowland. Each of the three daughters, and Harry Wisdom, the testator's brother, also received a parcel of meadow. The acreages are not stated, but the names are given, one of them being 'Hollond Mede', which in the Tithe Award was three acres. (There are two other meadows in the Award which are called Wisdom's Meadow, and these may be connected with the family.) Assuming that each meadow was two or three acres, Richard Wisdom had at least 20 acres arable, 16 to 24 acres meadow, 8 acres wood, as well as some other lands which are not described.

The fragmentation of the estate may have been the reason why the family did not become one of the more important families of Windlesham. In 1684 part of the Church lands was leased to Richard Wisdom, yeoman, but the lessee was apparently unable to write. The family persisted in the parish until the 18th century.

It was during the 16th century that many yeoman families achieved prominence. There was a great hunger for land as the rise in population and in prices speeded up the transition from medieval subsistence farming to farming for surplus and profit. Much land had moreover become available through the dissolution of the monasteries and the sale of Crown lands, and in the 16th and early 17th centuries land changed hands a great deal. Voluntary enclosure of open fields was being carried out for better production and there was much piecemeal enclosure by encroachment on commons and waste. In all these activities yeoman families of initiative and industry were conspicuous. At this period there was no typical yeoman holding: the size varied enormously and so did the nature, some yeoman having their lands scattered over the whole parish, some holding consolidated farms. Some land was held freehold, some copyhold, while many 'yeomen' did not own their land at all, but leased it on a long lease.

The Attfields, an important yeoman family, appear in Windlesham by the middle of the 16th century, but there were also Attfields in Chobham and other neighbouring parishes. John Attfield was a witness to several wills in the 1550s. William Molyneux released the manor of Freemantle to John Attfield in 1561,[31] and in 1588 John Attfield presented to the church as holder of the advowson.[32] There was more than one family of Attfields in the parish and it is not known whether this was the brother John to whom Nicholas Attfield of Windlesham left his house and lands in 1587.[33] Nicholas was comparatively well-off by the standards of the time. He was apparently unmarried and he gave legacies of, for example, £7 each to two children of a friend on their attaining 21 years of age. The Lay Subsidy return of 1593-4 gives an indication of the importance of the taxpayers and here a John Attfield was the highest valued at £8 in goods.[34] The Windlesham list for the 1596 Musters is headed by a John Attfield.[5]

In the 17th century the Attfields held land in all the manors. In his will of 1628 John Attfield the elder, yeoman of Windlesham, left his house 'in Bagshot called Holy Hull with all the lands belonging to it' to his eldest son John.[35] 'Holy Hull' (Hill) is said by Aubrey to be the old name of Bagshot,[36] but it seems possible that it was the name of the house. It is tempting to speculate that this was the house later called 'Hall Grove', which stands on relatively high ground, but the son, John Attfield, does not seem to have lived there. He was also to inherit, as well as the best bedstead, best feather bed and best brass pots,

> the furnace two great spitts all the standards about the house called Broadwaies as wainscotts portalls tables formes benches stands pondringe [?] tronghes and all other that may be standard to the house not named. Provided alwaies that my son John Atfeild shall leave behinde him at the house called Freemantells all the like standards as bee there and unfitt to be removed.

(The term 'standards' was used for the permanent furniture of a household.) It is interesting to see that the family owned or leased three houses. In 1637 a free tenant of the manor of Fosters was John Attfield of Broadways, presumably this son John who had moved from Freemantle Farm and was described in his will (1655) as being 'of Broadwaybridge'.[37]

John Attfield the elder had another son, Robert, and by the will of 1628 John the younger was to pay to his brother Robert £50, except that 'if Robert be preferred unto some spiritual living' the gift to cease. This may be the Robert Feild of Surrey, described as the son of a commoner when he matriculated in 1617, who became vicar of Woking in 1637 (and later vicar of Chobham),[38] and was named in connection with a court held for the manor of Freemantle in 1660. James Attfield, who seems to have been the son of John of Broadways, was probably living at Broadway Farm in 1664, but after he died about 1683 the farm went out of the family. It is not known who

occupied Freemantle farmhouse at the time of the Hearth
Tax, but it passed to the daughters of James Attfield after
his death, and in the early 18th century it, too, went out
of the family. In 1680 a John Attfield was one of the two
churchwardens, but as the family seem to have parted with
their houses not long afterwards, perhaps the main line
died out or moved away from the parish. From the 18th
century onwards, the representatives of the family were of
rather lower status.

Another yeoman family towards the end of the 16th century
was that of John Wise, who ranked slightly lower than John
Attfield in the 1593-4 Subsidy, having £6 in goods.[34] In 1606
John Wise, yeoman, who was brother-in-law to John Attfield,
left his land in Windlesham to his son John.[39] In 1694, however,
the current John Wise was a minor, and the family seems to
have died out soon afterwards, lands at Coopers Green passing
to Richard Sorrell, who had married Elizabeth, daughter of
John Wise.[40]

In Tudor and early Stuart times the average farmer might
possess one four-poster bed with a feather mattress. Secondary
beds would have only a flock mattress, but these were still
valuable enough to be mentioned in wills, together with the
sheets, bolsters, etc., which went with them. In 1592 a John
Attfield of Bagshot left to his wife Susan 'the best flock bed
in the parlour with all things that appertain unto the same
with a paire of sheets'.[41] The farmer would have only a few
brass pots and pans, a piece or two of pewter, a trestle table
and a form or bench in his living room. There are many
references to articles such as these in wills. For instance,
Thomas Edshaw, husbandman of Windlesham, in his will
(1604) left to his five sons and one daughter the following:
a great pan, a great brass pot, the best chaldron, a little pan,
a little pot, a great kettle, a round-bottomed kettle, another
kettle, and the pot 'which we customably use'. These would
be all the pots and pans which he had of any value, as several
of the items were not to go to his children until after the
death of his wife.[42]

As the earlier yeoman families disappeared or declined in
importance, others came to take their place by the later 17th
century. Edward Chitty, (three hearths in 1664) was probably
the farmer at Manor Farm, then on lease from the Dean

and Canons of Windsor to the Harward family; he was a witness
to the Harwards' lease of 1668, and about 1710 a 'Widow
Chitty' was the tenant. The inventory which would have been
attached to Edward Chitty's will, proved in 1684, is missing,
but if a note on the dorse of a figure of £331 relates to the
total value of his goods and chattels, these were quite substantial. The sum would no doubt include his farming stock, as well
as the furnishings of his house. By late Stuart times a prosperous yeoman would have a few pieces of silver. Edward
Chitty left a silver spoon to each of his two daughters, and
two pewter dishes each to his four sons and his unmarried
daughter. His eldest son, Roger, was bequeathed 'my great
Bible'.[43]

John Hamond (Hammond), who was also taxed for three
hearths in 1664, may have already been at Southhurst Farm,
which was farmed by a John Hammond in 1694.[40] There was
a Henry Hart (two hearths) among the third of the households
well off enough to pay the tax, and the Hart family were quite
important by 1694, when John Hart was joint lord of a moiety
of the manor of Freemantle.[19]

By the later 18th century we can identify families of important shopkeepers in Bagshot, by means of parish registers and
commercial directories. In 1763 an Edward Lewis, shopkeeper,
was buried, and in 1779 we find an Edward Lewis, grocer,
while in 1791 the family business had passed to Sarah Lewis.
The family can be traced as grocers into the 1830s. Another
family of grocers were the Everests. In 1779 Edward and Jane
Everest bought the *Black Bull* alehouse opposite the *King's
Arms* and converted it into their shop. The couple had had
three daughters, all of whom died within a few days of birth,
but their fourth child, Jane, survived, probably inheriting the
grocer's shop, which remained in the family up to 1838. The
Jenkins family of Jenkins Hill were butchers. After the death
of Richard Jenkins in 1785, his wife, Grace, was butcher as
well as alehousekeeper at the *Chequers,* and the sons, Richard
and Thomas, carried on the business to the 1820s. Another
butcher's business belonged to the King family. The burial
of Thomas King, butcher, is recorded in 1777, George King
ran the business in 1791 and the family were still butchers
till the 1830s. The Laird family, who were bakers, built the
attractive 18th-century building known as 'Laird House' (at

one time Bagshot Rural District Council Offices), and John Laird was a baker in 1832.

The Poor

About the poorer families next-to-nothing is known before the late 18th century. In early times the poor and sick had been dependent on alms given by the monasteries and on the charity of the better-off. After the dissolution of the monasteries, most parishes had some sort of alms collector. It was quite common for parishioners to leave money in their wills—the amount varying according to their means—to be distributed amongst the poor of their parish. There are many instances in Windlesham wills. For example, Nicholas Attfield left 20 shillings to the 'poor and nedde foulkes' in 1587;[33] Thomas Baker left 10 shillings to the poor of Windlesham in 1612;[44] John Attfield gave £5 in 1628, 20 shillings to be distributed at the time of his funeral, and a similar amount yearly during the next four years. He also provided for a 'pension' of 10 shillings yearly to be given to Anne Watts, 'a poor servant', unless his wife or his son kept her in their house.[35]

The office of overseer of the poor probably originated in that of alms collector. Under a series of Acts in 1572, 1597, 1601 and 1640, the responsibility for poor relief, the main recipients of which were widows and orphans, the aged and the disabled, was laid firmly upon the parish. Unpaid overseers were appointed annually by the J.P.s from lists drawn up by parish vestries, and their job was to maintain and (where possible) set to work the poor, the funds being provided by local taxation in the form of a poor rate. In 1662 the law of settlement and removal was introduced, and further Acts of 1691 and 1697 elaborated the provisions. Any stranger settling in a parish might be removed by an order from the J.P.s unless he gained a settlement in one way or another, or found security to discharge the parish from any possible expense. To gain a settlement it was necessary to rent a tenement of an annual value of at least £10, bear a parish office, pay a parish rate, be apprenticed to a parishioner, or serve one year in employment. Poor persons entering another parish were required to bring from their own parish, normally where they were born, a certificate agreeing to take them back if they proved a charge on the rates.

Unfortunately little remains to illustrate the working of the poor law in Windlesham before 1800. With regard to the number of poor people, in the Hearth Tax (1664) the average of non-chargeable entries in rural areas generally was about one-third of the total entries, whereas in Windlesham it reached two-thirds. Whether this was due to extreme poverty or to leniency in the granting of exemptions by the minister and overseers we do not know. Of the 61 non-chargeable entries (out of a total of 90), 31 were non-taxpayers, that is, too poor to pay the usual church and poor rate, while 30 were specially exempted from the hearth tax.[7] Exemptions were authorised if the house or any goods possessed were worth less than £1 and the occupier's annual income did not exceed £10. Some removal orders, settlement orders, and indentures for poor apprentices covering the 17th to 19th centuries were in existence up to about 1927. There were also some poor rate books with overseers' disbursements from 1717 onwards, and overseers' bills, etc., for late 18th and early 19th centuries.[45] All of these seem now to have disappeared, and parish records in connection with poor law administration begin with a rate book for 1800 and account book for 1804. Some earlier information can, however, be obtained from other sources.

Quarter Sessions Order Books provide examples of the sort of problems common to most parishes during the 18th century, when growing populations and rising prices led to increasing demands on poor relief. For example, disputes frequently took place between parishes as to liability for poor people, and the expenses which fell on the poor rate in connection with removal and litigation at court were considerable. In May 1729 Windlesham lost their case against Holy Trinity (Guildford), when they appealed against the removal of a certain Rachel Harris back from Guildford to Windlesham.[46] The job of unpaid overseer of the poor was not an enviable one, and parishioners would avoid it if they could. In October 1729 the appeal of Henry Procter (of Broadways Farm) against being made one of the overseers for Windlesham was allowed.[46] Parliamentary returns also contain some local information. In early days able-bodied paupers who were set to work by their parish remained as domestic outworkers in their own cottages, but in 1722 an Act was passed permitting parishes to buy or rent workhouses and to refuse relief to those declining to enter.

It is unlikely, however, that the workhouse at Bagshot Green was in use much before the last decade of the 18th century. A return was made by overseers of the poor in 1776 about workhouses in their parish, the number of people they could accommodate, and the rent paid for the building: Windlesham overseers made a nil return on these points.[47]

Charitable provision had, however, been made by some of the gentry for lodging the poor who were incapable of work. Six almshouses (to which the workhouse later adjoined) were built by James Butler, late an officer in the navy, 'at his own expense in the year 1761, for three poor widows and three poor widowers'.[48] Each cottage contained two small rooms.[49] In 1757 Lady Amelia Butler (of Bagshot Park) had given £100 for a pest-house to be built for the sick on the western outskirts of the parish. This was described in 1824 as having four rooms on the same floor, with three acres of land in front of it called Lambourn Moor. At that time the house and land were let to John Willmot, but he was bound to 'reserve one apartment for parishioners afflicted with small-pox, etc.'[49] The upkeep of the poor- and pest-houses did not fall on the poor rate. In 1768 a certificate was signed by the lords of the manors and the freeholders of the parish, agreeing to give up their right in two pieces of ground, one of which was behind the poor-house and one in front of the pest-house, so that the rents of these two pieces should go to pay for repairs to both houses.[49] The book of church rates and churchwardens' accounts for 1765–81 includes from 1771 onwards new receipts for rents of the lands referred to in the certificate. For example, rent for one year (£3 13s. 0d.) of land near the pest-house was paid by Richard Jenkins of the *Chequers*. There are likewise items of expenditure on repairs. In 1774 'pantiles and carriage for poor and pest house' cost 7s. 6d., and 9s. was spent on repairing the poor- and pest-houses. In 1776 a further 300 house tiles were purchased for the poor-house at a cost of 7s. 6d.[50] The pest-house, together with the piece of land on Lambourn Moor, was later sold to pay for the share of the parish towards building the new Chertsey Union workhouse (1836–7).[51]

There were other charitable gifts to the poor and needy. Following on his will of 1626, Henry Smith's charity was being distributed in Windlesham as in other Surrey parishes, and in 1788 this amounted to about £7 10s. 0d.[10] George Chewter's annuity (1754) was paid out of Daniel Moore's plantation at the west end of Bagshot (now forming part of Waterers' nurseries), 25s.-worth of bread being distributed on the first Sunday after quarter days.[49] In 1809 Mrs. Eleanor Strange gave the annual income on £100 to be outlayed in wearing apparel for six poor widows, which was to be distributed at Christmas.[49]

Meanwhile the problem of the poor had become acute. In 1776 the amount raised by the poor rate in Windlesham was £166,[47] and during the years 1783, 1784 and 1785 it averaged £211,[52] but in 1803 the amount raised had more than trebled to £720. It was now stated that there were 31 people in the workhouse, while 26 were being regularly assisted outside, and a further 31 had received occasional relief.[53] A schedule of documents which were once in the Parish Chest included an agreement dated 1800 between the inhabitants of the parish and Mr. Nathaniel Williams (of the *King's Arms*) for repayment of £302 advanced by him for building additional rooms in the workhouse.[54] (Overseers' accounts of 1823-4 show that the 'poorhouse'—presumably the workhouse is here meant—was then being rented from Williams at £1 17s. 6d. a quarter, and £100 was paid to him in addition during the year 'towards purchasing workhouse rooms'.) A 'manufactury of brooms' was being carried on at the workhouse, for which the poor pulled heath.[55] The amount of money expended on materials for the poor *in* the workhouse during 1803 was £13 3s. 4d. The amounts earned by the poor were as follows: *in* the workhouse, £29 11s. 11d., and *out* of the workhouse, £18 6s. 9d.[53] Broom-making continued as a village craft until late in the 19th century.

Early Schools

In the early 19th century, two school societies were founded: the nonconformist Royal Lancastrian Society, founded in 1808, re-named British and Foreign School Society in 1810, and the National Society for the Education of the Poor in the Principles of the Established Church throughout England and Wales, founded in 1811. Before this, however, elementary education in the rural areas was either non-existent, or at best haphazard. Small local schools came and went, and even the existence of a schoolmaster in a certain place at a particular time may not prove that there was a continuing school. In small villages like Windlesham and Bagshot, it is quite possible that there was no school much before the 18th century, A few boys may have been taught by the rector, but any other schoolmaster would have had to have a licence from the Bishop of Winchester. The first evidence of schooling which we have is that two Dame schools existed at the time of the visitation of Bishop Willis in 1724-5.[56] In reply to question No. 8 of the visitation inquiry made by the Bishop of Winchester in 1788, the rector stated that there were no endowed schools in the parish. There were, however, four day schools: the number of scholars was not given.[10] The 1791 Directory shows a James Harrison as schoolmaster at Bagshot, and in 1808 George Harrison was the occupier of a house, shop and school.[57] It is tempting to associate this with the fact that in 1803 there were 45 children in a 'school of industry',[53] and to wonder whether the items made by the children were sold in the shop. Schools of industry, where boys were taught such things as carpentry and cobbling, and girls were taught spinning, sewing and straw-plaiting, had become common in the 18th century. The schools were supposed to be self-supporting: the objects produced were sold, the money going to the maintenance of the child, who might be allowed to keep earnings in excess of the cost of his keep. Some of these schools did teach children reading and writing, but there was a natural tendency to emphasise the occupational aspect.

In 1807 the Rev. Edward Cooper left £5 5s. annually in his will for the purpose of teaching poor children reading, writing and arithmetic, and this was in due course applied in support of a National school (see Chapter 5).

Early Nonconformity

There is little evidence of the nonconformity which is often found in parishes without a strong resident 'squire', such as this one seems to have been. Perhaps the presence of royalty or its representatives at Bagshot Park cast, as it were, the shadow of 'the establishment'. As we have already seen, in the episcopal return of 1603 there was only one male papist

recusant and no other nonconformists, and in the Compton
return of 1676 there were two nonconformists and no papist
recusants.[2,3] From 1689 nonconformists, and from 1791
Roman Catholics, had to register their places of worship. If
such registrations were made for Windlesham before the end
of the 18th century, either with the clerk of the peace or with
the diocesan authorities, they do not seem to have survived.
The visitation of Bishop Willis (1724-5) does, however, provide
a little information. The papists then numbered four: George
Boteler, Esq., 'whose estate is in Ireland', the wife of Thomas
Paxton, Esq. (presumably Brigadier Thomas Panton of 'The
Cedars'), a weaver, and the wife of a labourer. There were
also 'seven or eight mean persons who call themselves Anabaptists'.[56] Two visitation inquiries (in 1764 and 1788)
asked about the number of papists and protestant dissenters,
and whether they had any meeting houses for divine worship
in the parish. The rector replied in 1764 that there were papists
and Anabaptists but no meeting houses.[58] In 1788 he said there
were no dissenters at all.[10]

Local Administration

During this period the Justices of the Peace held a central
position in local government as the county authorities. They
were generally responsible for law and order, and were concerned with an increasing variety of matters, such as the poor
law, highways, dissenters, and so on: we have already come
across some illustrations of this in connection with Windlesham.
Within the parish communities, vestries tended to become more
important from the end of the 16th century as the manorial
system declined but, owing to a complete lack of vestry
minutes, it is not possible to say much about the vestry in
Windlesham. There were several manors with lands distributed
about the parish, in some cases intermixed in the common
fields, and the power of the vestry probably arose at an early
date, as the only common source of administration of local
affairs, such as the regulation of common field planting, and
the use of waste land. The lords of the manors were seldom
resident, being in two instances (St. John's College, Cambridge,
and the Dean and Canons of Windsor) corporate bodies. It is
possible that the house at Hall Grove is most nearly to be

equated with the 'manor house', in which case the Attfield family in the late 16th and early 17th centuries (if they *were* at Hall Grove), and Ralph Leycester during his 40-odd years there from the later 18th century, would be the closest to resident lords, but there is really no evidence. In view of the weak manorial control, the villages (particularly Bagshot) were probably of an 'open' type, that is, one where settlers were not discouraged and there was reasonable freedom and social mobility. Cottages may have been put up fairly easily on the large area of unenclosed waste. Most of the houses were freehold, and the Earl of Onslow agreed in the early 1800s to enfranchise many of the remaining leasehold ones.

Reference has been made to the separate nature of the settlements at Bagshot and Windlesham, but it must be borne in mind that from Tudor times onwards, when responsibilities were laid on parishes in connection with the poor, vagrants, repairs to highways and many other matters, the appointment of overseers and surveyors would have tended necessarily to increase contact. By the time the names of overseers are known they seem to be appointed one from each place.

I (*above*) Windlesham church, lithographed by C. T. Cracklow (1823): the church as rebuilt in 1680, after it was struck by lightning.

(*below*) The church today, still looking much the same from the southwest, in spite of the alterations and additions of the later 19th century.

II From the water-colour by John Hassell *c*.1824. This must be the 'old parsonage', and may have been occupied by a curate, as at this time the rector lived elsewhere. The house was probably down Rectory Lane, where the new rectory was built in 1840.

III Cattle grazing on the old 'church path' which runs across the field from Bagshot. Windlesham parish church is just visible to the left o the trees.

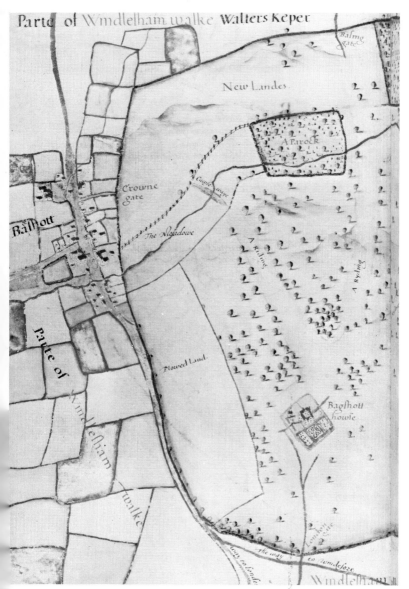

V The village of Bagshot, with the royal lodge and part of the park, as depicted by John Norden in 1607. A branch of the brook crossed the main road at the western end of the village and ran over the Guildford road in front of the *Red Lyon*, near the later *Three Mariners*. The large building on the right almost opposite the *Red Lyon* was the *Bell*, and the signs of both inns can just be seen hanging out into the street.

V Bagshot Park in the later 18th century.

VI This lithograph by G. F. Prosser makes an interesting contrast in style with the picture of the same house in plate V. The building was enlarged for the Duke of Gloucester in the 1820s.

VII Will of Richard Wysdome, husbandman of Windlesham, made in 1550. The second page of the will, bequeathing his house 'called copers' (Coopers) to his wife for life, and various meadows named 'warbroks', 'hollond', 'pendreds' and 'Jakegybbs' to his sons and daughters.

VIII Astagehill: *above* the old farmhouse *below* the granary. The house adjoined Eastersh (also called Eastridge or Eastage) and Ashington common fields. The earliest part of the building (on the right) is probably 16th century; a kitchen bay was then added (left rear), and finally the section in front of it which completed the square. The house is still in use, being occupied by staff of Fromows' nurseries. The granary about 12 ft. square was built much later than the house.

IX This water-colour by John Hassell, painted in 1822, is a bit of a puzzle. It may represent somewhere near Coopers Green and the junction of School Road, Church Road and Kennel Lane. (The latter was formerly called Dogkennel Lane: it was renamed by the new Windlesham Urban District Council in 1910).

X Bagshot Bridge, from the water-colour by John Hassell 1824. A 'new' brick bridge built by the turnpike trust in 1768 was rebuilt in 1777 after it had broken down. The bridge was replaced by the present concrete structure in 1925.

XI Hall Grove in 1832. The house with mansard roof built by Ralph Leycester about 1769 is here pictured from the south in a water-colour by H. Prosser. The roof was altered in Victorian times, when bays and a west wing were added.

XII Woodlands (Windlesham Park) in 1832, from the water-colour by H. Prosser. The house was built about 1790 and has been altered and enlarged on more than one occasion. It was renamed after the First World War.

XIII Grave of John Waterer the elder and his third son John Waterer the younger, in Bagshot old cemetery. Owners of the Bagshot Nurseries, between them they spanned some fifty years of the later 19th century. They were active in all aspects of local affairs.

XIV The old saddler's shop at Bagshot in the late 1880s. The shop, next door to the *Three Mariners*, was opened in 1780, and the Houlton family were associated with it for nearly a hundred years. In the picture are Henry (with the horse and cart) and Walter, sons of James Houlton, who then carried on the business for their widowed mother. The paving setts in front of the shop are part of the pavement of local heath stone laid by order of the turnpike trust in 1792.

XV The railway station at Bagshot, described when it was opened in 1878 as 'pretty and comfortable'. In the background, the iron footbridge carrying the 'old church path' across the line.

XVI The railway bridge over the Guildford road at Bagshot in the early 1900s, when the scene beyond was still quite rural. In the foreground (left) is the old police station — Bagshot was one of the first four stations of the Surrey Constabulary started in 1851.

XVII The stepping stones at Bagshot Bridge *c.*1900. Compare Hassell's painting (plate X).

XVIII The eastern end of the High Street at Bagshot in the early 1900s. The row of shops on the left (including not long before a beerhouse called 'Hit or Miss, Luck's All') is the site of the old *Bell* inn. Over the bridge is the house known as Hart Dene, which probably incorporated parts of the former *White Hart*.

XIX The Square in the early 1900s. The large premises of W. S. Stanley, draper and outfitter, had only recently been opened.

XX High St. Bagshot from the Square, looking west, early 1900s. The *King's Arms* was then still right on the road: it was rebuilt set back in its present position in 1938.

XXI High St. Bagshot, western end. Probably one of the earliest postcard views of Bagshot, postmarked 1904. Note the *Hero of Inkerman* in its original position before the bypass was opened. (There was a beerhouse in Broadway Road, Windlesham, called the *Alma* after another of the battles of the Crimean War.)

XXII A 'new' postcard view of Church Road, Bagshot, probably taken just before the First World War, when these houses had fairly recently been built. The card was apparently sent after war had broken out, and the writer mentions that there was 'plenty of traffic this way all day & night', referring no doubt to military traffic from the near-by camps.

XXIII The main road early this century, incredibly empty and still apparently with a gravel surface, before it was taken in hand by the County Council.

above London Road by the *Cricketers* at the east end of Bagshot: the board offers luncheons and teas.

below Jenkins Hill at the west end of Bagshot.

XXIV Updown Hill, Windlesham, in the 1920s. William Walter Lee's draper's shop and post office was opened by 1894.

XXV Windlesham Fire Brigade 1930.
l. to r. (*back row*) R. Reed (Fireman), P. Mills (Fireman), G. Potter (Ass. Engineer), E. Wallis (Fireman), C. Houchen (Leading Fireman).
(*front row*) T. Woodham (Chief Engineer), E. Hill (Fireman), A. Howland (3rd Officer), W. Eustace (Chief Officer), O. Street (2nd Officer), S. Underwood (Fireman), A. Hall (Fireman).

XXVI John Cree, author of *Note[s?]* *Windlesham Parish Church* (1927). Cree, who died in 1933, was one of [Win-]dlesham's best known and most remar[kable] personalities. Born into a Manchester [fam-]ily of cotton mill operatives, he entere[d the] service of Richard Copley Christie, C[han-]cellor of the Diocese of Manchester, [in a] humble capacity. His potential capab[ilities] were soon recognised and he cam[e to] Windlesham soon after 1890 as secr[etary] and friend to Mr. Christie, who in th[e pre-]face to his major work *Etienne Dolet* [paid] tribute to John Cree's invaluable assist[ance.] Mr. Cree was a parish councillor and di[strict] councillor, and was secretary of Windle[sham] Institute for over thirty years. His firs[t wife] Eden, whose plaque is in the church,[died] in 1905, and he subsequently ma[rried] Carrie Bullen, who came from a Windle[sham] family.

XXVII W. R. Oldham, J.P., Manager of Fromows' Windlesham Nurseries 1897-1937. A Yorkshireman of shrewd common sense, Mr. Oldham's judgement was highly respected by his associates in all spheres. For over forty years he was a prominent figure in local government. A born culti-vator, and one of the leading nurserymen of his time, he was a member of the Council of the Royal Horticultural Society and was awarded their Victorian Medal of Honour in 1937. Keenly interested in the affairs of the industry as a whole, he was three times elected President of the Horti-cultural Trades Association. He died in 1949.

PART THREE.—1800-1856

5 A Period of Expansion

AT THE END of the 18th century, England was still a land of predominantly rural settlement in nucleated villages or dispersed hamlets and homesteads. The 'pleasant little town' of Bagshot, which we saw developing in Chapter 3, would still strike the travelling stranger as fairly remote, although it was within 30 miles of London. On the great west road which crossed the vast expanse of heath he would have seen only a few small clusters of houses between Egham and Bagshot. After the welcome inns and village shops (three grocers, three butchers, a baker, three shoemakers, a tailor, and one or two other shops[1]), there were a few buildings on the western parish boundary at the *Golden Farmer*. Then it was just heath again for another two miles before the small settlement at the Blackwater river on the Hampshire border came into view. The village of Bagshot was to become even better known during the next 30 years or so when the coaching trade reached its peak.

A stranger was hardly likely to go to the village of Windlesham, which lay a mile off the main road, and was not yet mentioned by name in the commercial directory.[1] There was no direct road—only the old path across the fields—between the parish church at Windlesham and Bagshot village about a mile

| Year | Population | Increase or decrease % | | Number of inhabited houses |
		Windlesham	England & Wales	
1801	1,060	—	—	203
1811	1,148	8.3	14.0	208
1821	1,590	38.5	18.1	313
1831	1,912	20.3	15.8	384
1841	1,899	−0.7	14.3	381
1851	1,794	−5.5	12.7	388

Fig. 5.—Parish of Windlesham. Population and houses 1801-51.

and a half away. Rocque's map of 1768-70, viewed in con-junction with the enclosure map of 1814, shows a rather dispersed village pattern, still probably in part medieval, with groups of houses and smaller farms bordering the old common fields and some larger farms further out. There was one inn (the *Half Moon*), a wheelwright, blacksmith, carpenter, and brick-layer, but no proper shops. The enclosure of the large area of wasteland in the parish was to bring some changes.

The Increase in Population

The development of the coaching trade and the enclosure of the waste were apparently accompanied by a large increase in the population: details extracted from the printed census reports are given in Fig. 5. Between 1801 and 1811 the population increased by only 8.3 per cent. During the next 10 years to 1821, however, it rose by no less than 38.5 per cent.; the population of England and Wales as a whole rose by less than half as much, the national increase being partly attributed to the return of the armed forces from the Napoleonic wars. Between 1821 and 1831 the population of Windlesham rose by a further 20.3 per cent. (From the late 1830s there was a temporary decline in population and the circumstances in which this took place are discussed in Chapter 7.) The scale of the increase at Windlesham, especially over the decade 1811-21, is surprising, and if authentic must indicate an influx from outside the parish. Comparable growth is not found in other small Surrey villages, with the exception of neighbouring Frimley; here the population increase in 1811-21 is, in fact even more remarkable (from 702 to 1,284, no less than 83 per cent.), but is largely due to the establishment of 'New Town' later called York Town, near Sandhurst Military College after 1812.

It is necessary first to consider the evidence for the large increase in the population of our parish, the boundaries of which did not change over the period. The increase between 1801 and 1811 is below the national average, and it could be that in 1811 the male population of the parish was artifi-cially lowered. The natural increase over the period 1801-11 (shown by the parish registers) was 146,[2] whereas the census increase was only eighty-eight. This could, of course, be accounted for by migration out of the parish, but it could also be

explained by men being away temporarily. The fact that in
1801 there were 46 more males than females, only two more
in 1811, but 76 more in 1821, may also be an indication of
this. The Lieutenancy records for the period, which might
have given details of parishioners in the militia for instance,
have not survived. Militiamen were chosen by lot out of those
eligible—many would be exempt for age or other reasons—to
fill a quota, but substitutes could be arranged by payment and
these might come from a different parish.

Though the first three censuses (1801, 1811, and 1821)
give a fair indication of trends, they are not entirely reliable,
the fourth census (1831) being held to be a great deal more
accurate. Is it possible therefore that the census figure for 1811
was under-estimated, or that for 1821 over-estimated? While
there is, of course, no way of checking the actual size of the
population in 1811, the valuation of property made for the
poor rate in 1808 does provide some check of the number
of houses given in the census report.[3] The valuation was made
by an independent surveyor, a Mr. Pain: Mr. John Taylor,
overseer of the poor at the time, went to Horsell and Pirbright
in May 1808 to 'enquire after the character' of Mr. Pain.[4] The
total number of properties in Bagshot and Windlesham (the two
are not distinguished) was 195, to which must be added four
workhouse cottages and four other cottages not separately
assessed.[5] This makes a total of 203 properties in 1808, and
the valuation does therefore provide some support for the
contention that the census total of houses occupied in 1811
(208) was not grossly under-estimated. It is still quite possible
that the actual number of people may have been greater than
the number returned. There was in general considerable over-
crowding of houses by the end of the 18th century, and the
total number of people in the 218 family units living in the
208 houses may not have been counted properly by the
overseers in 1811. There is also the question of gipsies, of whom
there were no doubt quite a number on Bagshot Heath, as was
the case on most of the unenclosed commons. They were
probably not counted in 1811, but are more likely to have been
once the fencing of enclosures had taken place. Thirty-one people
living 'in barns and tents' were included in the 1841 census.

Turning now to the possibility of an over-estimate in the
census of 1821, some support is given for the figure of 313

inhabited houses by the poor rate books, in which were listed
occupiers of houses or land and the amount which they were
assessed to pay towards the relief of the poor. In the parish of
Windlesham a rate (usually 1s. in the £) was made several times
a year, the frequency depending on the expenses that had to
be met. It is unlikely that any two consecutive rates will have
exactly the same entries. The number of people rated fluc-
tuated, partly through natural causes (death, marriage,
removal), partly because it was more or less at the discretion
of the overseers. Some people would be omitted as too poor
to be worth the trouble of collection, and the overseers might
well prefer to leave out new residents of doubtful standing,
as paying a parish rate gave them a settlement in the parish.
Over the period 1808 to 1822 there were, however, two
'peaks' when exceptionally high numbers were rated. The
first peak was in December 1808, when there were 199 entries,
tallying closely with the valuation list of the same year. At
the beginning of 1822 the poor rate lists were revised, presumably bringing in most of those who had become occupiers in
recent years, and in April (the second peak) there were 297
entries, which suggests that there had been a big increase
in householders. Although the poor rate had reached as high
as 7s. in the £ in 1818–19, it had already fallen again to 4s.
by 1819–20,[6] and the extension of the rating lists in 1822 may
have resulted from the census return which had been made in
1821. Mr. John Taylor, overseer of the poor, paid two visits
to Guildford in 1821, the first in July 'to return population',
and a further visit in November 'on population'.[4] Both parish
and county authorities may well have been surprised by the
exact size of the population now revealed.

Natural Increase and Immigration

Assuming that this very considerable increase did take place
in the population, how far can it be accounted for by natural
growth as distinct from immigration? Over the 10 years 1811–20
inclusive, the excess of baptisms (449) over burials (231) was
218, equivalent to 19.0 per cent. on the population of 1,148
leaving about half the census increase unexplained. Over the
following 10 years 1821–30, the excess of baptisms (625) over
burials (286) was 339, equivalent to 21.3 per cent. on the

population of 1,590, and here the whole of the census increase could be accounted for, though there would obviously have been some movement both into and out of the parish.[7]

The parish registers cannot of course be regarded as an exact record of births and deaths. Some allowance must be made for under-registration, particularly before the opening of the new chapel at Bagshot in 1821. It is unlikely, however, that the numbers of baptisms and burials recorded in the registers were greatly affected by nonconformity. There were certainly Baptists in the parish in the early 19th century, but their numbers were small, as they met from time to time in various houses occupied by one of their members. By his will proved in 1816, Henry Bartholomew, yeoman of Windlesham, bequeathed his 'building or meeting house used as a place of public worship by a society or congregation of protestant dissenters called Independent Baptists with the burial ground thereunto belonging', together with a second house, on trust to four persons.[8] Both these houses seem to have been in Chobham, but the burial ground may have been used by Windlesham people. One of the trustees named was Richard Chapman (cooper) of Windlesham, who in 1810 had registered a house in the occupation of Henry Bartholomew in the parish of Windlesham as a meeting place for Baptists, Chapman being the minister. A few years later a house at Hatton Hill in the occupation of William Ives (who was then the minister) was registered, and subsequently a house in the occupation of James Styles, landlord of the *Red Lion* at Bagshot. As might be expected, many of the Baptists were craftsmen and small shopkeepers. Those applying for registration included Mark Lawrence (grocer in 1832) and William Hayward (tailor in 1826). Wesleyan Methodists, among whom can be recognised Samuel Hayter (blacksmith in 1826), met in a room on the ground floor of a house at Bagshot in 1817, but presumably they continued to have baptisms and burials performed at the established church.[9]

A substantial element of immigration seems quite likely. Round about 1817 the baptismal rate shot upwards, followed shortly afterwards by the burial rate, which had tended to fall since the 1790s. Both rates then more or less stabilised at considerably higher levels, suggesting a distinct increase

in the population. This may be partly due to men returning
from the war in 1815, but in the revised rate lists of 1822
there appear a fair number of new surnames, which have not
been met with in either the 1808 valuation or the 1812
enclosure claims. Some of these people were merely taking the
place of other occupiers, and it may also be that some names
were not mentioned in earlier records because the bearers lived
in houses along with other occupiers, but were now getting
houses of their own, as a result of the new building. New
surnames do, however, continue to appear in rate books and
commercial directories right through to the mid-1830s, more
especially in Bagshot. In the 1841 census report, the numbers
of people born outside the county were 215 (out of 828)
in Windlesham, and 378 (out of 1,071) in Bagshot. The position
of the parish in the north-west corner of Surrey means that
newcomers did not need to have come very far to have been
born outside the county, but the point is that a considerable
proportion of the population at that date could not have been
born in the parish. This of course raises the question as to how
some of them were allowed to settle—the law of settlement
remained in force until 1876—but the settlement records which
once existed cannot now be traced.[10]

The population in the 1820s and 1830s must have been a
youthful one, the average number of baptisms a year being well
over 60, though not all the children survived infancy. In the
1831 census report the number of males aged under 20 (females
were not specified) was 475, as compared with 488 over 20,
whereas in 1841 there were 436 under 20 and 536 over twenty.
Although by 1841 the population of the parish had fallen to
1,899, earlier in the preceding decade it had no doubt been
higher. Ten people are known to have emigrated between
31 December 1840 and the taking of the 1841 census in June
1841. The total number of houses in the parish (inhabited and
uninhabited) was nine more in 1841 than in 1831.

Houses and Other New Building

The total number of houses in the whole parish increased
from 208 in 1811 to 402 (381 inhabited and 21 uninhabited)
in 1841. Separate figures for Bagshot and Windlesham are not
usually given in the census reports, and the first problem is

to decide where the growth was taking place. It must be emphasised that by Windlesham is here meant all the rest of the parish (the larger acreage) apart from the tything of Bagshot, which was centred on the junction of the London and Guildford roads. First of all how were the 208 houses divided in 1811? We know that in 1808 the peak number of 199 poor rate entries was split on the basis of 119 in Bagshot tything and 80 in Windlesham. Some people were rated for more than one property, some for land or stables only, but we shall not be far out if we allocate the 208 houses on the basis of 124 to Bagshot and 84 to Windlesham.

By 1821 there were already 315 houses in the parish (313 inhabited and two uninhabited), an increase of 107 since 1811. A road book for 1826 gives the number of houses in Bagshot in 1821 (the figure is said to be taken from the census) as 171,[11] and this would leave 144 houses in Windlesham. The poor rate books provide a rough check of these figures. As already explained, the next peak number of entries after December 1808 was in April 1822, when the total of 297 was split into 166 Bagshot and 131 Windlesham. (It must be remembered that Windlesham, although it had most of the bigger houses, had also most of the poorer ones, and one would expect to find more properties there not chargeable to rates than in Bagshot, which was more 'middle class'.) We may, therefore, assume that by 1821 the number of houses in Bagshot had increased by about 47 (from 124 to 171) and the number in Windlesham by about 60 (from 84 to 144). It seems that so far as house-building was concerned, Windlesham had grown at a faster rate than Bagshot over this decade. This is perhaps a little surprising, but it is in line with the census report, which shows a large increase in the number of families engaged in agriculture.

In 1831 there were 393 houses (384 inhabited, nine uninhabited), an increase of 78 since 1821. After the peak of 1822 the number of people rated to the poor dropped again, and the rate books are of no help in dividing the additional houses between the two places. However, the census report for 1841 does show that out of the total number of houses at that date (402), 225 houses were in Bagshot and 177 in Windlesham. There were only nine more houses since 1831 and as so little is involved we may allocate five to Bagshot and four to

Windlesham. We can thus arrive at an estimated number of houses at the different dates:

	1811	1821	1831	1841
Bagshot	124	171	220	225
Windlesham	84	144	173	177

After 1821 Bagshot had grown rather faster than Windlesham as a result of the coaching trade.

A very rough idea of where houses were built in the earlier part of this period can be gained from Bryant's map of Surrey (June 1823), but as the scale is only one and a half inches to the mile, it is not possible to count the houses in the built-up part of Bagshot or to distinguish with certainty between houses and other types of buildings such as barns. The distribution of new building in Windlesham is fairly general, consisting in the main of an infilling of space near the church and at Hatton Hill. However, on two different areas of newly-enclosed land several houses have been built. On Windlesham Road (School Road) near its junction with London Road and along the latter towards Broomhall, a number of new houses are shown, some of which could be connected with nursery gardening as they were near Henry Hammond's grounds (see Chapter 6). Quite a few new houses had also been built at the eastern end of the village on Updown Hill and along Chertsey Road. So far as Bagshot is concerned, most of the additional houses must have gone to build up the village. There is only a scattering on the outskirts down the Guildford road, while on the main road towards Basingstoke there are half-a-dozen buildings regularly sited near John Taylor's nursery.

No attempt can be made to identify the majority of the houses built between 1823 and 1841. By the time of the first large-scale O.S. maps (1869–70), a further 76 houses had been built in the parish, so that the earlier building cannot be distinguished. However, it is unlikely that any significant building took place in entirely new areas of the parish in the later 1820s and the 1830s, for little such building is shown on the 1870 maps and even cheap cottages would hardly have been pulled down in less than 50 years.

The ratio of families to houses occupied did not change measurably between 1811 and 1831, but the average size of a family dropped from 5·27 persons to 4·73. This may just mean that a family was identified throughout with a related group of people living in the same house, but as time went by more families were set up as more young couples had a house of their own. Some of the house-building of the earlier 19th century was probably a corrective to the over-crowding of the late 18th century. There were nine unoccupied houses in the parish in 1831, but these may have been dilapidated ones no longer required. Over the decade 1821–31 the number of houses in England and Wales increased at a faster rate than the population for the first time in the century.

In spite of the fact that this seems to have been a time of fever of cottage building, it has not been possible to find out what sort of place was built, nor by whom. The very fact that few houses have survived is evidence that they were very cheaply constructed. A high proportion of the new poor rate entries were for small amounts, indicating a low rateable assessment. The majority of the houses, intended for general or farm labourers, would probably only have had two or three rooms, and may have been of lath and plaster or thin brickwork. Out of eight houses belonging to John Taylor, nurseryman, which were put up for sale in 1828, seven were stated to be 'brick and tiled'. Some of these houses were probably late Georgian, but one at least was described as 'a new built brick and tiled messuage now used as two tenements'. The houses were on plots of between a quarter and half an acre, with rents varying from £8 to £14 per annum, and probably therefore of a better type.[12] Tiles were presumably hung on the upper storey covering a softwood timber framework, the brickwork being halted halfway up so as to effect a saving in the brick tax, which was in force from 1784 to 1850. Another construction which was common in Surrey by the 1830s had the advantage of beating the brick tax altogether. Softwood cottages (deal-framed with external weatherboarding) were built in pairs for housing farm-workers. The pair shared one central chimney-stack; each had two rooms on the ground floor (one behind the other) and either a full storey or attics above.[13] Fir or pine for such cottages could have been obtained from plantations which had been made earlier in the parish or its neighbourhood. The interior of a typical cottage of the period was thus described by William Howitt:

His naked walls; bare brick, stone or mud floor, as it may be: a
few wooden or rush-bottomed chairs; a deal or old oak table; a
simple fireplace, with its oven beside it, or in many parts of the
Kingdom, no other fireplace than the hearth; a few pots and pans—
and you have his whole abode, goods and chattels.[14]

Some increase in larger houses, particularly in the later
1830s, is suggested by the number of 'gentry' who are shown
in the 1839 directory.[15] 'Erlwood', the home of Edmund
Currey, Controller of the household of the Duke of Gloucester,
which was one of the first of the new houses, was built in
1825-6.[16] 'Windlesham Hall' was the seat of the Rev. Dr. Giles,
who gave the eastern window when Windlesham parish church
was rebuilt in 1838. The Hall, described in 1841 as a 'new and
handsome building',[17] was of red brick in Tudor style.

National School

In the 1820s and 1830s there must have been a large number
of children of school age. A yearly sum of £5 5s. 0d. left in
trust by the Rev. Edward Cooper in 1807, for the purpose of
teaching poor children reading, writing and arithmetic, was
being applied in support of a National school.[18] According to
the *Victoria County History,* the school was founded in 1814
and a new building opened in 1825.[19] The records of the
National Society show it received an application in 1818 from
the then rector (Rev. Thomas Snell) for aid towards the fitting
out of a building *at Bagshot* which he had purchased for £50
for a school, the total cost of the undertaking amounting to
£250; the Society made a grant of £50 and its annual reports
indicate that about 100 children attended the school.[20] At
the time of the 1833 Education Inquiry the master and
mistress received a joint salary of £80.[21] Pigot's directory for
1832 mentions the National school at Windlesham—Robert
and Judith Nicholas being master and mistress—and by this
time the school was almost certainly on the site of the present
school in School Road, Windlesham.

New Chapel and Enlargement of Parish Church

For a very long time there had been no church building for
worship in Bagshot, and the increase in population must have
been a major factor in the construction of a new chapel of

ease in Chapel Lane in 1821. The cost was £2,200, which was raised mainly by public subscription, £200 being given as a grant under the Act for promoting the building of additional churches. There is a picture of the chapel, a plain rectangular brick building, in Cracklow's views of Surrey churches.[22] The chapel, which stood on the site of the present mortuary chapel, could accommodate 600 to 700 people, and was in use until St. Anne's church was build in 1884. The accommodation in the parish church at Windlesham was doubled in 1838 (from 257 to 503 sittings) by the building of the new north transept (see Chapter 2) which, it was said, 'on account of its size may almost be regarded as the body of the church'. At the north end of this transept was a large gallery for children belonging to Sunday schools and for the poor, and there was another gallery in the tower at the end of the nave.[23]

New Road

Meantime, in 1835-6, a 'new and very convenient road' had been built to the parish church from Bagshot.[17] The road cost £517 3s. 3d., and many of the gentry subscribed, the Duke and Duchess of Gloucester giving £150.[24] In the late 19th century this road, which is still called New Road today, was sometimes referred to as 'the Gloucester Road or the Duke's Road, he having been instrumental in its construction'. The road, which leaves Bagshot Green near the almshouses, was of course of gravel and was built on faggots laid on what was virtually a bog.[25] James Restall, bricklayer, was paid £94 13s. 4d. for building a bridge with seven arches over the Bourn brook. There were advantages to the new road, apart from better access to the church. The list of subscribers includes a number of tradesmen and others, who did not contribute to the subsequent rebuilding of the church. John Lane (farmer) obviously benefited from improved access to some of his land. Mr. Robert Heynes (surgeon), Richard Hudson (corn-chandler), George George (plumber), Henry Houlton (saddler), and Michael Waterer (nurseryman) no doubt anticipated speedier business. Waterer was, in fact, paid £14 7s. 6d. for supplying the quick to be planted in the hedgerows.[24] The interest of Mr. Ramsbottom (owner) and Mr. Samuel Woods (landlord) of the *Half Moon* inn, which up to that time had been on a dead-end corner below the church, needs no explaining!

6 Economic Factors

The Enclosure of the Waste

MOST OF THE GOOD FARMING LAND was already in separate enclosed farms before the Enclosure Act of 1812,[1] which enclosed 156 acres remaining in open common fields, as well as some 3,700 acres of waste and heathland. The common field holdings, though scattered over several fields, were mainly in the hands of the larger landowners,[2] and it is unlikely that the enclosure of these aroused much interest or opposition. On the other hand, it seems that the enclosure of the large area of heathland was a controversial question, though the book of vestry minutes covering the years 1800–13 (which apparently still existed about 1927[3]) is now missing.

Partial enclosure had in fact been contemplated some years before 1794, when James and Malcolm were unable to find out why it had not been carried out.[4] The Earl of Onslow, lord of the manor of Fosters, had wanted the waste to be enclosed for some time, as is shown by two letters written to him in 1805 by Ralph Leycester of Hall Grove. Leycester advised the Earl that some of the leaseholders and copyholders wished to purchase the enfranchisement of their property, and if allowed to do so, they might thereby be induced to concur in the enclosure of the waste. Two or three of the farmers, however, 'had been active in their canvas against the enclosure, and in solliciting house to house signatures to a paper'. He suggested a partial enclosure of, say, 3,000 acres as a possible compromise.[5] It may be that the farmers were conservative and preferred to keep their common grazing rights. They may have been turning out more than their fair share of livestock to graze, or encroaching on the waste by unauthorised enclosures, and feared to lose more than they would gain by a general enclosure.

There were good arguments in favour of enclosure, such as the present unproductiveness of the heath round Bagshot. Stevenson referred to the local women's practice of cutting heath for besoms and gathering whortleberry for sale as 'the miserable productions and trifling employment which these heaths in general afford'.[6] There were also encroachments by people who had no right to be there. The papers of the Clerk to the Enclosure Commissioners contain an undated draft of an agreement among the parishioners relating to enclosure, and this refers to the fact that the commons and wastes 'have for many years past been enclosed and trespassed on by temporary occupiers of tenements in Windlesham and others to the great detriment as well of the commoners of pasture and turbary . . .'.[7] William Knight's new brick and tile kiln, for instance, gave cause for complaint because the quantity of heath it consumed denuded the area to the detriment of the poor, who 'work thereon in cutting turves and digging peat as well for themselves as their neighbours to whom they sell at 18d or 2/- thousand'. An increase in the poor rate was feared by causing the poor to purchase coal or other fuel instead.[8]

An authorisation to the solicitor, John Mears, to communicate opinion in favour of enclosure to the lords of the manors and other interested parties was signed by 26 persons, a few of them farmers.[9] Some people calling themselves 'friends to the inclosure of the waste lands' produced a printed notice assuring all concerned that in any Bill the interests of the smaller proprietors would not be forgotten. Among other things, they would recommend that land on the outskirts should be sold to pay expenses and if possible for the outside fencing of every man's allotment. 'After a full allowance to the Poor, to the Lords of the Manor, the Clergyman, the Cottages and for the Expences, they verily believe each Inhabitant will be entitled to twice as much Waste as they have Inclosed Land.'[10]

The draft prospectus of a Bill (dating to about October 1811) provided for (a) land to be enclosed—not more than four acres per house in the parish—for cutting of turf, and (b) not less than one acre of heath to be allotted to each cottage not let for more than £5 per annum, for the exclusive benefit of the renter for the time being.[11] However, the Act merely allocated not more than 500 acres where the poor occupying houses of a yearly value of not more than £6 could cut turf. The Act also provided that enclosures and encroachments made within the past 20 years were to be deemed part of

the waste, and to be divided and allotted accordingly. An exception was, however, to be made for enclosures which poor
persons had been allowed to make within the last five years
for the erection of cottages.

By the Award made 29 December 1814, nine public roads
were laid down. Four started on the north side of the London
road and were denoted as Sunninghill, Windsor, Bracknell and
Oakingham (Wokingham) respectively. The five roads on the
south side were Guildford, Chertsey, Chobham, Hook Green
and Windlesham. These were all more or less on the line of
existing gravel roads and lanes, but several small pieces of old
wayside common (Coopers, Broadway, Hook, Westerley, and
Bagshot Greens) were enclosed in the process of laying down
the wide, straight roads. Twenty private carriage roads for
access to properties, and eight public footpaths were also
defined.

Between 300 and 400 acres were sold to defray the cost
of the Act. The rector received 32 acres in the common fields
and 382 acres of heath in respect of tithes and rights of
common. Tithes were extinguished from all commonable
grounds, heath and waste lands, and from open and common
fields, allotments and sale lots, but rights to tithe on the old
enclosed land were maintained. St. John's College, Cambridge,
and the Earl of Onslow each received approximately 166 acres
as lords of the manors. The overseers of the poor claimed
that there were 111 houses whose value did not amount to £6,
and asked the Commissioners to allocate as much land to the
poor as they were empowered to, as even this would be found
'greatly inadequate' for the demand.[12] In the event 220 acres
of heath were allocated, equivalent to about two acres per
house, and the land, which consisted of 31 acres on the East
Common and 189 on the West Common, was right out on the
fringes of the parish. It must, however, be remembered that in
the majority of enclosures none of the waste was left at all.

A small minority of the cottagers owned their property and
thus received an allocation of land; some of the new houses
seem to have been built on land allocated in this way. Two
reports throw some light on assistance given to landless
labourers after the enclosure. In a report of the Charity Commissioners in 1824, it was said that the portion of Henry
Smith's charity assigned to the parish (amounting for the

year 1822 to £8 15s. 0d.) was laid out 'partly in providing implements of husbandry, which are distributed by the church-wardens among the industrious poor'. It appeared that this course had been adopted after the enclosures, the supply of tools having been found to be of great benefit to the poorer cottagers, by enabling them to labour on the waste, 'a great part of which has been annually broken up . . . and brought into a state of cultivation'.[13] In another report made in 1833 one of the Assistant Poor Law Commissioners said that, thanks to efforts made by Col. Currey (manager of the Duke of Gloucester's affairs), the rector, and other gentlemen and farmers, a Labourer's Friend Society had recently been formed in the parish. It was the aim of the society

> to assist the labourers of the parish in obtaining small parcels of land at a low rent: for which purpose ground will be provided in various situations so as to offer every man an opportunity of having 40 or 50 rods of land not far from his residence, and if required money will be advanced to the labourer to help him in the purchase of manure and seed, thus hoping he will be able to procure for himself the possession of a few pounds at the close of every autumn.

Through the liberality of the Duke of Gloucester, the society had been enabled 'to commence its benevolent intentions with a pleasing prospect of increasing the comforts and adding to the moral happiness of the labouring class in this parish'.[14] The beginnings of the allotment system can be traced back to the late 18th century, but it was not until after the agricultural riots of 1830 that the practice became common, two Acts being passed (in 1831 and 1832) to facilitate the provision of allotments.[15] The Labourer's Friend Society had headquarters in London and published a magazine giving advice about the organisation of allotments.

The Use of the Land

The land sold for expenses and allocated to the lords of the manors, the rector of Windlesham, and the poor, accounted for some 1,300 to 1,400 acres. The allocation of the rest of the waste to land and property owners in proportion to their existing holdings worked out rather more like acre for acre than the 'twice as much' that had been suggested by the 'friends to the inclosure'. It is not possible to see in any detail how the

newly-enclosed land was put to use during the period following
enclosure. The land was never brought into account in the Land
Tax returns, and the Tithe map (1843) only shows the old
enclosures. Any new farms established before the later 19th
century were probably fairly small. Rectory Farm is shown on
Bryant's map of 1823 on the 277 acres of land allotted to the
rector north of Windlesham village, but this land had, in fact,
already been sold by the rector, who had acquired the older
Ulliams Farm, then re-named Rectory Farm.[16]

Nursery gardening was to take a more and more important
place in the economy of the parish as the 19th century went
on. Most of the hitherto unenclosed waste was Bagshot sand,
and it is reasonable to suppose that there was some increase
in nursery gardening as a result of the enclosure, although
the real development does not seem to have taken place right
away. John Taylor, the Bagshot nurseryman, received some
45 acres in the Award and part of this was probably devoted
to nursery grounds. He owned a number of houses, some of
which may have been occupied by his employees.[17] John
Taylor died in 1828 and in May 1829 most of his February
poor rate assessment (£2 3s. 6d.) was debited to Michael
Waterer, who had opened his first nurseries at Knaphill
(Woking) about 1800.[18]

Another nurseryman, Richard Dare, who died in the early
1820s, had acquired 91 acres of heathland at the enclosure,
having purchased a good deal in addition to his allotment.
Some of this land was later occupied by Henry Hammond (of
Windlesham, not to be confused with the Rev. Henry Hammond
of South Farm, Bagshot), whose nursery garden is shown on
Bryant's map of 1823 just off the London road. Henry was
probably the son of Edward Hammond, whose original nursery
seems to have been near Cooper's Green, now part of Messrs.
Fromows. Poor rate books give some indication of the development of Henry Hammond's business. In January 1822 he was
assessed for rates at 12s. 6d. Subsequent entries are as follows:

March 1823	£1	(addition for land late Beauchamp)
November 1823	£1 6s.	(addition for J. Lane's ground)
November 1826	£2 5s. 7d.	(addition for Gloucester, late Birt)
April 1827	£1 12s. 3d.	(reduction for Lane's, Birt's)

By 1832 the assessment had risen again to £2 2s. 7d., but
in July the same year 12s. 6d. was deducted for house and

nursery not occupied. He may not have been using the original site of the nursery any more, as 4s. was added for 'new house'.

Much of the enclosed heath was sooner or later planted with trees. Already in 1820 a sale notice for land allotted to the rector on Windlesham West Common said that some of it was planted.[19] By 1841 there were 'many extensive and thriving plantations of larch and Scotch fir' in the parish.[20] A large number of houses were of course built, but most of them were small. It seems likely that the potential of the heathland did not really begin to be exploited until after the railway came to Sunningdale in 1856. From then on prosperity led to an increasing demand for high-class housing, a development for which the land was very suitable.

The Peak of Road Travel

During the first 30 years or so of the 19th century before the railways came, road travel of all kinds reached a peak that it was not to know again until the era of the motor car. The coach guides show the increasing numbers of coaches and waggons on the roads, and Bagshot was getting a good share. In 10 years from 1808 the number of coaches from London calling at Bagshot trebled, and there were 10 daily coaches in 1818. Between 1818 and 1829 the number trebled again, and there were now 30 coaches from London calling every day.[21] A directory for 1826 gives details of some of them:

> To and from London, pass through Bagshot nearly every hour during the day.
> To Barnstaple, from the White Hart, every afternoon at five.
> To Exeter, at six, eight, and half-past-eight, and eleven evening.
> To Southampton and Salisbury, at half-past-ten morning, and Weymouth at nine in the morning.[22]

The directory for 1832 shows even better the extent of the coaching services:

> To London, coaches call at the King's Arms or the White Hart Inns every hour during the day—& several coaches call at the Bell & Crown during the night time.
> To Alton, Basingstoke, Devonport, Exeter, Farnham, Gosport, North Devon, Salisbury, Southampton, Warminster, Wells, Winchester, and all intermediate places, coaches (from London) call at the King's Arms and White Hart Inns, every hour during the day—and several coaches call at the Bell & Crown during the night.[23]

The number of coaches in 1829 (60 altogether in both directions) is probably the maximum ever, as the 1838 guide shows only 25 from London. (*Kelly's Directory* for 1845 stated that there had been 'upwards of 70 coaches formerly passing and repassing daily', but they may not have all stopped at Bagshot.) Assuming the journey of 26 miles to take two and a half to three hours—the mail coach took three and a half to four hours at the end of the 18th century[24]—the timetable suggests the arrival of 15 coaches from London in the short space of time between 8.30 a.m. and noon! No wonder the village was later described as having been a 'scene of continual bustle and animation'.[25]

The stagecoach provided the country dweller with a daily spectacle of unfailing interest. After the horses had been changed and the travellers refreshed, there would come what Cobbett called 'next after a fox-hunt, the finest sight in England', a stagecoach just ready to start. For the travellers on our route it must have been exciting to reach the two short straight stretches of very good road along which a coachman would regularly gallop his team. One of these was the Hartford-bridge flats on the way from Bagshot to Basingstoke; an even more famous one on the way to London between Staines and Hounslow was known as 'the galloping ground of the western coaches'.[26]

With regard to the carriage of goods, the Bagshot district was of course entirely dependent on road transport. Places further south and west were also served by the Basingstoke canal as far as Basingstoke (where goods were transferred to carriers), although in 1832 there were waggons daily from Bagshot to Southampton, Winchester, Farnham and Exeter.[23] Waggons only carried an average of four tons of general goods at a time, and proceeded at a walking pace of two to four miles an hour. As the population of the Bagshot district increased, the number of goods waggons from London to Bagshot had grown from three a week at the beginning of the century to nine in 1828.[27] In 1826 James Cowdray went up from his own house at Bagshot every Monday and Thursday at 6 a.m. to the *New* inn, Old Bailey.[22] He left London on the return journey Tuesdays and Fridays at 7 a.m.[27] In 1832 William Taylor, waggonmaster, was making the trips to London;[23] the number of waggons from London calling at

Bagshot went on increasing right through to 1838, when there were 12 a week with two more which ran daily, making presumably 24 waggons altogether.[28]

Apart from its position on the main highway, Bagshot had links with Guildford and Chobham to the south, and with Windsor and Reading to the north. In 1832 John Hockley went to Guildford (12 miles) weekly and to Reading (16 miles) once a fortnight.[23] There was considerable commercial traffic with Reading (which was one of the larger towns in the southern part of the country) and with Wokingham. It was for this reason that a road to Wokingham was laid down at the enclosure as far as the parish boundary, though when the enclosure of Easthampstead (Berkshire) was carried out three years later the continuation of this road was stopped up. In 1837, when it was learned that several highways in Easthampstead were to be re-opened, a petition was got up by the inhabitants of the parish of Windlesham to persuade the Commissioners of Woods and Forests to re-open this direct road to Wokingham. It was pointed out that it was three miles shorter than the one via Bracknell and avoided two turnpikes, but the Commissioners were not convinced that sufficient reason had been shown for the re-opening of the road after 20 years. The petition stated that the greater part of the corn which was consumed at Bagshot was supplied from the corn markets held at Reading and Wokingham. Meat was also purchased at the beast market at Loddon Bridge near Wokingham, and among the depositions made was one by George King to the effect that he had been a butcher for the past 50 years and that he always used to go by the direct road across the heath to Loddon Bridge.[29]

The Turnpike Trust

Strangely enough, Paterson's road book of 1826 does not show a turnpike at Bagshot. The toll bar is, however, marked near the *Cricketers* on the Enclosure map of 1814 and on Bryant's map of 1823. The adjoining field was referred to in the Tithe Award as Turnpike Gate Field. When the tolls were put up at auction for three years at £725 a year in January 804, they fetched £1,080, and, although the trustees pointed out that this was due to 'an extraordinary competition', and could not be relied upon for the future, in January 1807 the highest bid was £1,060.[30, 31] Three years later Henry Bartholomew even bid £1,350, but vacated the lease early, entering into a new contract for £1,005.[31] An Act was obtained in 1816 by which the tolls laid down in 1728 were virtually doubled.[32]

Every horse drawing a carriage, wagon, etc.	3d. (Sun. 4½d.)
Every saddle horse	1½d. (Sun. 2d.)
Oxen per score	1s. 8d.
Sheep per score	10d.

When the next auction was held in June 1816 the tolls realised £2,260. The lessee (an associate of Lewis Levy, the Jewish stockbroker friend of the well-known coachmaster, Edward Sherman), then found that he had over-estimated and applied to the trustees for relief on the grounds that he was losing a lot of money, but they would not release him. In January 1823 Lewis Levy himself began to farm the tolls, and as the sums fetched tended to stabilise round about £1,500 to £1,600, presumably no one tried to outbid him.[33] (At one time Levy contracted for half a million pounds a year, one-third of the aggregate toll revenue of the whole country.)

In January 1819, apparently as a result of Post Office criticism of the condition of the road, it was resolved to place it under the direction of James McAdam, son of John Loudon McAdam. At the end of the year the trustees were so pleased with the improvement made by macadamizing the road, they voted to pay him one hundred guineas a year. This was continued until 1828 when McAdam himself suggested that as the improved condition of the road no longer required so much of his attention, his salary might be reduced, and 50 guineas was agreed upon. In 1820 a side bar was erected in Bagshot High Street near Mr. Everest's house, opposite the *King's Arms*, in order to prevent evasion of tolls by people driving animals, presumably into or out of the Guildford road.[33]

An Act obtained in 1833 virtually doubled the tolls for many wheeled vehicles, and after this the amount bid for the tolls, which were being auctioned annually, reached its highest point in December 1835, when a bid of £1,955 was made. From this time onwards the amount realised fell.[34] The purpose of the 1833 Act was to carry out improvements at the east entrance of Bagshot by straightening and widening the road from Bagshot Park to Bagshot Bridge.[35] The work which had been deferred, was in fact never carried out, the trustees deciding in February 1838 that they were not justified in undertaking it.[34]

With the increases in permitted tolls and in the traffic on the road, receipts might perhaps have been expected to rise higher than they did over the period up to 1835. The obvious explanation for their not doing so is some form of cheating. Farmers of tolls were often secretive about the amount produced the previous year and were known to form 'knock-outs' among themselves. However, on at least one occasion (January 1832) when the trustees took the tolls into their own hands after the prospective lessee failed to complete a contract following on a rather high bid, their own receipts must have been down, as they put the tolls up for a much lower sum a year later.[34] Lessees and trustees alike were cheated by their own collectors, who did deals with travellers and pocketed their share.

Bagshot Village and Its Coaching Inns

Bagshot must have been quite an attractive little place in the 1820s, when the directory comments:

> In the vicinity of this place is Bagshot Park . . . other respectable residences give a consequence to this village, which added to the advantages it receives from being a considerable thoroughfare, renders it a pleasing, lively and well-doing village.[22]

There were lights in at least part of the high street, which would be unusual at that time in a smallish place. The turnpike trustees had resolved in July 1812 that—at their own expense— as many lamps should be provided and lighted along their footpath 'as shall be necessary for the convenience and safety of the public'.[31]

The *King's Arms* and the *White Hart* were described in the 1832 directory as 'large Inns and extensive posting establishments'. Harriet Scarborough, the licensee of the *King's Arms*, was a coach proprietor. The Scarboroughs had begun to pay the rates on the inn (rented from the Williams family) round about 1821; they remained there until 1838.[36] It may have been at this period that certain alterations, which can be seen by comparing the Enclosure map (1814) and the Tithe map (1843), were made to the buildings, probably augmenting the accommodation for travellers and stabling for horses. Prior to

conversion to a private house (after 1854) the accommodation
of the *White Hart* included nine bedrooms (apart from servants'
rooms), two dining rooms, and a 'neat sitting room with bow
window' on the first floor. There was a double coach-house
and stabling for 40 horses. The *Bell and Crown* at the western
end of the village, formerly the *Chequers,* was re-named in 1812
when it was leased by the brewer, W. B. Parfett, to T. Fagg,
coachmaster, of the *Bell and Crown* in Holborn. The stipulation
was made that all Fagg's coaches were to stop for refreshments,
and that only Parfett's Bagshot ale and beers, or wines and
spirits supplied through the brewery, were to be consumed
there. The lessee was moreover to spend £400 on improving
the premises within a year. When the *Bell and Crown* was up for
sale in 1854, it was said to have seven bedrooms, billiards room,
tap room, bar and bar parlour. According to licensing records
for 1826 and 1827, there were still only four other inns, the
Fighting Cocks, Red Lion, Three Mariners, and *Cricketers.*
The last-named was described about 1850 as a brick-built house
with eight bedrooms and three parlours.[37] Soon after the
Beerhouse Act of 1830, beerhouses began to proliferate, as
it was now possible for any householder to sell beer by payment of excise duty of two guineas.

A great number of post and coach horses were naturally
kept at Bagshot. In December 1828 Edward Sherman, who
had large stables at the *Bull and Mouth,* opposite the G.P.O.,
London, was charged poor rate on a stable at Bagshot, and the
coach guide for the following year shows two of Sherman's
coaches calling there for the first time. In December 1831 the
item was entered as late Sherman, now Nelson. Mrs. Nelson was
another well-known coachmaster, whose business was based
on the *Bull* in Aldgate; she was also paying poor rate for a
second stable. In July 1834 both stables were stated to be
empty, and as we have seen, the peak of the coaching trade
seems to have been reached by 1829.

Occupations

The printed census reports for 1811, 1821 and 1831 divide
the occupations of families in the parish into broad categories
of agriculture, trade, and 'other' employment; the numbers
shown in the three categories are not altogether reliable, and

Occupations by (a) FAMILIES, 1811–31 (percentages in brackets)

Year	Total	Agriculture	Trade	Other occupations
1811	218	63 (28.9)	54 (24.8)	101 (46.3)
1821	326	153 (47.0)	92 (28.2)	81 (24.8)
1831	404	167 (41.3)	134 (33.2)	103 (25.5)

Occupations by (b) PERSONS, 1831

Males, 20 years of age and over:

Agriculture: Occupiers employing labourers	21
Occupiers not employing labourers	—
Labourers	243
Manufacture	—
Retail trade or handicraft (masters or workmen)	154
Capitalists, bankers, professional or other educated men	12
Labourers employed otherwise than in agriculture	39
Other males, except servants	7
Male servants	12
	488
Male servants under 20 years of age	5
Female servants	54

Fig. 6.—Parish of Windlesham. Occupations 1811–31 (information by persons available for 1831 only).

as pointed out in the introduction to the 1831 report, the method of allocation to categories in 1831 may differ from the two earlier census years. The 1831 report also gives actual numbers of individuals in particular categories: these details are probably more satisfactory. The census information is summarised in Fig. 6. Commercial directories for the years 1826, 1832, 1838, and 1839 give more detailed information about individual shopkeepers and craftsmen, many of whom can be identified in the property valuation of 1808, the enclosure claims of 1812, and in poor rate books. By means of all these sources we can see something of how the economic changes of this period were reflected in the occupations of parishioners.

Agriculture

The proportion of families in agriculture increased from 28.9 per cent. in 1811 to 47.0 per cent in 1821, dropping slightly to 41.3 per cent. in 1831. Most of the new houses built in Windlesham by 1821 must have been for farm labourers, and there may also have been more Bagshot families in agriculture, owing to expansion by John Taylor the nurseryman. In 1817 a new corn mill—a brick building three storeys high—was started at Bagshot (Church Road). It may also have been at this period that a windmill was built on land off London Road (where the *Windmill* inn was opened before 1855), which had been allocated to the Humfrey family of Hook Mill at the enclosure.[38] In contrast to many other agricultural parishes, the 21 agricultural occupiers were all employing labourers (243 altogether) outside their own families in 1831: 264 out of 488 males over 20 years old were thus employed in farming in 1831.

In considering the large increase in agricultural workers, the enclosure of the heath must be borne in mind, for enclosure did not invariably lead, as is sometimes suggested, to unemployment. Jobs such as hedging and ditching of new enclosures, clearing of scrub and planting of trees, would furnish temporary work over the first few years. A more intensive cultivation of any of the common field now enclosed, by courses of turnips, beans, etc., or the adoption of such improved methods elsewhere, would require more labour, while nursery gardening would absorb far more men than mixed farming, possibly one man for every acre. Moreover, much employment in agriculture was seasonal and men classified as farm workers could have been otherwise employed—building their own houses, for instance—from time to time. (Although it might have been expected that a fair number of labourers, as distinct from craftsmen, would be required for constructing new houses at this time, the numbers in 'other' employment fell between 1811 and 1821.) The proportion of men in agriculture was apparently higher in 1801 than in 1811 and part of the large increase after 1811 may be due to the fact that men who had been away at the war returned to agriculture.

Trade and 'Other' Employment

The proportion of families in trade increased steadily from 24.8 per cent. in 1811 to 28.2 per cent. in 1821 and 33.2 per cent. in 1831. Almost all this increase will have been in Bagshot. No commercial directory has been found for a date between 1791 and 1826, but a comparison of named shop-keepers and craftsmen in the 1808 valuation and the 1812 enclosure claims with those in the 1826 directory suggests that the number had nearly doubled. There were as many as 10 grocers, and William Page had opened up as pastry cook and confectioner. It is possible that some of the six shoemakers and four tailors were supplying the cadets at the Military College, which was transferred from Great Marlow to Sandhurst in 1812, although there was a bootmaker (Mr. John Stallwood) among the Marlow and Wycombe tradesmen who moved with the College.[39] At the end of 1830 Edward Robinson, shoe-maker, began to pay poor rates on a new house which he had built adjoining the turnpike road on the site of Stephen Robinson's old shop. By 1832, however, the number of shoemakers had reduced. So had the number of grocers, though there were two beer retailers.

Although the growth in trade over the decade 1821 to 1831 was broadly similar to that of the previous decade, most of it seems to have already taken place by 1826. We have noted that the peak of the coaching trade had been reached by 1829, and most of the people who came to Bagshot were probably connected with coaching. There was a considerable turnover of population during the period. It is interesting to see, however, that representatives of several of the family businesses opened in Bagshot in the early 19th century were still to be found in the village 100 years or so later. Among them, for example, were Evans (farrier and ironmonger), Frimley (baker), Copas (baker, with premises opened in 1803). Henry Houlton had his saddlery business next door to the *Three Mariners*. The shop had been established in 1780; it was continued on the same premises by Henry's son, James, and afterwards by James' widow and his two sons, Henry and Walter, until *c.* 1900, when the former opened a new shop further up the high street.

In Windlesham (as distinct from Bagshot) the increase in population between 1811 and 1821, being mainly of farm workers, did not immediately lead to the development of shops and services. Though these began to appear in the village about 1821, they did not amount to much before the late

1830s. The list of traders and craftsmen in the 1826 directory
(under Bagshot) does not mention Windlesham, but Mark
Lawrence (grocer) and Daniel Christmas (baker), who were at
Windlesham in 1832, first appear in poor rate books in 1821
and 1824 respectively. In 1832 the directory is headed Bagshot
and Windlesham, and there were two beer retailers at Windlesham. In 1838-9 there were two more grocers, John Attfield
and Henry Temple, and John Becket had set up as tailor. Daniel
Christmas (now baker and grocer) had opened a receiving house
for letters, which went to and from Bagshot by foot post. The
Christmas family were to be associated with the post office in
Dogkennel (Kennel) Lane for nearly 100 years.

Two commercial directories of the late 1830s show the
effect of some larger and better houses being built in the parish
at this time. James Restall, bricklayer in 1832, now described
himself as bricklayer and builder. There were now three
plumbers in Bagshot, two of them plumbers and glaziers, the
third a plumber, painter, and paperhanger. The number of
domestic servants, presumably included in 'other' occupations,
may have increased with the larger houses. The Duchess of
Gloucester maintained an active interest in the parish and was
probably often in residence at Bagshot Park, keeping a sizeable
number of both indoor and outdoor staff.

Comparative Prosperity

For various reasons—the rising population, the effects of
enclosures and industrialisation, a labour force swollen by
disbanded servicemen, agricultural depression, some very bad
harvests—the period between the end of the Napoleonic Wars
and the accession of Victoria is considered to have been a
particularly difficult one for the rural labourer. The riots in
the countryside in 1816 and 1830 were the result, but authorities differ as to the relative importance of the causes, and it is
not clear that the situation was universal even in the south,
which was the area worst affected. Poor relief expenditure was
certainly extremely high. The year 1812-13 was a peak one
generally in England and Wales: the average expenditure per
head of population was 13s., this being also the average for
Surrey.[40] In Windlesham expenditure in this year reached the
sum of £1,163, which is equivalent to just over £1 per head

of the population of 1811; there were 16 people in the parish
workhouse at Bagshot, 48 people were receiving regular relief
outside and 50 people received occasional relief.[41]

Expenditure fell over the country as a whole in the two
following years, but another peak was reached at some time
between 1817 and 1820. Subsequent to this there was again
a fall in expenditure in line with the fall in the price of wheat,
but also due no doubt to economies made after a House of
Commons Select Committee had complained of maladminis-
tration in their report of 1818. From 1815–16 Windlesham
expenditure had been rising again, and in 1818–19 it reached
£1,301. In 1819–20 it fell very sharply indeed to £745.[42]
The accounts at Windlesham were normally kept by two overseers, who seem to have been responsible for alternate months.
In 1819–20, however, while John Lane and Will Denyer
prepared accounts for the first half of the year, Nathaniel
Williams took over in November from Denyer, who died early
in 1820. Pages of detailed expenditure are missing for some of
the winter months, normally the heaviest. However, it can
be seen over the next few years that weekly outside relief
had been substantially cut. There may have been a Friendly
Society: in 1815 there was a society with 216 members[41]
(no doubt a fairly high proportion of the working men), and
there are some later references to 'Club' in books of weekly
relief.

Some of the reduction may have been due to more
efficient administration. In 1819 a Vestry Act had authorised
the appointment of select vestries and paid assistant overseers.[43] It is possible that a select vestry or committee to deal
specifically with poor relief was appointed in Windlesham at
this time. There are no proper vestry minutes covering the
period, but several books of detailed 'Weekly relief to the
Poor' include some badly-written notes of meetings held at
the workhouse. These now survive only from 1827,[44] but
such books did exist from 1819 onwards.[3] John Willmot was
appointed assistant overseer (paid) for 1820–1, and he was
followed in 1822–3 by Henry Houlton.[45] By the latter year,
expenditure was as low as £680, that is 8s. 6d. per head of
the population of 1821.[46] (At the same date the average cost
per head in England and Wales was 10s., and in the county
of Surrey 11s.[40]) The cost of poor relief remained round about

£600 to £700 throughout the period to 1834, in spite of the rise in population, and there is no sign of the peak commonly found in 1833.[47] A comparison may be made with the parish of Walton-on-Thames (Surrey), the population of which was considerably larger at the beginning of the century, but had grown relatively little by 1831, when the two places were much the same size. In 1812–13 the expenditure per head was nearly as great in Walton as in Windlesham, and it remained high over the whole period. Walton Vestry rejected proposals for a select vestry and a paid overseer in the early 1820s, though there was a paid overseer by 1834.[48]

It is conceivable that the farmers were spreading the employment over more labourers than they required at rates of pay just high enough to keep the workers off relief, for this sort of thing did happen at some places later in the century.[49] It would be the opposite of the supplementing of low wages from parish funds which is supposed to have been usual. In a report made in 1833 an Assistant Poor Law Commissioner stated that throughout the whole of the agricultural parishes of Surrey few labourers with families were not in receipt of parochial relief in some shape or form.[50] Windlesham was not of course entirely an agricultural parish, and it may be that it was cushioned to some extent by the prosperity of Bagshot at the peak of the coaching trade.

The difference between the number of houses occupied in 1821 according to the census report (313) and the peak number of occupiers rated in 1822 (297) is very small, which would suggest that at that time the number of people receiving outside relief—who would obviously not be rated—was pretty low. However, in 1831 it looks as if about a quarter of the occupiers in Bagshot and rather more than this in Windlesham were not paying poor rates. Generally speaking, all the harvests from 1828 to 1831 inclusive had been poor, and during these years bread was being distributed fairly regularly at the Bagshot workhouse,[44] although the quantities were small compared with those supplied in 1843 (see Chapter 7). The troubles among agricultural workers in the South East may not have been wholly avoided. When the riots of 1830 were at their worst, the Duke of Gloucester 'came to Bagshot to be at the head of his household, who are all armed. The threats have been very dreadful against his residence'.[51] The exact direction from which the threat came is doubtful, as one of the worst affected counties was Berkshire and Bagshot Park was on the boundary.

The poor of course included those receiving occasional help from time to time on account of illness, etc., and also old people, widows and orphans in the workhouse. Under the old Poor Law methods of workhouse management varied. The care of the poor might be farmed out to a contractor, who would be paid either an annual sum or on a weekly 'per capita' rate. It was then left to the contractor, who probably lived elsewhere, to make what he could out of it, an arrangement which can hardly have been to the advantage of the occupants. The workhouse at Bagshot seems to have been very small, and this is no doubt why the alternative method was adopted whereby workhouse needs were supplied by local traders and paid for by the overseers. A workhouse master or mistress received a small salary for looking after things on the spot. Although open to obvious abuses, this sytem must have given a less regimented atmosphere, especially if the master or mistress was of an old local family, like Mrs. Attfield, who was paid six or seven shillings a week in 1829.[44] Vegetables were grown in the garden and in 1824 £5 9s. 0d. was received from William Cherryman (the Bagshot miller) for the 'growing crop of rye in the workhouse garden'. In 1823 Henry Houlton, assistant overseer, made several journeys, first to Wokingham and them to Sandhurst, Frimley, Ash and Chobham 'respecting parish girls'.[45] Presumably this was in connection with apprenticing out for domestic service.

It was not a wealthy parish, though there were well-to-do individuals: in 1831 there were just twelve 'capitalists, bankers, professional or other educated men', according to the census report! What was the everyday life of the ordinary person like in this period of transition? R. J. White describes it as a time of vulgarity and gusto, with something still radically untamed about it. He takes the view that this is 'perhaps the last truly historical age in the sense that it is divided from us by a real chasm in time. The chasm came with the railways'.[52] Maurice Quinlan, however, pointing to the increase in church building and church attendance, the spread of education, and the improvement in manners, suggests that there was already something in the nature of a Victorian prelude by the 1820s and 1830s.[53] Certainly the peaceful, if far from idyllic, scene of work and spare-time hobbies described by William Howitt in the early 1830s would support this idea. Howitt does, in fact, say that within the last 30 years a change in the leisure pursuits of the working man had taken place, the rather archaic sports and somewhat brutal pastimes of previous centuries giving way to games such as cricket—'. . . it is the game of cricket which shows whither the mind of the people is tending and what will be the future character of English sports'.[54] We have as yet no details of the leisure activities of the folk of Windlesham, but something of a Victorian flavour may perhaps be detected in the entry in a parish book of poor relief which reads 'Owen Duff reproved for impertinence'!

7   A Temporary Depression

The Early Railway Routes

WITH THE OPENING of the Stockton and Darlington Railway in 1825, followed in the 1830s by lines between Liverpool and Manchester, Liverpool and Birmingham, and London and Birmingham, a new era in passenger communications began. Greville, one of the early travellers on the new form of transport, was of the opinion that it rendered 'all other travelling irksome and tedious by comparison'. On 18 July 1837 he comments in his diary ' . . . The first sensation is a slight degree of nervousness and a feeling of being run away with, but a sense of security supervenes and the velocity is delightful. Town after town, park and chateau one after another are left behind with the rapid variety of a moving panorama, and the continual bustle and animation of the changes and stoppages make the journey very entertaining . . .'.[1] It is curious that the words 'continual bustle and animation' are the very ones used by Brayley (in 1841) to describe the scene in the village of Bagshot before the decline of coaching.

The first line in the southern part of the country, the London & Southampton (later South Western) Railway, was opened from Nine Elms, Battersea, to Woking Common on 21 May 1838, and a year later the line reached Basingstoke, Winchester and Southampton. Francis Giles, who was responsible for surveying the line finally adopted, had made earlier surveys of the area as engineer for the Basingstoke Canal, and this is no doubt the main reason for the line which he chose.[2] The line more or less followed the Thames and the Wey to the Basingstoke Canal, and then accompanied the canal for much of the way to Basingstoke, difficulty over purchase of land being presumably less over the parts where the railway ran alongside the canal. A branch line from Woking to Guildford was opened on 5 May 1845. The route decided for the main line was to be a major factor in the development of at least two villages in north-west Surrey, Woking and Walton-on-Thames, but the effect on other places like Egham and Bagshot was just the opposite.

After the initial railway mania there was a depression in railway building, which accounts for some of the other branch lines which were proposed in the area of north-west Surrey never having been built. On 25 June 1847 the Windsor, Staines & South Western Railway Company obtained an Act for a line from Staines through Egham to join the London & South Western main line at Pirbright.[3] The line was expected to ease the pressure on London & South Western main line stations, but it was not built and the powers expired after three years. The line would have run down the parish boundary between Chobham and Windlesham, but on the Chobham side.[4] The Act provided for a station only at Egham, and possibly at points where certain roads were crossed. No place on the line would have been much nearer to the village of Windlesham than the station later built at Sunningdale, but it is possible that such a railway might have led eventually to more building on the eastern side of the parish, which even today is quite rural. No other railway building affecting Windlesham and Bagshot was undertaken until the Staines, Wokingham & Woking Junction Railway Company obtained an Act on 8 July 1853 for a line from Staines to Wokingham (see Chapter 8).[5]

The Fall in Road Traffic

It has been shown, in connection with the London to Birmingham railway, that the coming of a railway brought a rapid decrease in the traffic and revenue, not only on roads which were parallel and adjoining to it, but also on those which were parallel at a short distance away.[6] So it was with the great west road through Bagshot. Already by 1838 three of the main coachmasters had one coach fewer calling daily at Bagshot than in 1836.[7] A coach list which included the 'Devonport Mail' and others of the main coaches was still given in one of the commercial directories for 1839, but this was a re-issue of parts of a volume published in 1838, probably before August of that year.[8] It is likely that by the end of the summer of 1838 several of these coaches were already off the road. The 'Devonport Quicksilver', which left from the Gloucester Coffee House in Piccadilly, was horsed by

William Chaplin. Chaplin had quickly seen the way things were going when the London to Birmingham railway was opened, taking his coaches off the road and entering instead into co-operation with the rail by transporting passengers to and from stations. He had taken shares in the London & Southampton at the start and became a director in 1837.[9] The following advertisement for the sale of horses by auction on the premises of the *King's Arms* at Bagshot, appeared in *The Times* in September 1838:

> Forty superior, good-sized, strengthy, short-legged, quickactioned fresh horses and six sets of four-horse harness which have been working the Exeter 'Telegraph', Southampton and Gosport Fast Coaches and one stage of the Devonport Mail . . . The above genuine Stock for unreserved sale, entirely on Account of the Coaches being removed from the Road to the Railway.[10]

In 1839 it was still claimed that coaches to and from London, Exeter, Barnstaple, Southampton, Portsmouth, Farnham, Salisbury, and places on the western line of road, passed through Bagshot almost hourly, some of them calling at the principal inns.[11] In 1845, however, there were only two coaches calling at Bagshot (one daily and one every other day) and by 1855 all the stagecoaches must have been off the road; an 'omnibus' left Bagshot at 8.30 a.m. (return 6.45 p.m.) to meet the London omnibus at Shrubs Hill.[12] The carriage of goods by road from London to places beyond Bagshot must have also been vastly reduced, although the area itself would have continued to be supplied by road at least until the railway came to Sunningdale in 1856. For most of rural England, the disappearance of the stagecoach meant a serious loss of contact, and we may imagine the sense of isolation which had descended on our district by this time.

The accounts of the Bagshot Turnpike Trust show a dramatic fall in revenue received from tolls:[13]

Year	Revenue (£s)	L. & S.R. line
1837	2,069	
1838	1,654	Opened to Woking May 1838
1839	1,071	Opened as far as Basingstoke, and from Winchester to Southampton, by June 1839
1840	655	Opened Basingstoke to Winchester throughout May 1840
1841	444	

Receipts were thus cut by more than three-quarters in 1841, the first full year of railway operation. The effect of the railway was anticipated in that from the end of 1838 no bidders appeared when the tolls were auctioned. One lessee did take the gate in January 1841, but before the end of the year he had refused to pay the rent and had given up the gate. In May 1840, by agreement, James McAdam's salary was reduced to 25 guineas, and in July 1841 he relinquished it altogether. In May 1841 the trustees decided that they could no longer afford to water the roads, as they had been doing since 1832, and the water carts were sold. We may presume also that for the first time in nearly 30 years the street lights went out in Bagshot.[14]

Receipts continued to fall steadily, and in March 1844 the turnpike trustees notified the vestry of their intention of erecting side bars at the south entrance to Bagshot in order to protect their revenues.[15] Travellers were, it appears, taking advantage of the new road constructed between Windlesham church and Bagshot in 1835, to diverge from the turnpike road through Windlesham and so avoid the tollgate at the *Cricketers*. The new road passed through a few yards of a meadow owned by the Dean and Canons of Windsor, and in 1832 Edmund Currey (then Chairman of the Trust), anticipating this sort of abuse, had asked them to preserve this stretch as a private road and grant permission only to parishioners to pass along it. He was apparently given authority to lock the gate on this piece of land, but it must surely have been difficult to do this effectively.[16]

As soon as notice was received of the proposed side bars, the inhabitants of Bagshot and Windlesham presented a petition with 143 signatures. This pointed out that they were already penalised by the present tollgate being so near to Bagshot that they had to pay toll when travelling only a short distance on the turnpike road by horse or carriage in the course of their daily business, being in many cases 'prohibited from the indulgence of horse or carriage exercise for the purposes of health'. If now side bars were to be erected as well, inhabitants of the same parish would be unable to pass from one part to the other without paying toll. They would not have access to any of the parish roads, for the repair of which they paid, except through a toll bar. Worst of all, the trade of Bagshot which had been 'very seriously injured' by the advent of the railway, would sustain further injury if the village were to be boxed in by tolls on every side. The trustees nevertheless issued two orders on 3 April 1844 for erection of side bars across the highway to Guildford. One bar was to be near the *King's Arms,* and the other bar near the house of Mrs. Cox at the junction of Mariners Lane with High Street. On 27 April a meeting of parishioners resolved that the bar on the road leading from Bagshot to Windlesham should be closed except for parishioners from 1 May, and on 10 July the parish authorities told the turnpike trustees that the regular traffic had in this way been preserved to the turnpike road, no evasion having taken place by means of the new road.[17] They obviously hoped the new side bars would not be erected, but the trustees were not satisfied and the orders were put into effect.[14]

In spite of such precautions, in 1849 the revenue of the trust was only £234,[13] and in 1850 the Western District run by the Egham and Bagshot Trust was reunited with the Eastern District to form the United Bedfont and Bagshot Turnpike Trust. In 1852 the Windlesham vestry complained to the trustees about the serious nuisance caused by the bar in the street of Bagshot with the 'unsightly' caravan attached. The nature and position of the bar were considered very annoying, while the payment of toll by parishioners passing from one part to another was again called 'an unusual and unfair burden'.[15] An order for the removal of the *King's Arms* bar and Cox's bar was made by the trustees on 8 July. The side bars were, it seems, no longer profitable since the recent erection of a gate at Virginia Water—the amount received in tolls over five months was £12 18s. 8d., while £10 9s. 0d. had been paid out in wages![18]

Effect on Bagshot and Windlesham

Contemporary reports and comments give evidence of increasing depression in Bagshot from 1839 to the early 1850s; the population declined, shops and inns were closed, unemployment was high. (It must at the same time be borne in mind that these were difficult times in the country as a whole, during which emigration reached a peak, with an average of 250,000 in 1847–9). Towards the end of 1840 Richard Jackson, the assistant overseer, defending his administration of out-relief, and comparing expenditure favourably with that of Chobham, summed up the situation by saying that Chobham 'is not in any way affected by the Railway, while Bagshot is completely crippled'.[15] In 1841 Brayley refers to Bagshot in the following terms:

> . . . very recently noted as a posting town, and regarded as a place of considerable importance . . . but its trade has been entirely ruined by the opening of the Southampton and Great-western railroads; and its numerous inns and public-houses, which had long been profitably occupied, are now almost destitute of business . . and a deplorable depreciation of property has in consequence taken place.[19]

In March 1840 the *York Courant* had described the distressed inns at Egham. The annual rent of the 30-bedroomed *Catherine Wheel,* for example, which had been £250 in 1837, had fallen to £50.[20] At Bagshot (where the tenants of the three main coaching inns, who had all been there for a considerable time, had already departed by September 1839), Mr. Jones, licensee of the *Bell and Crown,* applied in April 1841 for a reduction in his poor rate assessment, his rent having been reduced by half on account of part of the premises having been pulled down. The vestry agreed to reduce the rating from £22 10s. 0d. to £12, and Mr. Graham (of the *Cricketers*) also had his assessment reduced because several of his stables were unoccupied.[15] In 1845 the *White Hart* was the only 'posting house', the *King's Arms,* which Nathaniel Williams had sold to Neville Reid & Co. (brewers of Windsor) before 1843, being designated as a 'commercial inn'. In April 1848 the assessment of Mr. Attride, landlord of the *King's Arms,* was reduced, the 'greater part' of the premises being shut up.[15] A large portion of the inn was pulled down not long afterwards, leaving the building fronting the road which remained until 1938. In 1852 the assessment of Mr. Finch at the *Red Lion* was reduced. The *Bell and Crown* fetched only £410 when it was up for sale in 1854,[21] and the *White Hart* is missing from the list of inns in the 1855 directory. The drop in trade was very noticeable by 1845: the shops were not nearly so numerous as in 1832, the reduction being mostly in grocers and general stores. In

1855 a number of tradesmen were dealing in more than one type of goods or service.

The population of the parish of Windlesham had been in 1831 very similar to those of Walton-on-Thames and Woking, places which were, however, now on the main railway line. By 1841 the population of the parish had actually fallen at a time when the population of the country as a whole was continuing to rise, albeit more slowly. (See Fig. 5.) The fall was only by 13 persons from 1,912 to 1,899, but 42 of those enumerated could hardly be considered as part of the normal population. They were 'attending Ascot races', so there were probably some house parties at the big houses! The census report for 1851 shows a further drop in the population to 1,794, with the following note:

> The parish of Windlesham has decreased in population owing to many families having left Bagshot, since the removal of the coaches from the great west road.

In 1841 there were 21 uninhabited houses in the parish, and in 1851 the number had gone up to twenty-six.

Was there another side to this picture of depression? Although many reductions were made in poor rate assessments, there were also instances of increased assessments. In July 1842 reference is made in the vestry minutes to some new and improved premises since the last valuation in 1838: James Draper, grocer, improvements—Stephen Evans, blacksmith, new building to house—John Collins, shop erected. In 1850, a number of people having asked for a reduction in their assessments, a new valuation was mooted. It was decided, however, that instead the parish officers should be empowered to add to or diminish rates, aggrieved parties being entitled to have their rates reduced to a minimum of four-fifths of the actual rent paid.[15] Windlesham would not, of course, have been directly affected by the loss of the coaching trade, except for the fact that the farmers could no longer procure abundant cheap stable dung for manure![22] Unemployment in this part of the parish was probably due to the general situation. The census report shows that eight of the 21 houses which were uninhabited in 1841 were in Windlesham, but the number of shops in the village remained much the same in the 1840s and 1850s as it had been in 1839.

Alternative Occupations

Presumably the more skilled of those who were displaced from their occupations in connection with the coaching trade moved away from Bagshot to find jobs elsewhere if they could. What could other forms of employment contribute over this period of depression towards filling the gap for those who remained? According to Brayley, the immediate source of employment was 'a large tan yard'.[23] Habbakuk Robinson had apparently retired from the job of tanner towards the end of 1830 when Edmund Nicholls began to pay rates as occupier. Nicholls remained until at least 1845, but there is no tanner indicated in 1855,[12] and it may be that the yard was closed after the death in 1851 of Habbakuk Robinson, who probably still owned it. Some of the earlier demand for leather for harness, saddlery, etc., would have disappeared with the reduction of the horse traffic on the road. The number of shoemakers had already gone down. It is most unlikely that the tan yard was still working in the 1870s, although it is referred to in the same terms as before.[23]

Farming remained of course the main occupation. In many areas farmers had experienced difficulties in the period since the end of the Napoleonic wars. A better period for farming was about to start, but we have no information about the state of farming in Windlesham specifically. Nursery gardening had by the later 19th century assumed a position of major importance in the economic life of the parish, but there are indications that this further expansion did not start before the 1850s. In 1842 Brayley devotes a whole paragraph to Michael Waterer's Knaphill (Woking) nursery, which then extended over about 120 acres.[24] Under Bagshot, however, he merely says that most of the gardens in the neighbourhood were stocked with the finest specimens of American plants, and that there was 'a very celebrated American garden' at Bagshot Park.[22] (The term 'American plants' was at that time given to hardy shrubs like the azalea and the rhododendron which needed a moist peat soil.)

In 1844, after the death of Michael Waterer, the Bagshot nursery, which had till then been run as one business with Knaphill, became a separate concern owned by John Waterer the elder.[25] In 1848 John Waterer's American nursery covered 30 acres.[26] There were two other nurserymen at this period, but the extent of their grounds is not known. An advertisement by George Baker in the *Gardener's Chronicle* shows that he had taken over Hammond's nursery at Windlesham before 1845.[27] John Standish, who had previously been foreman at Bagshot Park, had set up on his own at Bagshot about 1840. By 1848 he was joined in partnership by Charles Noble, and their business became important horticulturally.[28] Their nursery, which adjoined Bagshot Park,[29] was later known as Royal nursery.

Another factor in Bagshot life was the continuing interest of the War Office in the surrounding heath. One of the first camps for combined training of soldiers had been held on the northern boundary of the parish at Wickham Bushes in 1792, there being 5,000 men under canvas. Coachloads of visitors came to see the camp, and there was a great review on 7 August in the presence of George III.[30] After the Royal Military College was moved in 1812 to Sandhurst (Berkshire), next door to Bagshot, the suggestion was made that the College 'comes so near to this . . . that it will occasion other improvements here however barren the land'.[31] At this date Bagshot village was the nearest place of any size, but the subsequent growth of a community of shops and other premises known as New Town (later York Town) will have reduced the business brought to Bagshot traders; several tradesmen did in any case move with the College.[32] A second camp was held near Chobham in 1853, and again attracted many visitors; stalls were put up by many local publicans, Mr. R. Brooker of the *Bell and Crown* at Bagshot advertising his 'spacious booth' opened for refreshments near Highams Lodge. It is unlikely, however, that the military presence had much real effect on the parish before Aldershot Camp was built in 1854. The 1861 census report attributed the increase which had taken place in the population to the nearness of the camp.

Unemployment

The vestry minutes throw some light on unemployment in the parish in the early 1840s.[15] In December 1842 a committee was set up to find work 'for poor labourers now out of employment'. Some idea of the size of the problem envisaged can be gained from promises of employment then given. The

Duchess of Gloucester undertook to take six labourers for 10 weeks each; Thomas Dumbleton (Hall Grove) and the Rev. J. C. Lucena undertook to take four labourers, Rev. T. Snell (rector) and George Breton ('Hatton House') two labourers, Rev. H. Wood, one labourer, all for 10 weeks. Others promised employment up to a certain amount of money. Admiral Sir Edward Owen ('Windlesham House') and J. C. Fyler ('Woodlands') promised £10 each, John Mears (solicitor) and John Lane (farmer) £8 each, Nathaniel Williams and Mr. Smith between them £6, Dr. Giles ('Windlesham Hall') and William Perrin (farmer) £5 each, while Major-General de Butts gave £4 10s. 0d. The men were to receive 9s. per week, and a superintendent was to be engaged at 12s. per week. The total promised was thus equivalent to about 30 labourers for 10 weeks.

Arrangements were also made (from 2 January to 3 April 1843 inclusive) for bread to be supplied to the married men 'at day or task work', the scale laid down (4lb. loaves weekly) being as follows:

Man, wife and one child	1 loaf
Man, wife and two children	1½ loaves
Man, wife and three children	2 loaves
Man, wife and four, five or six children	3 loaves

Tenders were asked for, that of Daniel Christmas for 5½d. per 4lb. loaf being accepted. The total number of loaves provided was 449, at a cost of just over £10. The average number of men receiving bread was 13 a week.

By 30 January 1843 employment had already been provided for an average of 19 men each week over seven weeks. Most of the gentry had helped, but few farmers. There was obviously some resentment over those who were getting away without giving anything. A meeting of Proprietors of Lands and Tenements was arranged for 10 February, in order to 'find employment', but no one besides the original committee seems to have turned up! At the usual committee meeting on the following Monday it was resolved that 'some of the inhabitants should call on the landowners and ratepayers that have not given employment to the poor nor contributed towards paying for the bread . . .', but the outcome of such visits, if paid, is not stated. The record of employment given, which continues up to and including 27 March, is not always specific, and the final numbers cannot be totalled. With the end of the winter, no doubt the situation eased.

Considerable effort and expense were thus incurred to help the unemployed poor, though one cannot tell how far the situation was directly due to the decline in the coaching trade. The only reference throughout to the Board of Guardians of Chertsey Union (who had been responsible for the poor of the parish since the new Poor Law of 1835) was when two men were told to report to the guardians. There is nothing in the guardians' minutes, and parliamentary returns in connection with the poor now relate only to the area of Chertsey Union as a whole.

Emigration and Unrest

The census reports show that the number of men over 20 in the parish was 536 in 1841, a noticeable jump from 488 in 1831, the total number of males having only increased by nine over the period. Thus the unemployment problem may have been aggravated by the rise in the birthrate which had occurred some 20 years earlier. The situation would presumably tend to get worse, unless people moved out. Ten people had in fact already emigrated early in 1841. In October 1849 the vestry resolved that Chertsey Board of Guardians should sanction the expense, not exceeding 11 persons altogether, of £5 each (£1 deposit, £3 outfit, and £1 to be given on arrival) for poor persons emigrating to the Cape of Good Hope. The guardians' minutes refer a little later to £50 having been advanced for 10 persons.[33] In March 1850 a meeting was held at Bagshot to consider the suggestion that a fund of £200 should be established to enable those having settlements and willing to emigrate to do so. The plan was rejected, however, only four people being in favour.[15]

Other problems with which the parish had to deal over these difficult years were those of tramps, incendiary fires, and robberies. Tramps were a familiar and longstanding burden owing to the position of Bagshot on the great west road: in 1803 162 people not parishioners had been given poor relief.[34] In 1839 Chertsey Board of Guardians complained about the bill for tramps, having already ordered that all such applying for relief before 4 p.m. were to be sent to the workhouse.[35] The incendiary fires and robberies were probably not peculiar to the parish, but symptomatic of the unsettled state of the country. On 4 May 1839 a meeting held at Bagshot, which was 'numerously attended', resolved that active measures should be taken for protection against incendiary fires, and 'for the discovery of the wretches already guilty of these diabolical acts, in burning the poor man out of his cottage, and in the indiscriminate destruction of Plantations and Property by the Firebrand'. A subscription was to be got up for necessary expenses and rewards to be given for information. Several adjacent parishes where fires had also been caused were to be recommended to appoint committees, and it was felt that a central committee should be set up.[36] Nothing further has been traced on the subject, however.

In February 1849 the vestry reversed a decision taken in 1843 *not* to have a paid constable, because there had been so many robberies in the parish, though it seems to have been mostly petty larceny of foodstuffs. Adelaide Currey, daughter of Sir Edmund and Lady Currey of Erlwood, comments in a diary written in her late 'teens on incidents which had taken place at Hall Grove and at Mrs. Usborne's (Woodlands), where 30 bushels of potatoes were stolen one night. On 18 November 1848 she writes:

> We open the dining room window after dinner, but as I do not think it right in these days of robberies that we should all leave the room when any one from the Garden might enter through the window, I sit down here to keep guard.[37]

8 Renewed Growth

IN 1865 A SURREY GUIDE-BOOK remarked that the village of Bagshot, which had 'long been almost as desolate as the great road which passes through it', had of late 'shown symptoms of revival'.[1] By 1891 the joint population of Bagshot and Windlesham was well over half as much again as it had been in 1851. Some of this growth must be related to the opening of railway stations at Sunningdale (1856) and at Bagshot (1878), though growth probably followed the coming of the railways as there does not seem to have been any great local demand for rail facilities. In the census report for 1871 it was noted that 'the increase in population is attributed to building operations in the neighbourhood of Sunningdale station'. In 1898 the guide-book commented that now Bagshot had a station of its own 'fresh residents are attracted by the extreme salubrity of the district'.[1]

The Railway Lines

The opening of Sunningdale station on the Staines and Wokingham line in 1856 meant that heavy goods such as coal and provisions could now be brought in by rail instead of by road waggon, while nursery and farm produce, particularly meat, milk, and vegetables, could be despatched to London and other areas more easily. For the convenience of passengers, the *Sunningdale* hotel was opened near the station, and the proprietor owned a 'fly' which they could hire to carry them on to their destination. Passenger services were, however, not very good. In April 1860 the first train up did not reach Waterloo until 9.55 a.m., and the last train down left Waterloo at 6.35 p.m. In August 1864 the railway allowed a 10 per cent. season ticket reduction for seven years to occupiers of new villas at Sunningdale rented at £60 or more per annum.[2] In 1865 some building speculators entered into an agreement with St. John's College for development of land

in the immediate vicinity of the station, but the scheme fell
through because no offers for purchase were received,[3] and this
particular area was not developed until considerably later.

Sunningdale station in the north-east corner of the parish
was, of course, some three or four miles away from Bagshot
village. The lack of railway facilities was meanwhile proving
very inconvenient to the fast-growing settlements at York
Town and Cambridge Town (later re-named Camberley), where
the Staff College had been opened in 1862. Legislation was
promoted by the Sunningdale and Cambridge Town Railway
Company to build a railway which would run from the Staines
and Wokingham line at Sunningdale to Cambridge Town,
passing through Bagshot on the way. The scheme seems to have
aroused little interest in Bagshot. Evidence in favour of the two
Bills put up in 1864 and 1865 was given to House of Commons
committees on behalf of the Staff College and the Military
College (at Sandhurst), but the only person from Bagshot to
give evidence was Frederick Waterer, son of John Waterer
the elder. Waterers' nurseries were much further from Sunningdale station than were the other nurseries in the parish, and
they were, therefore, very interested in securing better rail
transit outwards for their trees and shrubs, and inwards for
coal and other items. When asked about other possible advantages to the Bagshot neighbourhood, he referred to the great
quantity of timber grown (there were now steam sawmills
for timber at Bagshot) and the considerable amount of coal
consumed. Replies to the enquiry made of landowners, lessees
and occupiers of property in the parish through which the
proposed line would pass, show that many were neutral, some
failing even to answer the letter. Some of the major landowners
—Henry Dumbleton (Hall Grove), James Hodges (Penny Hill),
Lady Currey (Erlwood), and St. John's College, Cambridge—
dissented from the project. They did not, however, go so far
as to be represented at the hearing in order to press their case.
The London & South Western Railway lodged a petition against
the first Bill, but withdrew their opposition during the committee stage.[4]

The first plan deposited envisaged a No. 1 railway from
Sunningdale to Cambridge Town, and a No. 2 railway on to
Farnborough, where it would join the London & South
Western.[5] The No. 2 railway was, however, abandoned, and the

Act obtained in July 1864[6] was for a line between six and seven miles long, terminating in or adjoining High Street Cambridge Town, for which capital of £70,000 was to be raised. The company was to run three passenger trains to and from Cambridge Town daily. The *Surrey Advertiser* of 16 July 1864 commented, referring to Bagshot, that the railway was 'about to find out this charming place'. Meanwhile the Military College and Frimley residents had not given up their pressure for a further extension with a station at York Town and a link with Blackwater. A further plan was deposited in November 1864,[7] and a second Act obtained in June 1865 (capital £20,000) carried the No. 1 railway on through Frimley and a No. 2 railway to Blackwater, where it was to join the South Eastern.[8]

On 19 November 1864 the *Surrey Advertiser* had reported the ceremony of cutting the first turf which was carried out at Cambridge Town and followed by a 'dejeuner' at the *Cambridge* hotel for nearly 100 ladies and gentlemen. By March 1865 about one mile of the railway had been made, with the exception of laying the metal track, a heavy cutting to the depth of 50 feet having been successfully carried out.[4] (On 2 September 1865 the *Surrey Advertiser* carried an account of an accident to three navvies at the railway cutting between Cambridge Town and Bagshot, owing to a fall of earth.) Early in 1866 the directors of the Staines, Wokingham and Woking Junction Railway Company (which owned the line through Sunningdale) were still looking forward to the increase in their own traffic which they anticipated would follow the opening of the line to Blackwater, but very soon afterwards delays with contractors and the engagement of new ones were reported. It was 'trusted that the unissued share and debenture capital would be sufficient'.[9] No minutes of the Sunningdale and Cambridge Town Railway Company seem to have been preserved, but presumably it was owing to financial troubles that the railway was never completed.

A line was finally built by the London & South Western in 1878, an Act being obtained in 1873.[10] There was at least one other abortive attempt in the interval, and the L. & S.W. directors considered that they must build in order to protect their own interests in this area between Ascot and Aldershot.[11] No minutes of evidence before a parliamentary committee can be traced, and there may well have been no opposition to the London & South Western. Between Bagshot and Cambridge Town the line appears to be almost identical with that of the Sunningdale and Cambridge Town railway, but the connection with the Staines and Wokingham line was made at Ascot and not at Sunningdale. At the other end the line connected at Ash Vale with the branch to Aldershot. The railway was originally single track as far as Frimley Junction, and double from there to Sturt Lane Junction, where there was a connection with the main line from Waterloo via Woking. In 1879 the line was doubled between Frimley Junction and Frimley station, but it was not until 1893 that the rest of the line was doubled to Ascot.[12]

The *Surrey Advertiser* of 23 March 1878 commented that the opening of the new branch on 18 March was 'quite an event' for Bagshot, which had 'suffered the greatest inconvenience for many years' owing to the lack of rail facilities. Twenty-one people attended a celebration dinner at the *King's Arms,* Mr. Sumpster (the new stationmaster) contributing 'some choice songs' during the evening. The station was described as 'both pretty and comfortable'. The 'liberal service' of trains—six each way daily—had been 'most liberally patronised' during the previous week. As the guide-book of 1898 points out, the passenger from Bagshot to London had the choice of travelling via Ascot or via Woking, the time occupied being nearly the same in each case.[1] The first train up in the morning, which achieved the journey in one hour 19 minutes, left Bagshot at 8.21 a.m. The City businessman could return on other trains with a fast connection, the 4.45 p.m. via Ascot arriving at Bagshot at 6 p.m., while the 4.10 p.m. and the 5.50 p.m. via Woking arrived at 5.19 p.m. and 7.07 p.m. respectively. Other trains during the day usually took between one and a half and two hours.[13]

The Increase in Population

The highest rate of increase in population was immediately after the decline, between 1851 and 1861, and following this there was a fairly steady but slightly diminishing rate of growth, not dissimilar to that of the country as a whole (see Fig. 7). Separate data for Bagshot and Windlesham are not given in the printed census reports for 1851, 1861, and 1871, but in 1881

Year	Population	Increase or decrease %		Number of inhabited houses
		Windlesham	England & Wales	
1851	1,794	−5.5	12.7	388
1861	2,090	16.5	11.9	425
1871	2,364	13.1	13.2	478
1881	2,669	12.9	14.4	515
1891	2,965	11.1	11.7	604

Fig. 7.—Parish of Windlesham. Population and houses 1851–91

the populations of the ecclesiastical parishes are quoted. The parishes of Windlesham (St. John the Baptist) and Bagshot (St. Anne) covered most of the population of the civil parish of Windlesham, though there were also small numbers within the ecclesiastical parishes of St. Saviour, Chobham (formed in 1868) and Holy Trinity, Sunningdale (formed in 1841). So far as can be seen, the area of the new Bagshot parish constituted in 1874 was more or less the same as that of the old Bagshot tything for which the population was given in the 1841 census. Over the second half of the century Bagshot and Windlesham had somewhat differing patterns of growth. The information in the census reports can be supplemented from *Kelly's Directories* (1867, 1882, 1890, 1895), and from the six inch O.S. maps which were first surveyed in 1869–70 and revised in 1894-5.[14]

Growth of Bagshot

In 1881 the population of Bagshot ecclesiastical parish was 1,209, and the number of inhabited houses 248. Bagshot would have had some leeway to make up after the fall in its population in the 1840s: in 1841 the population had been 1,071, but in 1853 a petition against the granting of a spirit licence to the *Bird in Hand* said that the population of Bagshot had dropped between 1841 and 1851 by 127 persons.[15] By the 1860s there were again more shops in the village, but the character of the place must have been very different at this time, more self-contained like that of Windlesham. Now that the stagecoaches had gone, the main road was freer of through traffic than for a long time, although there would be quite a lot of local horse and foot traffic, especially to and from Sunningdale station and later Bagshot station. Some more large houses had begun to appear: on the western outskirts of the village, 'Penny Hill House' (where the famous holly hedge was described in the 1907 directory as 40 feet high in parts) had been built by the mid-1850s, following soon by 'Lambourne House' across the main road.

In the 1880s and early 1890s the population of Bagshot was growing quite fast. By 1891 it had overtaken that of Windlesham once again, having increased by some 20 per cent. during the previous decade. Mr. F. B. P. Lory, whose father (Rev. Frederick Aylmer Pendarves Lory) became the first vicar of the new Bagshot ecclesiastical parish, calls Bagshot in the '80s a 'picturesque place'.[16] Before 'Sycamore Villa' and 'Chestnut Villa' were built in the early 1890s, there were no buildings on the south-east side of the high street from Webbs, the butchers, near the *King's Arms,* right up to 'The Cedars'. The stream still ran open alongside the road under a row of fine horse-chestnuts, and the fields stretched to the railway line. Drinking fountains had been installed in a number of places along the street. Houses of this period include 'Pinewood' (near St. Anne's new vicarage), where Lady Elphinstone lived, 'Grove End', by Hall Grove, and 'Failthe', down the Guildford road. 'Florence Villa' (1888) and other new houses were built in Church Road. In 1882 the village had about the same number of shops as in the coaching days of the late 1820s, and these now included a chemist. The post office now dealt with telegrams, the telegraph system having been taken over by the G.P.O. in 1870. By 1895 there were also a tobacconist, a stationer, and an agent for W. & A. Gilbey, Ltd., wine and spirit merchants.

We can get some impression of the village community in the earlier part of this period from fairly regular reports in the *Surrey Advertiser,* which was first published in 1864. The centre of many events was the Bagshot Institute, founded in 1862 by James Hodges of Penny Hill, and given by him to the public.[17] During the later 19th century many similar village institutes were established by members of the gentry as a means of self-improvement for the working classes. The Institute comprised lecture, reading and billiards rooms and was managed by a committee of five residents. The varied activities that took place there during the early years well illustrate the

capacity of mid-Victorian society for providing its own entertainment and education. In 1864 'all ranks and classes of its
members' were 'uniting most heartily in supporting not only
with their money but also with their personal services'. Local
talent was well displayed. On one occasion, for instance, Mr.
Frimbley gave two comic recitations, Mr. Poulter read two of
the Ingoldsby legends, and Mr. Robertson two humorous
extracts from 'Charles O'Malley', while Messrs. Cranham, Hone
and Knight rendered the 'Canadian Boat Song' and other songs,
accompanied by Miss Mears on the piano. Another evening two
plays ('Honesty the Best Policy' and 'Boots at the Swan') were
performed by the Misses James of 'Lambourne House' and
their friends, while John Waterer junior obliged with a song
in the interval. When the village choir gave their second annual
concert in connection with the Institute, the room was
'crowded to excess', while as many as 500 people were present
at a 'conversazione', when there was an extensive display of
natural and other curiosities.[18]

There were also regular lectures at the Institute on a great
variety of subjects, often by speakers who came down specially
from London. At a lecture on 'The Management of Bees',
there was 'a considerable number of the working classes present,
for whom the lecture was specially intended'. In January 1865
the Secretary was able to announce that the lectures would be
resumed 'under a more *enlightened* arrangement', a little joke
referring to the fact that gas had been specially laid on in time
for a lecture on 'Coal Gas' to be given by Mr. H. McLeod of
the Royal College of Chemistry! On this occasion it was
reported that the room was 'brilliantly lighted up and filled
by a numerous and fashionable audience'.[18]

For those whose tastes were less elevated, there were of
course the numerous beerhouses, places said by William Howitt
to be 'kept by people without capital, often without character;
their liquor supplied by the public houses and adulterated by
themselves'.[19] Some people thought that there were too many
inns and beerhouses in the parish. In 1865, when two further
applications were made for a full publican's licence in Bagshot,
a memorial against the granting of such licences pointed out
that the parish had 2,100 inhabitants, while there were 11 inns
and 10 beerhouses, two-thirds of them in Bagshot! Both
applications were refused.[20]

Cricket was a favourite sport, the teams often having dinner and a convivial evening together afterwards at one of the inns. Athletic sports held on the cricket field on three evenings in May 1866 were said to have attracted an average attendance of 700 people each evening.[18] The first annual Musical and Horticultural Fete and Poultry Show took place at Bagshot Park in 1870, and the event was still being held in 1884.[21] After the station was opened in 1878, the links with Camberley (which had a population of over 5,000 by 1891), Woking, and Aldershot probably meant more to ordinary folk than the more expensive connection to London. Some may have enjoyed a day at Ascot races!

The special census of church attendance which was taken by the civil authorities for the first and only time in 1851 gives us some information about churches in Bagshot. Returns were called for from the Church of England, and also from other denominations, of the numbers attending services on 30 March and the average attendances during the past year. The form for the Anglican chapel in Chapel Lane was signed by the rector, but the figures may have been inserted by the curate. On 30 March morning attendance was 120 in the general congregation, with 35 children attending Sunday school; afternoon attendance, 145, with 40 in the Sunday school. It is not known, of course, how many people attended more than once in the day. Free sittings in the church were said to number 225, other sittings 300.[22] It was not till 1884 that the present church, also dedicated to St. Anne, was erected in Church Road. It was built of red brick in the geometric style at a cost of £6,000, 450 sittings being provided.[23] A mortuary chapel was built on the site of the old chapel.

Brayley says (in 1841) that both the Wesleyans and the Baptists then had chapels in Bagshot.[24] The only nonconformist return made in 1851 was for a Baptist chapel, but it is known that not all ministers completed a return. The Baptist return was signed by a James Wells of Camberwell, who described himself as 'occasional preacher with others', and it did not specify any particular sect. The building, the whereabouts of which was not given, had been erected about 1838, there having been no previous chapel on the site. It was used as a place of worship and as a Sunday school; the latter had been started six months before. There were free sittings for 150

people and other sittings for a further one hundred and fifty.
On 30 March 1851 the morning congregation was 36, including
19 Sunday scholars. In the afternoon there were 23 scholars,
and a general congregation of 67 attended in the evening.[22]

The Baptist chapel is not mentioned in directories after 1855.
In the early 1860s Bagshot was the centre of a Primitive Methodist Mission, which covered not only Bagshot itself but places
as far away as Guildford (which had 20 society members in
March 1862) and Compton. Bagshot seems to have been the
only place with a chapel building, shown in 1870 (25 inch O.S.
map) in the Guildford road between the *King's Arms* and the
gasworks. The following account was given in the Primitive
Methodist magazine early in 1862:

> A short time since the inhabitants of Bagshot were generally
> opposed to Primitive Methodism, but the success which our mis-
> sionary collectors have lately met with, proves that a good impres-
> sion is being made in the place. Bagshot is hard soil, but God is
> working, our congregations are improved, and on Sunday evenings
> the improvement is very great . . .

This was the only nonconformist church recorded in a return
made to Parliament in 1882.[25] However, some time before
1894, when the chapel no longer appears on the map, the
Primitive Methodists must have given up. A Wesleyan Methodist
church was built on Jenkins Hill in 1886 (by G. Kemp, a
builder from Aldershot, at a cost of £1,088 8s. 8d.) and continues until the present day.[26]

Growth of Windlesham

In 1881 the ecclesiastical parish of Windlesham was a little
larger than that of Bagshot so far as population was concerned;
the two parishes had almost the same number of houses, there
being 246 houses in Windlesham. The population of Windlesham had grown from 828 in 1841 to 1,336 in 1881, much
of this growth being probably in the late 1860s and the 1870s.
In 1867 Windlesham was for the first time given a completely
separate directory entry; the number of shops there (including
two coal merchants at Sunningdale station) had noticeably
increased since 1855. Before 1882 the village had acquired a
fishmonger-cum-poulterer (John Boyce) and there was enough
work for a plumber. In addition to the post office at the shop

of Samuel Christmas at the corner of Church Road and Kennel
Lane (which was now a telegraph office as well), by 1894
there was a second post office at the shop of William Lee,
draper, at Updown Hill. Updown Hill also had a butcher's
shop (George Hobbs) and a grocer and wine and spirit dealer
(Richard Arrow & Sons). Henry Greenfield (carpenter in 1882)
was now a builder, and there were two estate agents and auc-
tioneers at Sunningdale station.

The population had not been growing so fast after the 1870s,
but the development of shops and services must have been
encouraged by the building of a considerable number of large
houses. 'Woodside' (on Hatton Hill), 'Windlesham Court', and
'Northhill' were there before 1869, and by 1882 we have
'Ribsden' and 'Gunners' along the Chertsey road. Several large
houses were built about this time along Westwood Road, for
example, 'The Camp' and 'Westwood Lodge', and in 1888 the
vestry agreed that this road should be adopted by the parish.
By 1894 there were also a number of large new houses on the
main road towards Sunningdale: one of these was 'Woodhay',
build by Sir Ernest George in Queen Anne style, with typically
small bricks quarried locally. Others were 'The Pines', 'The
Towers', and 'Lavershot Hall', the home of H. H. Longman, J.P.

We know rather less about village events in Windlesham
during the later 19th century, as Windlesham is mentioned
less often than Bagshot in the newspapers, only achieving
fame when really startling things occurred, such as a suicide,
an accident, or a mad dog loose in the street! Most of the
social activities, organised and unorganised, were centred on
the inns and beerhouses. In 1867 there were as many as six
beerhouses, but by 1882 some of them had obtained a full
publican's ⊥licence, maybe because the Wine and Beerhouse
Act of 1869 had made it much less easy than before to get
a simple beerhouse licence. The *Sun* and the *Surrey Cricketers*
are on the map by 1869, and by 1882 the *Bee* had also been
opened up School Road. On a Saturday in early February
1866 the local scene was 'enlivened . . . by a spirited and
well-contested running match' between Louis Chennel of
Windlesham and James Norris of Sunningdale, both of whom
enjoyed 'somewhat of a local celebrity'. The match was held
at the *Windmill* inn (on London Road), of which Ann Chennel
was the landlady. Four hundred people saw Chennel put on a

spurt about halfway in the 120 yards distance to win by three yards. Later that year when a case of assault was up before the bench at Guildford, the complainants seemed rather confused as to whether this took place in the *Half Moon* or the *Sun,* thus giving the magistrate an opportunity to remark, amid laughter, that they 'did not seem to know the difference between the Sun and the Moon'.[18]

A room at the Board School was sometimes used for more sober public entertainments: for example, in November 1872 permission was granted for Penny Readings to be given there on certain evenings during the winter.[27] In 1880 a small brick building was opened for use as a Working Men's Institute and Reading Rooms.[23]

The only return for Windlesham in the religious census of 1851 was that of the parish church, and there does not seem to have been any nonconformist chapel until after the end of the 19th century. The form was filled in by the rector, Rev. Edward Birch. Numbers were entered under average attendance for the past 12 months—200 in the morning, 130 in the afternoon—and a note added to the effect that, because many of the parishioners lived at a great distance from the church, the number of the congregation 'depended greatly on the state of the weather'.[22] The church was extensively rebuilt in 1874 (see Chapter 2).

Occupations

Apart from the growing number of shops and businesses of both old and new kinds, the main occupations of the parish were agriculture and nursery gardening.

Agriculture

Up to about 1880 this was in general a good period for farming in England, but subsequently arable farming for itself became less profitable with the opening up of vast new areas of grain cultivation in America. The demand for meat and dairy products and vegetables was in any case increasing, while less bread was being consumed. There was a tendency to change to a mixed farming in which foodstuffs were grown for feeding to animals, which were the main end product. This sort of pattern can be seen in the farming practised in Windlesham. The area devoted to arable crops (including fallow ground and rotation grasses) was at its peak in the 1870s, amounting to nearly 1,500 acres in 1875, but it then began to decline. In 1895 the area under wheat was only about one-third of what it had been in 1875. In the later 1880s there was a big increase in cattle and in permanent pasture for grazing. Returns of livestock show over 500 head of cattle in 1885 and 1890, but the number began to fall again slowly in the 1890s. There were nearly 500 sheep in 1890, but less than half that number in the following decade. Before the end of the century farming was beginning to decline in importance in the parish.[28]

In an essay published in 1853, the soil on the Bagshot sand was described as 'generally of a useful kind' except on the worst sands. It varied from a good dry loam (bearing every kind of corn and roots) to a sharp, blowing sand, which produced only rye and poor turnips. The average size of the farms was 200 to 400 acres, but there were many of only 50 to 100 acres,[29] and farms in Windlesham continued to fall mainly in the latter category. The opening of the station at Sunningdale (1856) may have encouraged the establishment of new farms, a number of which are shown on the first edition of the six-inch O.S. map (1869–70). There were 18 farmers in the 1867 directory, twice as many as in the previous decade. Lavershot, Broomhall Waste, Lightwater, and Bellevue farms were entirely on land enclosed in 1814. Two farms may be partly on old enclosed land: Bagshot Green Farm, and New Farm, which had previously been part of James Lane's land, but was now marked as a separate farm. Broadley Green Farm was on land up to now part of Rectory Farm. One of the older farms near Coopers Green, belonging to Edward Hatch at the enclosure, had been split up into various lots; William Perrin (the farmer) had moved to Hill House Farm on Marsh Hill, which had been bought by Henry Dumbleton of Hall Grove after the death of John Lane about 1846. (For location of farms, see Fig. 3.)

A sale of growing crops, livestock, and implements belonging to Randle Jackson of Manor Farm, which was held in 1864, shows that this farm still went in for growing wheat as in earlier times. Out of 35¾ acres of growing crops, 16¼ were Chidham wheat, the rest being horse beans, barley, rye and white oats. Livestock for sale consisted of six working horses, seven dairy cows, and two Berkshire sows with litters.[30] Some farms seem to have been more devoted to animal husbandry. Immediately before Christmas 1865 the *Surrey Advertiser* carried a note of the excellent provision made for the festive season by Thomas Webb, the Bagshot butcher. Local supplies consisted of oxen from Webb's own farm at Broadway Green, sheep from Bagshot Park Farm, and pigs from the farm on the Hall Grove estate. The previous month a report of the Chobham, Windlesham, Horsell, and Bisley Agricultural Society annual show (probably its third) gave evidence of a lively interest in farming in the district.[31] This may have been stimulated by the existence of the model farms at Windsor and Bagshot Park with which the Prince Consort had had much to do. Farm implements at Randle Jackson's sale, which were listed as first-class and recently purchased, included a Ransome & Sims haymaking machine, Corne's No. 2 chaff-cutting machine, and Barrett & Exall's two-horse-power threshing-machine.[30] Although such agricultural machines had been available since the late 18th or early 19th century—threshing-machines were often the target for destruction in the 1830 riots—it was not until the later 19th century that machinery became generally used.

The number of farmers had begun to fall again by the 1880s and more of the old farms disappeared. Hill House ceased to be a farm with the advent of the railway, and Humfrey's farm was partly absorbed into nursery gardening. On the 1894 map Hook Mill was shown as disused and the large barn used for storing corn at Manor Farm nearby was pulled down not long afterwards. The remaining farms in the parish were increasingly oriented towards milk and meat. Of the newer farms, in fact, only Broomhall Waste, Bagshot Green, and Broadley Green remained on the map by 1894, and some of the buildings at Broadley Green had been pulled down before 1912. It was impossible about 1895 to find a tenant for Broomhall Waste, which was otherwise known as Starveall Farm, no doubt an apt description.[32]

Nursery Gardening

There is little doubt that the opening of Sunningdale station gave an impetus to the development of nursery gardening. At the beginning of 1857 Charles Noble announced that he was leaving Standish's nursery next to Bagshot Park and was setting up a new nursery of his own near the station. George Baker was advertising his American nursery as only a mile and a quarter from the station.[33] In 1857 Waterers acquired land off Thrift (Swift) Lane, which had belonged previously to the *Three Mariners* estate,[15] and by 1864 they were shown (on a plan deposited in connection with the Cambridge Town railway) occupying further extensive grounds off the main road nearly opposite John Taylor's original nursery. Somewhere about this time Richard Mason opened nurseries at Hatton Hill.

By about 1870 nursery gardens covered rather more than 200 acres. Waterers was, of course, the largest nursery, extending over something like 80 or 90 acres. Royal or Duke's Hill nursery (Standish) and Sunningdale nursery (Noble) each covered about 40 or 45 acres. Lavershot nursery (Baker) and Mason's nursery were smaller, the former being of 25 acres and the latter at this stage probably only about 10 acres.[34] As has already been pointed out, all the other nurserymen were much nearer to Sunningdale station than Waterers; John Standish and Charles Noble did not reply to the letter notifying them (as lessees of land which would need to be acquired) of the proposed railway from Sunningdale to Cambridge Town (1863). Frederick Waterer was asked at the committee hearings about the extent of his business and the number of men employed. He claimed that over the busy period from August to June, on average between two and three tons of goods were taken to Sunningdale every day. Some days there might be as much as 10 tons—'we have had five, six and seven waggons at a time at the station'. Besides this, considerable quantities were taken to Blackwater or Farnborough stations for shipment to Sussex, Kent, and the Continent. The firm owned eight horses and hired other waggons as necessary. At present they had to send some goods by road, but they would send more by rail if the station were nearer. Their traffic was in hardy plants (American principally) and forest trees, everything, in fact, except fruit trees. They traded with all parts of the United Kingdom, America, and India, and held an annual exhibition in Regent's Park. With regard to men employed, Frederick Waterer said that they generally had about 100 hands, but he was not particular whether there were 100 or 200, for at this time (April) they put on all they could.[4]

The acreage devoted to nursery gardening reached its 19th-century peak in the 1880s (279 acres), falling again slightly by 1895.[35] Some old enclosed farmland was now being used for nursery gardening, which hitherto had been almost entirely on the heathland. In the 1882 directory Richard Mason's Windlesham nurseries were said to be extensive. Mason was a grandson of James Humfrey, and his nurseries now occupied some of the land belonging to the old farm near Coopers Green and next to the church. In 1894 James Jabez Fromow and Joseph Fromow started Messrs. Fromows' Windlesham nurseries with the purchase of 15 acres of land from Mason[36] (see Chapter 10). By 1894 Lavershot nursery had disappeared and Sunningdale nursery had reduced in size, some of this land being swallowed up by new houses. Meanwhile Waterers had acquired more land on the south-east of the main road near the railway. It was probably at this period that they bought Duke's Hill nursery, John Standish having moved away to the Ascot area. In 1882 Waterers were one of the four principal landowners in the parish, and their nurseries may by then have covered some 150 acres, though it is unlikely that the reference to 250 acres in the 1895 directory is correct. Some 60 acres were devoted to the culture of rhododendrons, which were largely shipped to America. John Waterer the elder had died in 1868, and his son, Frederick, in 1871. The business was now run by John, third son of John Waterer, who was a well-known figure in the life of Bagshot until his death in 1893. The *Surrey Advertiser* commented on the occasion of his funeral: 'He will be remembered for his genial manner, cheery words and charitable acts, his workmen and dependents especially feeling acutely his loss'.[37]

9 The Beginnings of Public Services

DURING THIS TIME of renewed growth in Bagshot and Windlesham in the later 19th century, the activities of the vestry were increasingly affected by the powers of other authorities, although, broadly speaking, it continued to be responsible for parish affairs. Until 1894 there was in existence no proper system of local government which could be applied to urban and rural areas alike to deal with certain important new problems, and the device of *ad hoc* specially constituted bodies was consequently employed. A big change had already taken place in one of the traditional spheres of local administration, when in 1835 the parish vestry lost direct responsibility for its own poor to the new board of guardians. Special bodies were later set up to deal with two other matters which came to be considered of paramount importance: sanitation and elementary education.

Windlesham Vestry and Chertsey Board of Guardians

At this period some of the most prominent people at vestry meetings were the nurserymen: George Baker, Charles Noble, John Standish, and, above all, the Waterer family. From the time that John Waterer the elder was first made an overseer of the poor in 1844, he and his sons played an important part in parish affairs, being concerned with a variety of subjects, from schools to gas supplies. Certain of the farmers also took an active share, a prominent and popular vestryman in the 1860s and 1870s being Thomas Webb, who also had a butcher's shop in Bagshot. The numbers attending vestry meetings were not very large in the earlier part of the period, and meetings were held mostly at the old workhouse at Bagshot Green, the vestrymen often dining together afterwards at one of the inns. On occasions when a special vote was to be taken and more people were expected, the meeting would be held at the Bagshot Institute, Windlesham Board School, or (after 1880) at the Windlesham Institute. In 1890 the question was raised as to where future meetings should be held, as there was not sufficient space in the old workhouse room for the number then attending (which seems to have often been between 40 and 50), but the problem was of course solved by the change to a smaller elected parish council in 1895.

The vestry elected two guardians who represented the parish on the Board of Guardians for Chertsey Union. The Windlesham guardians apparently did not attend the meetings of the board very regularly, and special notices had to be sent to them when anything of importance affecting the parish was to be discussed. In June 1879 it was stated in the vestry minutes that much inconvenience was caused by the meetings being held at Chertsey, over nine miles from Windlesham. The Windlesham representatives would of course have to go on horseback or drive a trap, and as meetings were held in the daytime, their own affairs would take priority.

Gas Supplies and Street Lighting

From the mid-1860s gas was being supplied on a private basis to some of the residents of Bagshot. The promoters of the Bagshot Gas and Coke Company, Ltd., which was incorporated 2 May 1864, were James Hodges (of 'Penny Hill House'), Jabez and Frank James (of 'Lambourne House'), Frederick and John Waterer, Thomas Webb (farmer and butcher), and Thomas Attride (*King's Arms*). The nominal capital was £1,250, divided into 250 shares of £5 each. The objects of the Company were stated to be the manufacture of gas and the supplying of the town of Bagshot, the sale of coke and other material obtained from the manufacture, and the supply of pipes and fittings required by consumers.[1] The 34 shareholders, more than half of whom held five shares or less, included all the more important shopkeepers in the 1867 directory. In July 1864 the Company was given permission by the United Bedfont and Bagshot Turnpike Trust to lay down pipes in the turnpike road,[2] the gas works being just down the Guildford road south of the later railway bridge. The *Surrey Advertiser* commented on 16 July 1864: 'the march of improvement has not left this good old place behind'. No accounts of the Company have been preserved. In October 1877 a special resolution was passed winding up the Company voluntarily, the gasworks, plant, and everything connected with it being sold to Mr. Richard Kemp (coal and coke merchant, gas works proprietor and gas engineer in the 1882 directory), for £600.[1]

The following year (January 1878) it was resolved in vestry (26 for, 11 against) that Bagshot streets should be lighted by gas at the expense of the ratepayers living within a radius of one mile from the post office. A Bagshot Lighting Board consisting of seven inspectors was appointed to carry out the provisions of the Lighting and Watching Act.[3] A tender made by Richard Kemp to erect and supply gas standards and lamps complete at £3 13s. 6d. per standard and £2 18s. 6d. per bracket was accepted. Mr. Kemp also undertook to supply gas and oil, and to light, clean, repair and make good breakages for £3 per lamp per annum. The inspectors reported that a sum of about £100 would be required for the ensuing year, which for the district to be rated meant a rate of 9d. in the pound. The figures suggest that something like 15 lamps were erected at this time.[4] According to the parish council minutes, there were 21 lamps in 1895.

However, not all ratepayers are in favour of the latest improvements when they have to pay for them! Once the Act had been adopted its provisions remained in force for three years, but at any time thereafter it was possible to decide not to continue. In 1881 a resolution was put that the village should _not_ be lighted with gas at the expense of the ratepayers. This was lost, but in October 1885 a similar proposal was carried. In the December, however, a lighting committee which had been got together was given permission to use the existing lamps and columns, placing them where they thought best for lighting the village, the cost to be met by voluntary subscription. Whether this was in fact forthcoming is not clear, but in 1892 a proposal in favour of adopting the Lighting Act was again carried in vestry. Nine inspectors were appointed and a rate of 3d. in the pound approved for the coming year.[5]

Parish Roads

The General Highways Act of 1835, which repealed all existing highway legislation except that dealing with turnpike trusts, had left the individual parishes responsible for all their other roads, the repair of which was to be met from a highway rate. In Windlesham two waywardens or surveyors were appointed annually to see to the repair of roads and bridges, an additional waywarden being later found necessary after the return to parish care of the stretch of turnpike road. For the four years 1865-8, control of parish roads passed to a highway district board set up under the Highway Act of 1862, under which parishes could be forced to amalgamate for road repairs. This board, based on Chertsey, was not popular because of its expenditure: parishes were always convinced that they could repair their own roads cheaper (if not better) than any district authority. Under the Highways and Locomotive Act of 1878, the functions of existing highway boards were transferred to rural sanitary authorities, which had recently been set up. A provisional order was made to again form a highway district for the Chertsey area, but the Windlesham vestry, mindful of past experience, protested at the Quarter Sessions Court on 1 July 1879 against the order being confirmed. Several reasons were put forward, first and foremost of which was the increased expenditure which the vestry anticipated under a district board, it being pointed out that repairs carried out under the waywardens for 1861-4 amounted to only £472, while under the previous board the total for 1865-8 was £717. The cost of repairs after 1868 was not quoted (presumably because it was higher), but the roads in Windlesham were said to be in a good state of repair, four new brick bridges having been built within the last four years. There were now nearly five miles of disturnpiked road to be cared for at additional expense. Other reasons given were that a surveyor from Chertsey would not inspect the roads as often as the waywardens did, and that the latter would be put to 'great difficulty and expense . . . to attend a Highway Board at such a long distance from the parish'.[5] Other parishes also protested, and the order was quashed.[6]

The United Bedfont and Bagshot Turnpike Trust maintained the turnpike road until 1 November 1875, when responsibility for repair reverted to the parish. The trust surveyors during this period were Thomas Jackson, his brother, Randle Jackson (farmer) and Charles Noble (nurseryman).[2] In November 1877 the Trust was finally wound up. The materials of the Bagshot

Gate were put up for auction on 11 October; it was described
as a brick-built house with slate roof and wood-built W.C.,
together with gate, posts, rails and fencing. A lease of tolls
(1872) lists the fixtures and goods inside the house, the rooms
consisting of bedroom (with corner cupboard, old bedstead
and deal table), kitchen and pantry.[7] In 1888 Surrey County
Council assumed responsibility for main roads, but maintenance
of the road through Bagshot was at first contracted out to
the parish surveyors. For a considerable time the upkeep of the
so-called 'great west road' once again depended solely on the
parish. The road was, of course, at this period still largely
free of through traffic, although in the 1880s the cyclists began
to herald in a new era.

Poor Relief

In-relief for the poor meant the Chertsey workhouse, and
there is not much information relating specifically to Windlesham in the Chertsey Board of Guardians' minute books of the
later 19th century. Unpaid overseers of the poor continued
to be appointed by the Windlesham vestry to authorise emer-
gency or medical out-relief, and to levy the poor rate. A paid
assistant overseer was appointed for the parish from year to
year, his duties being to act as clerk, make out the rate books,
and carry out any orders of the overseers. After 1861, contributions to the common fund were assessed on the rateable
value of parishes and not on their individual poor law expenditure.

Public Health

Concern with the problems of public health only goes back
to the decade or so preceding the Public Health Act of 1848,
which was passed as a result of the repeated cholera epidemics
of the 1830s and 1840s, and the investigations of the Poor
Law Commissioners into the causes of disease among the poor.
A Commission of Enquiry (1845) reported that the biggest
sources of disease were inadequacies of water supplies, drainage,
and facilities for disposal of refuse. The 1848 Act set up a
General Board of Health with powers to create local health
districts, and by adopting the Act the urban parts of poor

law unions could become local government districts with their own local boards of health.

In rural areas meanwhile, a Nuisance Removal Act (1846) recognised the boards of guardians of the poor as authorities for sanitary matters. On a certificate being signed by two medical practitioners, a complaint could be laid before the J.P.s to summon the owners of premises on which a 'nuisance' existed, such as an offensive privy, cesspool, or pigsty. In October 1848, as a result of a cholera epidemic, the vestry at Windlesham set up a committee to visit houses and see what required to be remedied in order to 'put the parish in a sanitary condition'. The *Red Lion* was to keep three beds in readiness in case of cholera. Notices were left by the assistant overseer at premises where a nuisance was found to exist, but little attention was paid by owners. Meanwhile Chertsey Board of Guardians had notified its intention to prosecute any nuisance properly reported. The vestry decided to print 250 copies of the board's notice, together with a further notice saying that the vestry was determined to act upon it if any nuisance 'decidedly prejudicial to health' remained unabated after 13 November, the notices to be affixed in public places and distributed generally. On 14 November it was resolved to report about a dozen cases (mostly privies) if the nuisance was not abated by 18 November, but only one privy was finally reported. Of the others, some had been cleansed and some were not thought to be bad enough! The committee was supposed to meet occasionally in future to look to the sanitary state of the parish, but there is no record that it did so.[8] In August 1866 during another cholera scare, a committee was set up to enquire into nuisances generally and to report them to the Inspector of Nuisances who had recently been appointed for the Union.[4]

Chertsey Rural Sanitary Authority

It is very unlikely that much action was in fact taken in rural districts, as there was little cause for satisfaction with that taken in urban districts. Following on the report of the Royal Sanitary Commission (1869–71), a new central department, the Local Government Board, was set up in 1871, and under the Public Health Acts of 1872 and 1875 England was divided into urban and rural sanitary districts. Rural sanitary authorities were empowered to provide their district (or any contributory place within it) with a proper water supply, by constructing or purchasing waterworks, or by contracting with any person for a supply. Similarly, an authority could construct or purchase sewers and sewage works, while most existing public sewers (and public cisterns) were vested in the authority. Every authority was allowed to undertake (or contract for) the removal of house refuse from premises and the cleansing of earth closets, privies, ashpits and cesspools, either for the whole or any part of its district; by order of the Local Government Board an authority could be *required* to do this. General common expenses of rural authorities were to be met out of the poor rates, but special expenses by a levy on the particular parish concerned. The Chertsey Board of Guardians became the rural sanitary authority for its area, which included (as well as Windlesham) the parishes of Chertsey, Walton-on-Thames, Weybridge, Byfleet, Chobham, Bisley, Pyrford, and Horsell. One of its first acts was to issue a general notice reminding householders of their duty to provide proper ashpits and see that cesspools were not offensive. Enquiries were also made of the individual parishes whether any works for drainage or water supply were already in progress there under the earlier Acts cited in the new Public Health Acts. The overseers of Windlesham replied that no such works were in progress.[9]

Water Supply

Towards the end of 1874 some fatal cases of enteric fever in Bagshot led to a report on sanitary conditions there being made by the Medical Officer of Health to the Chertsey Rural Sanitary Authority. He pointed out that there were no public sewers. Some houses drained into cesspools, but the sewage soaked into the sand and might pollute wells nearby. Other houses drained into the watercourses which ran through the village, while yet others had no drains and the occupiers threw slops on the ground or into a hole near the back door. So far as the water supply was concerned, some of the houses had shallow wells sunk in the sand, which were liable to pollution. A great many houses had no water on the premises at all, their only supply coming from their neighbours, the watercourses, or a small stream called the Butts at the bottom of the village. His view was that some system of drainage and an improved water supply were urgent. If some of the water which ran down from the high ground could be intercepted, stored in a small covered reservoir, and brought into the village in pipes, it would be 'a great boon' to the inhabitants.

The sanitary authority must, however, have been aware that such costly proposals would encounter resistance in the parish. Some attempts were made merely to remove the existing nuisances, and only after pressure from the Local Government Board was the M.O.H. asked to make a further investigation. In March 1875 he produced the following details about 51 houses:

> 44 houses had common privies, 7 had closets with trapped pans and cesspools. Most of the privies were offensive. 12 houses had no drains, 11 drained into ditches, 28 drained into watercourses or into cesspools which overflowed into them.
> 35 houses had no water, 16 had wells but the water in 4 wells was undrinkable, so that there were 39 houses effectively without water.[9]

The vestry at Windlesham became very alarmed at the possibility of having to fork out large sums of money. Mr. John Waterer doubtless recounted at the vestry meeting held in May 1875 the occasion when Sir James Clark (then physician to the Queen and residing at Bagshot Park) thrust his umbrella into the ground and said, 'In the circle of five miles round my umbrella you have the healthiest spot in the world'.[10] At any rate, they passed the following resolution:

> Bagshot as is well known being one of the most healthy villages in the County of Surrey according also to the opinion of the late Sir James Clarke . . . and it is well known Bagshot is a small scattered village that any attempt at laying on a water supply would be very expensive indeed to the ratepayers and benefit to none—The present water supply from the open stream being all that can be desired by the inhabitants . . .[4]

This resolution was read at a meeting of the sanitary authority and for the moment it was left to the parish to put in hand arrangements to improve the sanitary situation. Over the next few months the waywardens were very busy indeed cleaning out the stream and stopping up drains which ran into it. They pointed out, moreover, that the cases of fever in the village had been due not to polluted water but to infection from a contact in Liverpool. The M.O.H. insisted that in spite of all the activities of the waywardens, the water was still unfit for drinking. Although samples from above the village were fairly satisfactory, those from opposite the Institute and down by the Methodist chapel (near the gasworks) contained a large quantity of free ammonia and putrescible matter. Even if sewers were provided, the open stream would still be liable to pollution by dung, etc., washed off the fields.[9]

The Chertsey Sanitary Authority now called for advice from an expert, a Mr. R. Birch, who reported in December 1875 that with so many causes of pollution it was useless to try and protect the present sources of water and that the only way was to take a supply from higher ground. The principal source rose on the gravelly subsoil of Waterers' nursery next to the grounds of Penny Hill, and it could be intercepted here with a conduit of cast-iron pipes. The cost of mains and stand pipes in the street would be a little under £400. Birch did not recommend a system of sewers on this occasion, although he was convinced that it was the best method of refuse disposal. It would not overcome the water danger, and he was aware of the difficulty of carrying out any sewage scheme in the face of opposition. He therefore counselled delay, which must 'tend to overcome the difficulties resulting from prejudice and ignorance'.[9]

The Windlesham vestry returned to the charge, having had the water tested for themselves by Mr. C. W. Heaton, Professor of Chemistry and Joint Lecturer on Public Health at Charing Cross Hospital. From three samples he had reported it to be 'of good quality and uncontaminated with sewage matter to any appreciable extent', but as an extra precaution he recommended that all persons should be advised to filter it before drinking! At this point John Waterer declined to have trial holes for water dug on his land as had been proposed. The whole problem was then suddenly solved, to the obvious relief of all concerned, by an offer from James Hodges of Penny Hill in July 1876 to provide a water supply at his own expense. In the following October a vestry meeting was held at his request in order to decide 'the most desirable situations to erect the water fountains for supplying the inhabitants with pure water, a want so much felt in the village that it has been kindly laid on by him at his own expense . . .'. The sites proposed were four: opposite the *Hero of Inkerman,* opposite

Mr. Finch's (coal merchants), opposite the post office, and near Bagshot Bridge. The water works were handed over to the parish authorities and thanks were expressed to Mr. Hodges for saving the parish the considerable expense that must have otherwise been incurred to comply with the requirements of the sanitary authority.[4]

As a postscript to the long tussle described above, in September 1876 Chertsey Rural Sanitary Authority agreed that in order to meet the convenience of the guardians for Bisley, Chobham, Horsell and Windlesham, no subject by which a special charge would be occasioned would be discussed unless the parish guardians were present or a notice had been sent to them.[9] Attendance from these 'remote parts' was clearly somewhat irregular, as has already been noticed in connection with the meetings of the Chertsey Board of Guardians proper.

Over the years that followed numerous extensions and improvements were carried out to the water supply of Bagshot. In 1879 after the death of James Hodges, confirmation having been obtained that the water works had been 'dedicated to the public', the Inspector of Nuisances was instructed to take charge of them and a lease was signed with John Waterer at a nominal rent of 1s. per annum. In January 1880 the Inspector reported on the cost of extending the supply. He suggested that a water main be put in from the post office to the railway bridge in Guildford Road, where a standpipe would be erected, and the main then carried on for another 200 yards with a further standpipe. These two standpipes would supply 30 houses, the inhabitants of which now took their water from an open ditch, at an estimated cost of £60. The Inspector also proposed that the present three-inch pipe, which apparently only ran from the source as far as the *Hero of Inkerman,* should be extended to Bagshot Bridge, the two-inch pipe now in position over this stretch being taken out and used for the new extension. The expense involved was discussed at a vestry meeting, and the Chertsey Sanitary Authority having agreed that the parish could carry out the scheme itself, it was decided to ask for voluntary subscriptions. However, it was soon found that the necessary funds could not be raised locally, and the vestry could only express the hope that the authority would do the work with as little expense as possible. A tender for £70 from Mr. E. Spooner, builder and timber merchant at Bagshot mill, was later accepted, the suggested enlargement of the pipe obviously not being carried out.[11]

In July 1881 the Inspector of Nuisances made another report on the water supply. The mains now supplied 133 houses, there being six drinking fountains at intervals in the streets, and 44 houses having private supply pipes laid in direct from the mains. The estimated population of these houses was 665, requiring 13,300 gallons of water a day, but the present collecting tank and reservoir were failing to supply this quantity. He recommended that a new reservoir with contributory drains be constructed at the upper end of the nursery, and provided this supplied sufficient water, the three-inch main should be extended 700 feet to this reservoir, which would give an extra 15 foot pressure. The two lower fountains should be fitted with stoptaps instead of constant supply taps in order to prevent waste of water.[11] The work was duly carried out, the supply of water to the reservoir exceeding expectations. Meanwhile five residents who did not have the advantage of water supplies called on the sanitary authority to levy a water rate on those who did, and it was decided to levy a rate of 6d. in the pound for the year ending December 1882 on all houses situated within 200 feet of a standpipe.[12]

In 1885 the water supply failed again. The pipes were corroded with rust and the Inspector recommended that the main from the reservoirs to the *Inkerman* (440 yards) should be cleaned and perhaps renewed, and again suggested a larger main onwards from the *Inkerman* to replace the smaller pipes in use. It was, however, decided that what was needed was another new reservoir. The parish was required to pay £100 for special water supply expenses, and the further extension of the supply requested in a memorial from 15 Bagshot residents could not be entertained until arrears of special expenses were paid up. Soon afterwards the authority cancelled the demand for £100, deciding instead to levy a water rate again, but later on 'irrecoverable arrears' of water rates seem to have led to a return to the policy of charging the parish with special expenses.[12, 13] In February 1888 the Surveyor reported that the cost of enlarging, cleaning and repairing the water mains would be £120, but no details were given of the work actually carried out by Mr. R. Kemp for £98 10s. 0d.[13] In September 1890 the water supply was further extended to the almshouses.[14]

Sewage and Scavenging (Refuse Collection)

So far as a sewerage system was concerned, the counsel of delay given by Mr. Birch in 1875 seems to have been adopted, and the subject is hardly touched upon in the minutes of the Chertsey Sanitary Authority. Late in 1883 the Local Government Board asked what steps were being taken in Bagshot in view of an outbreak of fever there, and the Surveyor brought forward two schemes. The larger scheme, to drain 216 houses (out of a total of 248) at a cost of £1,500, was rejected outright by the inhabitants. A limited scheme to drain the lower part of the village only at a cost of £400 was not at first approved by the sanitary authority. Instead notices were served on a long list of occupiers for offences under the Public Health Act of 1875 in connection with ashpits, cesspools or the lack of same, but this seems to have led to an outcry in Bagshot for the notices were suspended almost at once. It was decided to undertake the smaller scheme and an application was made to the Local Government Board early in 1884 for an order constituting the ecclesiastical parish of Bagshot a Special Drainage District, for the purpose of charging exclusively on it (as a separate contributory place) the expense of works of sewerage and water supply. An Inquiry was held at the Bagshot Institute in July 1884 on behalf of the Local Government Board. A goodly attendance of parishioners then 'evinced considerable opposition' to a drainage scheme, Mr. John Waterer maintaining that it was unnecessary and that Bagshot could not afford it. John Waterer was at pains to draw an admission from the Surveyor that Bagshot was the healthiest of all the villages in the district, and when this was omitted from the *Surrey Advertiser* report, he made the paper put it in the following week![12, 15] Such was the current obsession with the subject that a subsequent report of the death of a village centenarian (William Skilling) was made the occasion for comment that the healthiness of Bagshot was proved by the fact that there were then seven or eight people living there who were over 80 years old.[16]

In October 1884 a public meeting passed a resolution to the effect that a large scheme was unnecessary, but that it entirely approved the smaller scheme. Further consultations took place with the government department, but no action was taken, the subject being continually postponed, in spite

of a memorial from 19 residents.[12] The sanitary authority
finally resolved in February 1886 that 'under existing circumstances and there now being an efficient public water supply,
a system of sewers in Bagshot be not undertaken, but that some
alternative plan for dealing with the condition of the village
be adopted'. The Surveyor was then told to order a sewage
cart and six pails for use in Bagshot, the cost not to exceed
£33, and a year later he reported the forming of pail closets
at seven houses, and the provision of cesspools at nine
others! The sewage from cesspools was now being emptied
regularly with the cart, and the authority agreed to pay £5
for one year for use of ground on South Farm as a depot
for scavenging. Meanwhile the Local Government Board had
conveniently lost their file on the subject of Bagshot sewerage,
and very little was heard from the central department over
the next few years![13]

Comprehensive scavenging arrangements had already been
started in the more populous districts subject to Chertsey
Rural Sanitary Authority. From 1880 Chertsey, and from 1883
or 1884 Addlestone, Weybridge, Oatlands, Walton, and
Hersham all had systems in operation whereby privy tubs were
supplied and emptied weekly, cesspools cleared at regular
intervals, and fortnightly collections of dry refuse made from
houses. This work had at first been done under contract, but
by 1884 it had been taken over directly by the rural sanitary
authority, which now hired horses and drivers only, itself
supplying all other labour as well as tub vans, sewage carts and
dustcarts.[11, 12] In December 1892 the Surveyor advised that
Bagshot should be scavenged on the same principle, except
that the work should be contracted for by some competent
person near the village. He would require additional plant,
consisting of one tub van (£42), one night cart (£28), one
dustcart (£22 10s. 0d.), 72 tubs, and 18 tub lids. It was
resolved to scavenge the parish of Windlesham for one year
from 2 January 1893, and to accept the tender of Mr. E.
Spooner to carry out this work in accordance with the
printed rules for £110, which would be charged as a special
expense to the parish. A year later a tender from George
Holmes for £100 a year was accepted, but the rate was
increased to £125 as from 24 June 1894, owing to increased
work in Bagshot.[17]

Elementary Education

The only schools for which the State had full responsibility in the mid-19th century were those run by the armed services and the prison and poor law authorities. It had nothing to do with a large number of schools run by religious organisations which either did not welcome State participation or were unable to conform to its requirements regarding standard of buildings and nature of management. For those schools, however, which did wish for help and were able to qualify for it, various provisions were made during the period between 1833 and 1870. Grants were available for building from 1833 and for teaching purposes from 1846, when State inspection was made a conditon of all grants. Otherwise the schools run by a variety of religious bodies were supported by voluntary subscriptions and by the 'school pence' which were contributed by parents. Attendance was, of course, entirely voluntary. The need for a more comprehensive system of elementary education led to the passing of the first Education Act in 1870. This provided for the setting up where necessary of a school board (with its own elections, officers and rates) to assess and meet local needs. The period during which this *ad hoc* system of school boards was in operation overlaps the period with which we are dealing, for it was not until 1902 that the system came to an end, all elementary schools being transferred to the control of the county councils.

Windlesham National School (Church of England)

Up to 1846 the National Society's school in School Road, Windlesham, seems to have served both Windlesham and Bagshot. The society's general enquiry of 1846-7 records that the school was held in two rooms. The master and mistress received a salary of £70, a house being provided. The total annual expenditure was about £80, which was raised by the children's pence and subscriptions. The school was attended by 112 boys and 93 girls, about half of them on weekdays and Sundays, and the rest on Sundays only.[18]

In 1864 the school was enlarged at a cost of £265 with the aid of a government grant, and an annual maintenance grant was received thereafter. To conform with the requirements of the Charity Commission, a management committee was set

up, consisting of the ministers of the churches at Windlesham
and Bagshot, and four other persons, who had to be members
of the Church of England, and subscribers of one pound and
upwards annually to the school. The rector was to superintend
religious and moral instruction and could use the premises for
a Sunday school under his exclusive control, but in all other
respects the management was vested in the committee. The four
original committee members were William Ashton (Windlesham Hall), James Hodges (Penny Hill), John Clark, and Sir
James Clark (Bagshot Park), but the last-named resigned almost
immediately, being replaced by Charles Hulse (Hall Grove).[19]

The school was inspected in August 1864, when the following report was made:

> . . . The Managers will have to suffer from the injudicious arrange-
> ment of the children by the Master, who offered for examination
> under the fifth standard those who were not sufficiently grounded
> to pass in the third and fourth standards under which no children
> were presented for examination. They will also suffer from the
> want of discipline as some children copied after repeated cautions . . .

The Committee of the Privy Council which supervised government grants warned that it would be compelled to make a
serious deduction from the grant next year, unless the inspector
was able to 'speak more favourably both of the discipline the
supply of books & the state of the privies'. This led to the
immediate sacking of the master and mistress and the engagement of a Mr. John Brewin and his sister, who commenced
duty in January 1865 at a joint salary of £70 per annum and a
house rent free. It was decided that after the summer holidays
the fee for a single child should be 2d. per week to be paid in
advance, with 1d. per week for every additional child in the
same family. There were to be seven weeks holiday: two at
Christmas, one at Whitsun, and four at harvest time.[19]

For the rest of its existence as a National school, Windlesham
school received very good reports under John Brewin. In
December 1866 the Inspector said that it was 'a good and
efficient country school, the younger children are particularly
well taught'. The average number of children attending
increased from 75 in November 1864 to 92 in November 1865
and 102 in December 1866. In 1867 the schoolmaster asked for
either a larger salary or a fixed proportion of the Government
grant to be given to him, in view of the favourable reports and

increased attendance. (This was during the period of 'payment by results' between 1862 and 1890, when the size of the grant, which was paid to the managers and not the teachers, depended on inspection reports and on the children passing an annual examination.) The managers found on enquiry that his salary was 'not inadequate' compared with other schools. They did not think it desirable to fix the proportion of the grant which he would receive, but they assured him that his total emolument would not be less than what he would get if half the grant were allocated. Whatever the form of words, Brewin did, in fact, receive one-half of the grant in subsequent years.[19]

A list of subscribers to the school in 1870 is headed by the Queen, and seems to consist entirely of the gentry. The sum raised was £33 3s. 0d. In January 1872 the managers voted unanimously to transfer the school to the new Windlesham School Board which had just been elected. They reserved only the right to use the premises on Sundays for religious instruction.[19]

Bagshot National School (Church of England)

An infant school which had been erected in Bagshot next to the chapel burial ground about 1847[18] was supported principally by the Duchess of Gloucester.[20] By her will of 29 January 1857 the Duchess left £25 per annum for the support of the school 'at present existing in the parish of Windlesham . . . known by the name of the National School so long as the same or a similar Institution . . . not disapproved of by the Rector, Vicar, or Incumbent for the time being of the said parish shall continue to exist'.[21] The site of the Bagshot school was legally conveyed to the National Society on 16 July 1857[18] and the money was applied in support of this school. There are no actual records of the school until 1870, the year of the first Education Act, when it was decided that it would be advisable to place the school under government inspection in order to secure a grant. Managers were appointed in accordance with State regulations, the first committee consisting of the following:

> Rev. J. Fyler (rector), Rev. F. C. Fitton (curate), Mr. Waterer, Mr. John Waterer, Mr. Hodges (Penny Hill), Mr. James (Lambourne House), Mr. Dumbleton (Hall Grove).[22]

The school was first 'opened and conducted conformably with government regulations' on 25 April 1870. The salary of the mistress was £25 per annum 'in addition to the school pence at not less than 4s. per week and the partially furnished school house'. H.M. inspector visited the school at Bagshot in June 1870, and reported as follows:

> This school has hitherto been uninspected. The building is good and sufficient, but the gallery is too high and occupies too much space. The attainments of the children are as yet low. The School should be taught as a mixed school with an infant-department under an assistant teacher. The teacher's residence ought to be enlarged.[22]

On 3 December 1870 a public meeting was held at the Institute to consider the necessity of enlarging the school in accordance with the Education Act. There were only 23 people present. The first resolution to appoint a school board was lost by 12 to four, while a second resolution that the money required (estimated at £250) should be met by voluntary subscriptions was carried by 10 to one. In the event, however, the attempt to remain more or less independent failed for lack of funds. In February 1871 application was made to the National Society and also to the Diocesan Society and the Ecclesiastical Commissioners for aid in connection with the enlargement.[22] The school consisted of four small rooms, and it was proposed to erect a much larger room and lobbies, together with two additional rooms for the teacher's house, at an estimated cost of £425.[18] In May 1871 the subscription list still amounted only to just over half this sum. In January 1872 a resolution to transfer the school to the Windlesham School Board was carried unanimously.[22]

Windlesham Board Schools

The first School Board met in January 1872. The five members elected were Rev. J. Fyler (the chairman), Rev. F. A. P. Lory (curate of Bagshot), Edward Webb (Roundwood), John Gillham (Hatton Hall) and Henry Dumbleton (Hall Grove). The first requirement was to have new plans drawn up to bring the school buildings at both Bagshot and Windlesham to the required standard to accommodate the numbers laid down by the Education Department. An entirely new building was needed at Bagshot, the cost of which was estimated at £803, and it was decided in September 1872 to hire the large room at the *Red Lion* for teaching the children while the work was in progress.[23] By 1893 it was necessary to enlarge the Bagshot school owing to the increase in the population, and new buildings were erected to accommodate 320 children altogether, the average attendance at the time being 250.[24] About £447 was spent on the school at Windlesham in 1873 [23] and it was enlarged again in 1889.[25] The average attendance there was about 150 in 1888, and about 220 in 1902.[26]

It was one thing to provide the accommodation for the growing population of school age. The board's other main problem was to get the children to school. Attendance at board schools was not at first generally compulsory (under the Education Acts of 1876 and 1880 it became virtually compulsory for those under 13, but with numerous exceptions), but boards could enforce attendance in their own areas. Byelaws issued by the Windlesham Board in December 1872 provided that the parent of every child between five and 13 years of age must send the child to school unless there was a reasonable excuse. Excuses accepted were sickness, some other efficient form of instruction being given, or the child not living within two miles of a school. A child between 10 and 13 who had passed the fourth standard examination was not obliged to attend. Children were to attend for not less than 25 hours a week.[23] During the 30 years of the board's existence, parents were constantly summoned to attend its meetings to show good reason why they should not be made to appear in court on a charge of failing to send a child to school.

Windlesham School continued for a year or two under Mr. John Brewin, and he was followed by a Mr. Corry. In 1877 Mr. James Simms was appointed headmaster, a post he was to hold for at least 40 years. His wife, Winifred, also taught in the school for 28 years, and the teaching was very efficient.[25] A report on Bagshot School just after it was taken over by Windlesham School Board refers to it having 'scarcely as yet emerged from the condition of an Infant's School'.[23] Mr. A. Rogers was engaged as master, and he remained in the post for 20 years and more. The board had, however, occasion to warn him in 1896 that he might be sacked if it was not satisfied with the condition of the school during the current year. In 1898, after a report from H.M. inspector had put the blame for the unsatisfactory state of the school entirely on the headmaster, the board sent Mr. Rogers a copy of a resolution regretting that it 'saw no reason for not concurring with the report', and warning him that he risked dismissal at the end of the school year. It was, however, not until the following year, after the election of a new board with two fresh members, that his resignation was called for, the school being then under threat of withdrawal of the Government grant. In 1901 both schools were working well and obtaining the highest grants.[27]

Soon after the school board was set up, it was decided to start night schools, to be held three times a week between October and March. A good report was given on the first school by the Windlesham master in April 1873, and a similar arrangement was then made at Bagshot for the following winter, when it was laid down that pupils were to be charged 2d. per week, and none were to be accepted under 13 years of age. In November 1875 the Windlesham master reported an increased attendance of 18 boys who were 'attentive and willing to learn', but attendance dropped and the school was closed in the following February.[23, 25] Night schools such as these which were tried from time to time were equivalent in rural areas to an extension of elementary education for young adults who had missed their schooling, and were not a form of higher education.

As has already been mentioned, board schools were supported by the rates, as well as by grants from the Education Department. For this reason the triennial elections to the board were sometimes contested, as local ratepayers sought control over the way their money was spent. At the second election held for Windlesham School Board in December 1874 there were seven candidates for five seats. Details of the poll are entered in the vestry minutes: Thomas Webb (Broadway Green Farm) came top, with James Bull, of Lightwater Farm, second. The rector, who came fifth, did not attend the first meeting, but sent his resignation. In the following March an unsuccessful attempt was made to regain some measure of clerical control. Applications were made to the school board by the rector and Mr. James, and by the vicar of Bagshot and Mr. John Waterer, to be appointed managers to the Windlesham and Bagshot schools respectively. Some boards did appoint managers for individual schools, but the Windlesham School Board did not consider that it was necessary.[25]

James Bull, who had been elected chairman, remained in this office for 13 years. In 1887 Rev. J. M. Freshfield (the new rector, who was now a member of the board) was elected chairman, holding the office until he resigned the living in 1900.[26] The vicar of Bagshot (Rev. F. A. P. Lory), who was also now on the board, died about this time, and to fill the two vacancies the two new incumbents were co-opted, an action which was said in the *Aldershot News* to have met with a certain amount of criticism locally. The newspaper report then then went on to say that an unusually interesting struggle for seats was likely to take place in the forthcoming elections among seven strong candidates, who included Mr. John Fyler of Woodlands. A week later the paper disclosed that there was to be for the first time a lady candidate for Windlesham School Board. (At the first school board election held in London, Dr. Elizabeth Garrett and Miss Emily Davies were returned, but social changes would have come much later in the rural areas.) The Windlesham candidate was Miss Soames of Hall Grove, the local organiser of the District Nursing Association, who would, it was suggested, 'make a most useful addition'. The lady was unsuccessful, but considerable sympathy was expressed with her, and her 'plucky fight' attracted a lot of attention. It was felt that the share of the votes which she obtained 'augured well for some future success', but this turned out to be the last election for a local school board![28]

10 A Residential District

The Increase in Population and New Development

NEARLY A HUNDRED YEARS after the exceptional population increase of the early 19th century, there was a second
period of unusual growth. Set this time against a diminishing
rate of increase in the population of England and Wales, and
bearing in mind the development of new centres at Sunningdale and Lightwater, this large increase clearly indicates a
substantial element of migration into the parish. The rate of
increase began to go up again between 1891 and 1901, and the
highest rate was reached between 1901 and 1911 (see Fig. 8).
The proportion due to immigration in this decade is not known,
but in view of the very large increase, it must have been at least
as high as it was between 1911 and 1921. The census report
for 1921 attributes the increase of 629 persons (14.8 per cent.)
since 1911 as follows: excess of births over deaths, 281 (6.6 per
cent); immigration, 348 (8.2 per cent.). By 1921-31 immigration had dropped to 3.4 per cent. out of the total increase
of 7.8 per cent. There must also have been a certain amount

| Year | Population | Increase % | | Number of inhabited houses |
		Windlesham	England & Wales	
1891	2,965	11.1	11.7	604
1901	3,415	15.2	12.2	729
1911	4,249	24.4	10.9	954
1921	4,878	14.8	4.9	1,109
1931	5,257	7.8	5.5	1,343

Fig. 8   Parish/urban district of Windlesham. Population and
houses, 1891-1931

of immigration before 1901 and all-in-all it seems likely that there was an influx of well over 1,000 persons between 1891 and 1931, the peak probably occurring just before the First World War.

The main reason for this influx seems to have been that land was available for building, and so houses to rent were cheaper and less scarce than in neighbouring districts. That this was certainly the opinion of the local authorities is clear from comments made on the housing situation in 1903, 1912 and 1918. Already in 1903 the parish was described as 'largely residential', and a great deal of building went on between then and the war, much of it consisting of small tenements of under £12 rateable value.[1] During the war building virtually ceased, but there was considerably activity in the 1920s, some of which was devoted to rehousing in better conditions. Between 1 January 1919 and 31 December 1931, 402 new houses were built in the district.[2] The census reports show a net gain of 272 dwellings (including both inhabited and uninhabited) between 1921 and 1931.

The development of the area led to the gradual introduction of amenities. Gas became available throughout the parish about 1900, piped water was supplied generally by the time of the First World War, and public sewers were laid down in the 1920s. A detailed account of these and other public services is given in Chapters 11 and 12. So far as electricity was concerned, the early years of this century saw the usual rivalry between companies to get the necessary powers to supply the area. Companies were, however, only keen to lay mains in the more profitable roads, such as the London road, while the parish council wanted to have electric cables made compulsory in all other roads, or at least to get more favourable terms for supply than those laid down in the Electric Lighting Acts. No compulsory area was actually specified for Windlesham in the Act which the Ascot Gas and Electricity Company obtained in August 1906,[3] and mains were not laid in Bagshot and the district generally until early in 1924.

How was the growth of population allocated as between the old village centres of Bagshot and Windlesham on the one hand and the newly-developed areas of Sunningdale and Lightwater on the other? The only divisions of the population in the printed census reports are the areas of the ecclesiastical

parishes. A very small section of the population of the civil
parish remained within the ecclesiastical parish of St. Saviour,
Valley End, Chobham, but the part of Sunningdale in the civil
parish was transferred back from the parish of Holy Trinity,
Sunningdale, to that of St. John the Baptist in 1904, the
numbers involved being only about 100 in 1901.[4] Lightwater,
which had only a few scattered houses in the early 1890s,
was partly in the ecclesiastical parish of Windlesham and partly
in that of Bagshot. We have, therefore, to rely for population
distribution mainly on the evidence of the six-inch O.S. maps
surveyed or revised in 1894–5, 1912–13, and 1934,[5] and on
commercial directories.[6] The papers of the Church Commissioners do, however, suggest that in 1925 the population of
the Sunningdale district (within Windlesham) was about 500,[7]
and that of the proposed Lightwater 'conventional district'
round about 1,500 in 1929.[8] Lightwater and Sunningdale
could thus account for an increase of something like 1,900
people between 1891 and 1931, and as the total increase in
the population was just under 2,300, increase in the old centres
was obviously on a much lower scale. There was some movement out to Lightwater with the building of council houses
there from the later 1920s onwards, and by the 1930s the
population of Lightwater was probably nearly one-third of the
total.[8] We can now take a look at the four population centres
in more detail.

Bagshot

Relatively few houses were built in Bagshot in this period
(see Fig. 9) and growth had clearly slowed down compared
with the later 19th century. In the village itself, there were
some more houses on the south side of Church Road by 1912,
and there were other new houses up London Road opposite
Bagshot Park. Down Guildford Road were two large new
houses, 'The Beeches' and 'Stone Hill House'. Shops and
businesses continued to expand in the early years of this
century. The first branches of multiple stores arrived with the
International Tea Stores and the London & Provincial Meat
Stores—multiples had steadily become more common round
the country since the 1870s. In Bagshot Square W. S. Stanley
had a large draper's shop, later Mason & Stennett, ladies' and

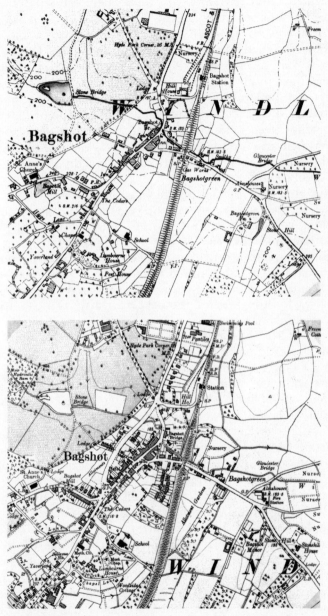

Fig. 9.   The village of Bagshot: *above* 1894, *below* 1934.

gentlemen's outfitters. A new coal merchants (later Morris Bros.) had opened in Guildford Road. An entirely new type of business now to be seen was that of cycle dealer and agent. Bagshot had a dentist, though he attended on Fridays only from 3 p.m. to 4 p.m. A branch of Barclays Bank had been opened next to the Institute. On 1 April 1907 Bagshot Wesleyan church on Jenkins Hill opened a new Sunday school building; a two-day bazaar (opened by Lady Elphinstone of Pinewood) had earlier been held in the Institute in order to finance the cost which was estimated at £650. Previous to the building of the Sunday school as many as 140 children were meeting in a small room.[9]

The character of the village must have changed yet once again, as the advent of the bicycle and the motor car re-introduced through traffic to the country districts for the first time since the end of the coaching era. It is clear from contemporary comment that Bagshot, with its pine plantations, was regarded as a healthy district and we may imagine the quiet lanes were popular with those in search of fresh air and exercise. By the turn of the century traffic through Bagshot was reaching sizeable proportions at certain times of the year, and the parish council applied in April 1899 for the high street to be watered during the summer months because of the dust. Surrey County Council, however, was only prepared to grant £2 for watering during Ascot week! In June 1903 the parish council complained about cars 'being driven so recklessly through Bagshot'. Two councillors paid for the hire of a stop-watch, several cars were timed, and the drivers summoned.[10] On 26 September 1903 the *Aldershot News* reported that motorists continued to make Bagshot a centre for excessive speed, suggesting that this might be due to the village being approached on either side by a hill. A further item entitled 'Baulking the police' told how one Bagshot resident had been doing his best to defeat the efforts of the police to catch offenders. The man, a car owner who was alleged to have been convicted more than once for speeding, had taken up his position on the London road the previous Saturday for at least an hour. He was 'armed with a roll of paper two feet square, and which was inscribed in large red letters, "Beware of the Police" '. This he held up as cars approached, and informed the drivers that there was a police-trap a little further on.

Consequently for part of the way through the village, cars went 'at something almost approaching a funeral pace'.

One of the chief complaints made about motor cars was the dust they created. Towards the end of 1905 a memorial was got up by the inhabitants complaining about the dust on the roads, particularly the main road, and a parish meeting was eventually called (April 1907) to discuss the estimated cost of watering the principal roads in the parish. One speaker claimed that on certain occasions something like 32 motor cars passed through the high street in two hours, and another suggested that toll-gates should be brought back! At their next meeting the parish council passed a resolution protesting against 'the present use of the roads by motorists to the detriment of the general public' and asking the district and county councils to consider what steps could be taken to 'again enable the public to use the roads with comfort and safety'.[11] The problem of dust was solved not long afterwards by the new tarring process (see Chapter 12), and in 1910 a visitor to Sunningdale commented on the 'straight tarred wide thoroughfare' along which 'the cycles and motors speed on incessantly'.[12] The Motor Car Act of 1903 had raised the speed limit for cars from 12 to 20 miles an hour, but on application by the local road authority, regulations could be made by the Local Government Board for a speed not exceeding 10 miles. In December 1908 the parish council asked Surrey County Council for a limit of 10 miles an hour between the *Cricketers* and Jenkins Hill.[11] A 10-mile speed limit through Bagshot village was made in 1911, but cars continued to go too fast. Windlesham Urban District Council asked for a 5-mile speed limit, but the county council did not agree (June 1914) that there were sufficient grounds.[13]

After the war there was a certain amount of further development in Bagshot. The by-pass road was completed in 1925 (see Chapter 12), and in the late 1920s and early 1930s shops and cafes sprang up on both sides. The car was now accepted as part of the way of life, the speed limit being abolished for cars by the Road Traffic Act 1930, and the *Camberley News* contained frequent accounts of serious accidents on the roads of Bagshot and Windlesham. Many garages were being opened up and down the country to carry out repairs and to sell petrol; petrol pumps supplying Pratts or Shell began to appear, petrol having so far been available only in two-gallon cans. There was now a motor garage on the by-pass and two others (Groves and Osmans) further along the main road at Jenkins Hill. There was also a garage in Bagshot High Street, and a motor car body painter, Alfred Parsons of Connaught Villas.

The mid-1920s saw the opening of both the Catholic Oratory of Christ the King in the Guildford road, and the Gospel Mission in The Square. The latter was founded as the result of a breakaway from the Methodist church on Jenkins Hill by a number of members. St. Anne's church built a new parish hall in Church Road in 1925. The main building firms were Geo. Church & Co. and Jonathan Corbett; there were no estate agents. In the 1930s one could buy almost anything in Bagshot. The village now boasted (as well as a large selection of food shops) a jeweller, a china shop, an optician, a ladies' hairdresser, two newsagents, and three tobacconists, while Alex. Papworth, in the Guildford road, sold a variety of goods from sewing machines to wireless sets.

Lightwater

The name Lightwater Moor is used by John Aubrey about 1700.[14] Rocque (1768-70) gives the name Whitmoor to the heath near Lightwater Pond, and 'light' may be a corruption of 'white'. Lightwater began to be developed in the late 1890s but the potential for building here had already been recognised 30 years earlier. Some 126 acres of heathland at Lightwater had been allocated to the Dean and Canons of Windsor in the Enclosure Award in respect of Manor Farm, and in 1867 when the property vested in the Ecclesiastical Commissioners a survey was made for them. The lessee of Manor Farm, Rev James Fyler, wanted to raise money for the purchase of the main part of the property, and he offered to sell his leasehold interest in the heathland to the Commissioners. He quoted the surveyor as saying that the heath property was valuable as building land owing to its position and the nature of the soil. The district was approved of by the medical profession, a lot of people having already been attracted to a sanatorium in the neighbourhood. The surveyor may have mentioned this to him privately, but the report to the Commissioners merely stated that the 126 acres had 'some additional value

Fig. 10. The Lightwater area: *above* 1894, *below* 1934.

beyond that which they realised as a run attached to the farm. The Commissioners declined to purchase the leasehold interest in the heathland, and Fyler later bought the whole property by means of a mortgage.[15]

No change is shown at Lightwater on the 1894–5 revision of the O.S. map, but the first development began about this time and Fig. 10 illustrates the remarkable change which took place over the next 40 years. No special reason has been found for the building of houses at Lightwater at this juncture apart from the fact that it was here that land was made available and, as already mentioned, it was comparatively cheap. It seems that originally the function of Lightwater was to meet the overspill needs of 'labouring people' from Bagshot itself and from neighbouring places like Camberley, Chobham and Sunningdale. Some of the earliest houses were built fronting the south side of the Guildford road on enclosure land allocated to Manor Farm and Harrishaws: the row of semi-detached brick cottages (originally some 25 pairs) between Macdonald and Grasmere Roads bear dates ranging from 1896 to 1902, the earlier ones tending to be nearer Macdonald Road. South of this area 53 acres belonging to Astagehill Farm came up for auction in 1895. In 1902 Lightwater was referred to in the papers of the Church Commissioners as an outlying poor part of the parish.[8] The employment of some of the first residents may have been in the nurseries of Messrs. Fromow, South Farm nearly opposite being acquired for nurseries between 1899 and 1902.

Before very long, however, people were coming to live at Lightwater from farther afield, often on retirement. By 1907 plots of land (for as little as £10) were obviously being advertised fairly widely: the minutes of Chertsey Rural District Council refer to building applications received, for example, from a Mr. Abel of north-west London for a house on the south side of Macdonald Road, and from a Mr. Ruddock of Wimbledon for two houses at 'Grassmere Hill'. A villa at 'Ambleside Hill' was mentioned in 1908, and in the same year the council's surveyor brought up the question of the state of the roads on the 'Grassmere Hill estate' then being developed. This was probably already part of what became known as the Brake estate: in the 1915 directory Henry William Brake, estate agent, had an office in Macdonald Road, and George

Cooper was a builder in the same road. There was no speculative building, though local builders might put up a pair of semi-detached cottages as an investment. By 1909 there were about 100 houses at Lightwater,[11] and pre-war directories name a number of the important residents at the larger houses. In 1911 there were three general shopkeepers, Walter Mann, James Street, and Charles Perry (who had the sub-post office), in Guildford Road, Lightwater. By the First World War the number of shops and businesses had increased considerably, now including baker, butcher, draper, chimney sweep, cycle dealer, cab proprietor, two laundries, a small nursery garden, and apartments for hire. Lightwater was still small enough, however, for most people to know one another.

All Saints' church, Lightwater, was built of brick in the Gothic style in 1903 at the expense of Mrs. Christie of Ribsden as a memorial to her husband, Richard Copley Christie, late Chancellor of the Diocese of Manchester and a distinguished scholar and author. The church served the Lightwater portion of Bagshot ecclesiastical parish as well as part of Windlesham, and had about 120 seats.[7]

A Primitive Methodist chapel was built on the corner of Guildford Road and Macdonald Road in 1913. Mission services had been started at Lightwater in July 1912, being held in a room at the side of the residence in Grasmere Road of a Mr. W. J. Alsford, one of the first trustees of the chapel. There was, however, only accommodation there for about 40 people, whereas twice as many wanted to attend. The church cost round about £600 (including £60 for the site), and a Sunday school was built not long afterwards at a cost of £250.[16] (Methodist services were held at Lightwater for 60 years, the last service in the church taking place in July 1972.)

Considerable further development took place between the two wars. In 1919 plots on the Brake estate cost £20 each, which was thought dear at the time.[17] Numbers of bungalows (many of them little more than wooden shacks, the plans of which were passed as temporary buildings) were put up in roads such as Curley Hill and High View. The papers of the Church Commissioners refer in 1925 to the district being built on 'to a considerable extent'.[7] A new cemetery was opened on land acquired by the Windlesham Urban District Council in 1921, and in 1925-6 the council built its first houses here, re-naming the road The Avenue. By 1932, 100 council houses and flats had been erected in Lightwater (see Chapter 12). There was more new building on the north side of Guildford Road, and the trees disappeared from the triangular area between All Saints' Road and Broadway Road. The number of commercial premises had doubled and now included newsagent, confectioner, shoe repairer, and two hairdressers. A dentist attended twice a week, 2.30 p.m. to 5 p.m. on Wednesdays, and 3.30 p.m. to 8 p.m. on Saturdays. There were two building firms, H. Hipperson and Miles Bros.

Windlesham

Early this century the village was thus described in the *Victoria County History*: 'almost entirely modern . . . the church is some distance from the village . . . The plan of the village defies analysis, and is of very recent growth'.[18] The change of emphasis, as the development of Updown Hill and Chertsey Road begun after the enclosure was concentrated more and more in this area, had tended to obscure the earlier plan. Rather more building for new houses occurred in Windlesham than in Bagshot during this period (see Fig. 11). By 1912 there were more houses on the south-west side of Updown Hill and on the east side of Chertsey Road. Parallel with the latter a new road—Pine Grove—had been laid out, with houses on the eastern side. New large houses further out from the village included 'Westwood' and 'Updown Hill House'. There were now two building firms, Bullens in Church Road, and Henry Greenfield in Updown Hill. A Wesleyan Mission chapel was started in a tin hut on Updown Hill in the early 1900s, services continuing to be held there until 1969.[9] Several new shops had been opened near the *Sun* inn, including another butchers (a branch of Grimditch & Webb, who were also in Bagshot), another grocers, in addition to Arrows (J. Chapman), a florist, and a newsagent. There were two cycle agents and a cycle repairer. Although it was not on the main road, Windlesham, too, was having some trouble with motor cars. In 1905 the parish council drew attention to the dangerous corners near the *Sun,* and Surrey County Council fixed notice boards warning drivers at the three road approaches.[19]

In the 1920s 16 council houses were built on the east side of Thorndown Lane, and there were a few more houses on the

Fig. 11. The village of Windlesham: *above* 1894, *below* 1934.

west side of Chertsey Road and in Woodlands Lane. More
of the larger type of house had been erected on the Sunningdale side of the village, particularly along Westwood Road.
The local builders were now Thos. Dale & Sons in Updown
Hill, and A. W. Viner in London Road. There were two motor
garages on the main road and also one at Updown Hill, while
Edward Matthews had a car for hire at the corner of Church
Road. Miss Louisa Bullen, court dressmaker in Updown Hill,
made dresses for Ascot and similar events for the ladies of the
big houses in the neighbourhood, employing a dozen girls
in her workshop. There was now a hairdresser in the village,
and two dentists attended part-time, one on Mondays, 11 a.m.
to 2 p.m., and the other on Thursdays, 10 a.m. to 1 p.m. By
the 1930s Updown Hill had also acquired a chemist and a
dairy. The Windlesham and Valley End Cottage Hospital
was opened, the foundation stone for a new range of buildings (as an extension to the existing house at Hatton Hill)
being laid by Princess Christian of Schleswig Holstein on
14 September 1921.

Sunningdale

As we have already seen, a certain amount of building had
taken place in the Sunningdale district over the second half
of the 19th century. The real era of development near the
station began, however, with the release for building of land
owned by St. John's College, which had over 500 acres in its
Sunningdale estate, of which some 250 acres were in the parish
of Windlesham. During the period of agricultural prosperity
part of the large area of barren heathland had been reclaimed
and cultivated, but as the effects of the subsequent depression
were felt, the tenants gave up, and a small syndicate then put
forward a scheme for leasing some of the land south-east of
the London road. Part of it was to be laid out as a golf course
(in Chobham parish) and part to be developed for building.
In 1899 the syndicate took a lease of some of the land, and
this was followed by other leases. Arrangements were made
for the development of the property for high-class housing by
the Ridgemount Company, who constructed roads, laid on a
water supply, and arranged for treatment of sewage. The
College agent at Sunningdale was Mr. T. A. Roberts, architect

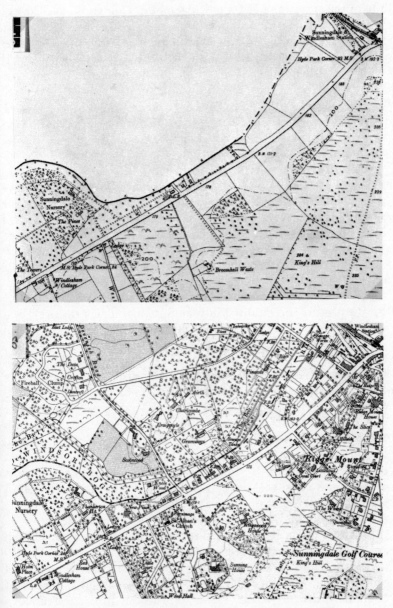

Fig. 12.   Part of Sunningdale: *above* 1894, *below* 1934.

and surveyor, who had his own office at Ridgemount. After the initial steps taken by the Ridgemount Company, the College continued to develop the estate, making further new roads. Lady Margaret Road in Windlesham parish (named after Margaret Beaufort, who founded St. John's College in 1511) was laid down in 1910–13.[20] Much of the development consisted of large houses each in a number of acres of land, such as 'Woodhall', 'Broomhill' (later named 'Sunning House'), 'The Moorings' (later 'Kingswood House') and many others on the map of 1912. Most of the houses had their own lodge or gardener's cottage (see Fig. 12).

The 1911 directory lists more than a dozen new shops and businesses on the London road at Sunningdale, whereas before there had been only coal merchants and estate agents at the station. There were two banks, branches of Barclays and of London & Provincial. The number of shops had increased further by the 1920s and 1930s, two firms of motor engineers and a firm of wireless engineers having set up business among others.

In 1902 the district church of St. Alban, a temporary iron structure originally built at Sunninghill (Berkshire), was re-erected on a site in the London road at the expense of Mr. C. D. Kemp-Welch. A new parsonage was later built next to the church, the whole site being leased from St. John's College at a nominal rent of £10.[21] Mr. P. G. Palmer of Guildford, who left detailed and evocative accounts of visits made to morning service at the churches at Windlesham, Lightwater and Sunningdale on summer Sundays in 1910, describes his walk of about seven miles to St. Alban's from Woking station. He obviously enjoyed these walking expeditions, but it would have been difficult for him to get there by public transport anyway, since there were no Sunday trains on to Bagshot. Having left Woking at 7.40 a.m., he reached Chobham church at 8.35 a.m. and Windlesham village at 10 a.m. He went on through the pine woods to strike the main road near the church at 10.30 a.m., when he saw 'quite a large number of well-dressed people' coming up the road from the direction of Sunningdale. The little cruciform church behind a screen of firs and quickset hedge was of corrugated iron painted deep red, with a thatched roof. The congregation numbered about 80, and Mr. Palmer again commented that it was 'quite a fashionable one', in contrast to the congregation at Lightwater, which he described as 'all villagers'.[12]

Communications

Railways

For travel up to London, railway services had improved considerably by the early years of this century, and in 1910 there were about a dozen trains in each direction from Bagshot, twice as many as in 1887. The first trains up left at 7.09 a.m (via Ascot) and 7.22 a.m. (via Woking), and several businessmen's trains took little more than an hour on the journey.[22] In 1938 trains ran at half-hourly intervals (apart from peak periods) in both directions between Woking and Ascot, but as the connections on to Waterloo were less frequent from Ascot, the Bagshot commuter had a better service via Woking and the main line.[23]

Until after the First World War the motor car was a rich man's luxury, and for ordinary people journeys within the area were still made mainly by horse and trap, or cart, by bicycle, or on foot. An 80-year-old lady recalls today how in her teens when coming from her Woking home to visit relatives in Bagshot and Windlesham she would take the train (via Camberley) to Bagshot station. A postcard would be sent home to report safe arrival. A fine day would be chosen for a visit to Windlesham from Bagshot, the nearest way to Updown Hill being a good two miles across the fields by the old church path. In the early 1900s there was a project started to provide a more direct rail link to Bagshot from Woking via Horsell, Chobham and Lightwater. We have already seen how a proposal 100 years earlier for a canal link from the Basingstoke Canal at Pirbright failed owing to lack of finance, and the scheme for a light railway along a parallel route seems to have met the same fate.

Messrs. Gardiner and Collinson Hall, the promoters of the scheme, attended a meeting of Windlesham Parish Council in November 1903 to give information about the proposed line, which would enter the parish at 'Rectory Cottage' in Black Stroud Lane, pass near All Saints' church, and cross Fromows' nurseries and New Road to join the London & South Western railway near Bagshot. Sidings would be provided at the nurseries and at other points,[24] and there was even the possibility of a station just south of Rectory Farm,[25] which would have been accessible from Windlesham as well as Lightwater. It was hoped to run special trains from Woking during the holidays to bring people into the district, and the promoters agreed that they had in mind 'booming the country passed through'. After much discussion a resolution was finally passed, but only by four votes to three, that the light railway would be of advantage to the parish. Those in favour thought that it would be an excellent thing for getting nursery and other produce to market cheaper and easier. The opposition view was that the railway would lead to the erection of small cottage property for an influx of labouring people from the Woking area, so increasing the burden on the rates without appreciable benefit to the parish, and that the larger houses in Lightwater would 'regard the rail with anything but pleasure'.[24] The council meeting was fully reported in the *Aldershot News,* which on 5 December 1903 published a letter from a Mr. C. C. Cannell of Heatherdene, Lightwater, saying that he had consulted the majority of residents of both large and small houses in Lightwater, and that most, in fact, favoured the scheme.

An Inquiry held by the Light Railway Commission on 22 January 1904 resulted in a Provisional Order being granted, although so far the London & South Western was not prepared to agree to junctions at Woking and Bagshot, obviously an important part of the scheme. Junctions were eventually arranged, and a further Woking & Bagshot Light Railways (Extension) Order was granted after a second Inquiry held at Woking on 17 July 1905. The scheme then went to the Board of Trade, which in spite of objections made by a landowner, who said that the financial resources of the promoters were inadequate and the populations of the places involved were not large enough to make it pay, confirmed the Order in 1906. It was reported that the promoters hoped to start work in October the same year, thus providing work for local people (there was some concern about unemployment at the time) during the winter. Work was to start at both ends simultaneously and to be completed within one year from the start. The promoters said that all the necessary capital had been subscribed, but as nothing more was heard of the railway, they must have been over confident![26]

Motor Buses

Light railways did provide sorely needed means of communication in many rural areas at relatively cheap cost, but they still required a track, and it was soon found that the real answer was the motor bus. The later phases of development of our parish after the First World War must owe much to the advances made by road transport, though public services followed the initial development and not the other way round. There had been at least one attempt as early as 1906—in competition with the light railway scheme—to start a motor bus service for Woking and the surrounding district, but the response was poor.[27] In 1916 the Aldershot Traction Company tried to get permission to extend its Aldershot and Camberley service (begun in 1913) to Sunningdale via Bagshot,[13] and although this seems to have been turned down, the company was running regular services on this route and on the Guildford–Woking–Bagshot route by the early 1920s. The services to and from Woking achieved at last the direct link with the main railway line.

There was also, of course, a connection by rail from Sunningdale with places to the north such as Reading, but to get to Windlesham from the station it was necessary to walk two to three miles over the golf course and the common, unless one went to the expense of a taxi. Some bus services through Windlesham were started in the earlier 1920s, but may have only lasted a short time. For example, on 1 May 1922 the Thames Valley Motor Company inaugurated a service from Woking to Ascot, which went via Lightwater, Broadway Road, Thorndown Lane, Updown Hill, and Bee Hill.[28] Mr. S. Tanner of Chobham commenced in 1926 a service from Woking station to Sunningdale station via Mimbridge, Chobham, Highams, *Sun* inn, *Bee* inn, Bagshot Square, and *Windmill* inn.[29]

The real rivalry developed between the giant Aldershot Traction Company and the very much smaller firm of J. R. Fox & Sons of Woking, who in 1924 extended their service from Knaphill to Bagshot. It must be appreciated that during these early years in which road transport multiplied there was no proper system of licensing. Buses were licensed by the various local authorities through whose areas they passed, but many urban authorities did not exercise their powers and few rural authorities possessed them. At first Windlesham Urban District

Council was content to rely on buses being licensed by Woking Council, but in March 1925 it decided to enforce its own powers. In the following year the threat of withdrawal of licences was used to persuade Aldershot Traction and Messrs. Fox to co-operate in providing a more convenient half-hourly service for the public between Woking and Bagshot, by adjusting their timetables. The struggle between the two companies continued however over the next few years. No one was ever keen on going out of their way to run buses through Windlesham because it did not pay, and there do not seem to have been many buses between Bagshot and Windlesham at any time. When Fox & Sons undertook (June 1927) to run a service from Knaphill to Bagshot via Windlesham, Aldershot Traction said this invalidated their agreement about the Woking to Bagshot run. They countered (September 1927) with a suggested service from Camberley to Sunningdale via Bagshot, New Road, and Windlesham, but this met with difficulties because of the proposed restrictions on the weight of vehicles using New Road. Aldershot now commenced to run a new service from Bagshot to Woking 10 minutes in front of Messrs. Fox, this being in retaliation for the latter having started one between West End and Woking timed 10 minutes ahead of Aldershot buses. Messrs. Fox next began to run buses on from Bagshot to Camberley immediately in front of those of Aldershot, and when the latter complained, Messrs. Fox slated the dangerous manner in which Aldershot buses were driven between Lightwater and Bagshot! Differences were sorted out again in February 1929, but Aldershot were, of course, the eventual winners and bought their rivals out after 1930.[29]

Meanwhile, the need for some co-operative action between local authorities had become obvious by 1928. A conference was held at Woking, and following on an interview at the Ministry of Transport, a local Joint Advisory Committee was set up, the representatives of Windlesham being the chairmen of the urban district council and its highways committee. Not long afterwards the Road Traffic Act 1930 set up the Traffic Commissioners to deal with the problem. Those who have to rely on today's services may care to know that in 1933 buses caused congestion in Bagshot Square, there being 'often three, sometimes four, even five' buses there at the same time.[29]

Occupations

The first occasion after 1831 when occupations in the parish of Windlesham were again given separately in the printed census report was in 1921. Although Windlesham had recently become an urban district, details of occupations were not given in 1911 because the population was under five thousand. We have, therefore, little information for the very interesting period at

	1921		1931	
Occupational category	Number of persons	Percentage of total	Number of persons	Percentage of total
Male:				
Agricultural workers ..	459	31.1	536	30.2
Transport workers ..	161	10.9	183	10.3
Commercial and financial	147	10.0	201	11.3
Builders and bricklayers..	105	7.1	166	9.3
Painters and decorators	39	2.6	49	2.8
Personal service ..	92	6.2	113	6.4
Professions	46	3.0	43	2.4
Public administration	44	3.0	17	1.0
Workers in wood ..	69	4.7	58	3.3
Metal workers	60	4.1	62	3.5
Professional entertainers..	19	1.3	53	3.0
Clerks and typists ..	34	2.3	48	2.7
All other occupations	202	13.7	247	13.8
Total	1,477	100.0	1,776	100.0
Female:				
Personal service ..	520	72.2	575	75.3
Professions	54	7.5	42	5.5
Commercial and financial	50	7.0	56	7.4
Clerks and typists ..	29	4.0	44	5.8
All other occupations	67	9.3	47	6.0
Total	720	100.0	764	100.0

Fig. 13.—Windlesham Urban District. Main classes of occupied persons 1921 and 1931

the beginning of this century during which the district became essentially residential. One point that must be borne in mind is the great increase in mobility which had resulted from the railways, and even more from the various new forms of road transport. Quite a number of the residents may have been working outside the district, and the reverse, of course, applies with regard to shops and businesses listed in commercial directories in that some employees may have lived elsewhere. The most important occupations of those living in the urban district in 1921 and 1931 have been extracted from the census reports for these years, and are set out in Fig. 13. Detailed comparison between occupations in the 1831 report and the reports of 1921 and 1931 is not possible owing to the changes in categories and method of presentation which had been made. Moreover, in comparing even 1921 and 1931 it must be remembered that in 1921 the total of occupied persons includes all those of 12 years of age and over, while in 1931 the limit was 14 years and over. Certain broad changes and tendencies are, however, clear.

Agriculture and Nursery Gardening

Whereas in 1831 54 per cent. of males (and this is only those of 20 years and over) were engaged in agriculture, in 1931 the proportion was only 30.2 per cent. Even more significant was the fact that although agriculture was still the largest single category, about 90 per cent. of those classified as agricultural workers were actually gardeners and gardeners' labourers. There were still 10 farmers in 1931, but they only employed 43 labourers altogether, as compared with 21 occupiers employing 243 labourers in 1831. It has already been pointed out that farming declined in importance from the end of the 19th century. In September 1903 it was stated at a public inquiry that there was little agricultural land and that the farming interest was very small.[30] There was a marked reduction in the area being farmed as Messrs. Fromow steadily increased the scope of their Windlesham nurseries, and the remaining farmers were engaged mainly in meat and dairy farming which required fewer hands.

Of those classified in the census as gardeners (341 in 1921 and 473 in 1931), no doubt the majority were at the nurseries where most of the work was still carried out by hand. In 1903

Waterers and Fromows together employed about 200 men,[30] and the earlier part of this century saw the area under nursery gardens rise to a new peak of 300 to 325 acres. About 1911 Waterers was combined with a business at Twyford owned by Mr. Bernard Crisp, the firm being re-named John Waterer Sons & Crisp. A policy of consolidation of the lands worked was followed, more land being acquired at Swift Lane, while Duke's Hill ceased to be a nursery by 1912. The business remained a retail one, round about 100 men being employed for approximately the same number of acres.[31]

Fromows' nurseries on the other hand were from the beginning almost entirely concerned with the production of stock for the wholesale trade all over the British Isles. The different types of soil in the various nurseries made possible a large range of stock. Owing to their having taken over old farming land, they had available not only peaty soil for rhododendrons and light soil for conifers, but also some of the heavier soil suitable for forest and fruit trees. It is interesting to note that roses do particularly well on the more clayey soil at Astagehill, the site of the old Eastersh common field. The Home Nurseries had been started in 1894 with the purchase of 15 acres, and this was followed by the purchase of Astagehill Farm (50 acres) in 1895. Further plots around the Home Nurseries were added, making a total of 50 acres there before 1903. South Farm Nurseries were purchased piece by piece meanwhile between 1899 and 1902, and Harrishaws Nurseries were acquired similarly between 1904 and 1912, the nurseries thus developing into an entire block on both sides of the Bourn Brook. The average number of men employed, which was only 20 at first, doubled within three years, and by 1906 had risen to 97 men working 180 acres. The peak of employment was about 1929 when Fromows employed some 125 hands for 200 acres.[32]

At the time the nurseries were first started, W. R. Oldham was employed at Fromows' Chiswick Nurseries. Mr. Joseph Fromow, recognising in him a young man of promise, made him manager at Windlesham. Mr. Oldham held this position for 40 years (1897–1937), during which time the business grew to become one of the leading wholesale nurseries.[32]

The classification of gardener also includes gardeners in private employ. The 1927 directory lists the names and addresses of some 50 gardeners, principally in Sunningdale and Windlesham with a few in Bagshot. All of them were employed at the large houses and most lived in lodges and cottages on the estate. To their number must be added the gardeners' boys and the jobbing gardeners.

Other Main Occupations

For occupied males, these were the building trades (including painters and decorators), commercial business, and transport. It is hardly surprising to find that builders, bricklayers, painters and decorators, constituted nearly 10 per cent. in 1921, and over 12 per cent. in 1931. Commercial and financial occupations (mainly retail business) accounted for 10 per cent. in 1921, and this had risen to over 11 per cent. in 1931. We have already noticed the number of new shops, particularly in Lightwater and Sunningdale. Transport workers represented between 10 and 11 per cent. in both census years. Over three-quarters of them in 1931 were in road transport, a category which included motor garage proprietors, haulage contractors, omnibus proprietors, drivers and conductors. Personal service, public administration (taken together with the professions), workers in wood, and metal workers, each constituted a substantial proportion of the total.

Women occupied at this period represented about one-third of the total number of females of working age. Both in 1921 and 1931 the predominant category was, of course, that of personal service, the majority being domestic servants. The big houses at Sunningdale and Windlesham must have generated a vast number of jobs of this nature, and even the more modest establishments often had a general servant. Some 72.2 per cent. in 1921 and 75.3 per cent. in 1931 were in this category. The next most important occupations for women were the professions (teachers and nurses), commercial occupations, clerks and typists. In 1921 there were 17 women in agricultural occupations, but there were none in 1931.

Unemployment

No details of those out of work were given in the census for 1921, which was taken when the period of unemployment which followed the immediate post-war boom was just getting under way. Before the end of the year there were two million unemployed in the country. This was not a distress area, but the number of unemployed was sufficient for a conference of local councils to pass a resolution to raise a 3d. rate for the purpose of providing work for them. Windlesham Urban District Council resolved in October 1921 to engage unemployed men, who must live in the district, for digging gravel at the Poor's Allotments. Payment was to be by the day (not the piece), the rate of wages to be the agricultural rate prevailing in the nurseries, which was round about £2 per week. On the first occasion as many as 41 men registered for employment, but only 17 were taken on, and after this married men only were employed. At the end of March 1922 the Surveyor reported that the council had employed an average of 14 men per week for 26 weeks, the total wages bill being approximately £660, £350 under the Unemployment Relief scheme and the rest debited to the General Highways account.[28, 33] The unemployment problem was subsequently taken care of by the commencement of the main drainage scheme in 1923: while this work was in progress the contractors remarked that there were only two men in the district unemployed, and they were unemployable! Subsequent sewer extensions and council house building must have helped to keep unemployment down. At a council meeting late in 1931, when reference was made to men from outside the district being employed on the current housing scheme, the Surveyor said that 19 workers—about half the total—were local.[34]

Leisure Activities

Only a brief mention can be made of a few of the varied leisure activities, which were now reported in the *Aldershot News* first published in 1894, and later on in the *Camberley News,* which followed it in 1905. The old village centres continued to have their separate clubs and societies, though there were, of course, occasions of combined activity. On 3 October 1903, for example, the *Aldershot News* contained a lengthy description of the Hospital Sunday Parade which had just taken place through Bagshot. The procession was headed by a detachment of the Bagshot Cycling Club, with their machines. Behind them came the Bagshot Military Band (brass and reed), and the Windlesham Fife and Drum Band with John Cree, its founder and bandmaster. Members of the friendly societies and slate clubs were present in force, a large number of the brethren of Bagshot Foresters Court walking behind their banner. After a service at St. Anne's church, tea was served to 120 people at the Institute.

Although a complaint was made at one club meeting that 'nothing answered in Bagshot', this being attributed to the unsociability of the village as compared with others, all tastes and requirements would seem to have been catered for there. A very special event—started in 1903—was the annual fete held by St. Anne's, which began with a church service. In 1905 the festival (reported in the *Aldershot News* on 28 July) took place on a really fine day, allowing the outdoor events which were held in the grounds of Penny Hill after lunch to be most enjoyable. The programme started with a cricket match, followed by sports and races; in the evening there was dancing to the Institute Band. There was frequent mention of the concerts of the Bagshot Choral Society, which were usually given to a crowded audience at the new Public Hall at the Institute, built at the expense of the Duke of Connaught (then at Bagshot Park) about 1900.

Sporting and social activities just before the war are described in the pages of the *Camberley News* (1913). On New Year's Eve 1912 a 'long-night dance' (8 p.m. to 3 a.m.) was held in the Institute by the Committee of Bagshot Social Evenings. About 120 people took part, the only trouble being 'too large a majority of ladies'. In February 1913 the Bagshot Miniature Rifle Club held its sixth Annual General meeting, but finances were in a bad way owing to there not being enough shooting members. There were regular reports of matches played by St. Anne's football club. Excursions by train were now a popular feature. In July 1913 St. Anne's choir outing travelled by train to Margate via Blackwater: a party of about 40 left Bagshot at 5 a.m. and returned by midnight (!), having enjoyed sea-bathing in glorious weather. The Sunday schools of Bagshot and Windlesham Wesleyan churches went to Bournemouth by special train for their annual treat. The most exciting event in the realm of entertainment that year must, however, have been the films shown at the Institute by the newly-formed Bagshot Cinematograph Company. There was a continuous performance from 6 p.m. to 10 p.m., with matinees on Wednesdays and Saturdays. For an admission price of 1s., 6d., or 3d., a selection of eight films could be seen. A typical programme, for 11 and 12 March 1913, was as follows:

> *Brittannicus.* Drama. Coloured.
> *The Deceivers.* Comedy.
> *The Vengeance that Failed.* Drama.
> *The Farm on Fire.* Drama.
> *The Rajah's Revenge.* Drama.
> *The Lady of Shalott.* Drama.
> *Jim and his Neighbour's Daughter.* Comic.
> *Bunny and the Dogs.* Comic.

Windlesham did not lack for entertainment. There were the regular social and cultural activities connected with the parish church and the Institute. The latter, of which John Cree was secretary for over 30 years, was enlarged in 1901 at the expense of Mr. Richard Christie by the addition of a new hall. Here on occasion a 'long-night dance' could be held, over 80 people attending such an event in the New Year 1913. Facilities for sport were provided by two golf clubs at Sunningdale, the Lawn Tennis and Croquet Club (which held regular tournaments at Lavershot Hall), the Football Club, and the Windlesham and Valley End Miniature Rifle Club. The fifth annual show of the Windlesham Poultry Society, held in the grounds of Sutherland House, was fully reported in the *Camberley News* of 9 August 1913.

In 1924 the *Camberley News* was re-named *Camberley News and Bagshot Observer* and coverage of events in Bagshot and Windlesham was extended. More provision was now being made for women's leisure hours. There was a branch of the Women's Institute in Bagshot, and to this body must go the credit for getting the Surrey County Library established there. In February 1929 the hours for the branch library, which was opened at Bagshot Council School, were Saturdays, 3 to 4 p.m. and Tuesdays, 6.30 to 7.30 p.m.[35] The Cedars Club for Girls held many social functions, while the Pantiles Tea Barn was opened opposite Bagshot Park in 1930 with the aim of making it a 'social rendezvous' for local people. Bagshot had clubs for bowls, tennis, cricket and football. The Bagshot Electric Theatre (Princes Cinema) now presented full-length films, which included, for instance, in 1925 'Bluebeard's eighth wife' with

Gloria Swanson, and a special showing for one day only of 'The Derby of 1925'. The hall was converted to a proper cinema with tip-up seats by the time the talkies arrived. Windlesham ran its own Amateur Dramatic Society, and a separate branch of the Women's Institute met in the infant school building in Chertsey Road, Windlesham.[36]

Until the *Red Lion* was opened at Lightwater (before 1934), it was necessary to go into Bagshot for a beer at the pub, and for a long time Lightwater men had no leisure time meeting-place of their own. In 1922, however, the Lightwater Working Men's Club and Institute was started in an ex-Army wooden hut, and not long afterwards proper premises were built. By the end of 1923 some of the local men who were not satisfied with the way the club was run decided to form a separate club, the Trades and Labour Club with premises on the opposite side of the road.

Education

Public Elementary Schools

Local participation in the running of elementary schools diminished after 1902 when Surrey County Council, as the new local education authority, took over the powers of school boards and became responsible for the expense of maintaining buildings. Four of the managers for Windlesham council schools were appointed by Surrey County Council, and two by the parish council, later the urban district council. In 1905 a new school was built at Bagshot to accommodate 460 children.[37] It was already being suggested that there would soon be a need for an elementary school at Lightwater. As the council managers' minutes show, parents of 16 pupils from Lightwater were concerned about the dinner hour arrangements for their children who had not time to walk home. Lightwater Ratepayers' Society was still pressing the county council for a school, without success, in 1928.[35] The school at Windlesham was improved and enlarged in 1925 with central heating.[21]

Private Nursery School

An infant school which had been built in School Lane, Chertsey Road (Windlesham) in 1884, largely through the efforts of the Rev. J. M. Freshfield, was enlarged in 1906. This expense was met mainly by voluntary subscriptions, the rooms being used for parochial purposes as well.[38] The school was still being held in 1927, when it was described as a voluntary nursery school for about 20 very young children.[21]

Technical Classes

Classes for further education were first held in Bagshot and Windlesham in the early 1900s. A wish having been expressed in Windlesham for classes of this kind (which were already being held in many other places in Surrey), a special meeting of the parish council was called in October 1903 to discuss the subjects to be taken. Though some of the classes may have been intended for young people who had recently left school, many were for adults. The first subjects decided upon were cookery and ambulance, though doubts were expressed about cookery classes, it being felt that these would be attended by the richer people rather than the poorer, 'to whom the instruction would have been most useful'. In 1905 classes at Windlesham included horticulture and home nursing as well, and in 1908 dressmaking was taught.[10, 11]

11 Local Government 1895-1918

The Local Authorities

DURING THE PERIOD of expansion in the district which we have just described local government was the subject of radical change. The various *ad hoc* bodies of the 19th century were dissolved and their functions transferred to district councils, county councils, and county boroughs, while after 1914 detailed control by the central government increased in all departments. Under the Local Government Act 1894 urban and rural district councils replaced urban and rural sanitary authorities. This was more than a change of name for the new councils were elected by democratic suffrage. Whereas the rural sanitary authority, being the guardians of the poor sitting in another capacity, had been the result of the election of two guardians by each parish vestry (where voting was according to property qualifications), now rural councillors represented their parish on the poor law authority. The rural council inherited all the powers of the rural sanitary authority, with a few urban powers in addition. For all parishes with a population of over 300, elected parish councils were also set up to which the rights and duties of the vestry were transferred. Between 1895 and 1909, three local authorities were concerned in the administration of the civil parish of Windlesham: Surrey County Council (set up in 1888), Chertsey Rural District Council, and Windlesham Parish Council. On 1 April 1909 Windlesham became an urban district and Windlesham Urban District Council replaced the two last-named authorities.

Windlesham Parish Council

The parish council took over the powers of the vestry in connection with the appointment of overseers, the management of parish property, village greens and allotments, and the provision of burial grounds, public lighting, etc. At the first elections for parish councillors for Windlesham held in

1894 there were 19 candidates for nine seats, and the following were elected: Charles Fendall (clergyman, elected first
chairman), William Bacon (retired butcher of Florence Villas,
Bagshot), Dr. Harold Osburn, Thomas Dale (builder), Thomas
Church (dairyman), Frank Waterer (nurseryman), Henry Irvine
(*Sun* inn), Wm. Walter Lee (linen draper and postmaster,
Updown Hill), and Frederick Hove (carpenter).[1] As usually
happens, there was much less competition for the seats on
subsequent occasions. After 1898, when Frank Waterer was not
re-elected to the parish council, the long involvement of the
Waterer family in the administration of the parish largely
ceased, although Frank Waterer did become chairman of
Windlesham Urban District Council in 1916. In the meantime the most important people in local affairs were Dr. H.
Osburn, Mr. W. R. Oldham, Mr. John Cree, and Mr. George
Fear, who succeeded one another as chairman of the parish
council between 1898 and 1908.[2, 3]

Chertsey Rural District Council

Rural district councils were concerned during this period
with a rather wider range of matters than they were later on,
including not only sewerage, scavenging, water supply and
housing, but also roads, gas and electricity. Such matters were
of course the subject of constant interchanges between
Windlesham Parish Council and Chertsey Rural District
Council, and parish council minutes are much more informative and detailed on certain things than those of the district
council. Relationships were not always harmonious: for example,
a misunderstanding over the lamp and fountain in Bagshot
Square, which dragged on interminably, caused the Rev. J. M.
Freshfield (district councillor) to assure the parish council in
1898 that 'as regards the lamps the District Council wish and
intend *to work in accord with the Parish Council, to make the
most convenient arrangements for the public*'. In October 1899
the parish council was very put out by the tone of a reply received
in connection with roadside waste, and regretted that 'the District
Council is always unable to give a courteous reply to the Parish
Council's requests for help in safeguarding public rights'.[2]

Three district councillors were elected for the parish. At the
first elections Rev. J. M. Freshfield (the rector), Stephen W.

Evans, and Frank Waterer were chosen from six candidates,[1] but casual vacancies occurred frequently as a result of resigna- tions, and elections were largely uncontested. The misunder- standings which arose with the parish authorities may have been due to poor attendance at the meetings of Chertsey District Council by the Windlesham councillors in the earlier years. The old problem of communication was blamed. At the Urban Powers Inquiry of 1903 it was pointed out that to get to the Chertsey district from Bagshot involved a rough drive of at least nine miles or a two-hour train journey via Ascot and Virginia Water. Only during the last two years, it was said, had it been possible to get gentlemen on the district council who were able to give the necessary time to the work of the parish.[4] The minutes of the two councils show clearly the sterling service rendered as district councillors by such people as Mr. George Fear (from 1898) and Mr. W. R. Oldham (from 1906). As soon as the representation improved, the idea of getting urban powers for Windlesham took root.

Windlesham Urban District Council

In January 1902 a parish meeting was called on the requisi- tion of 20 parishioners in order to consider the desirability of applying for urban powers. The main reasons advanced in favour were the long distance which the local district coun- cillors had to go to attend meetings, and the lack of proper supervision of roads and sanitary arrangements, which was held to be due to the distance from which it was exercised. In the ensuing discussion the opinion was expressed that these two items, which were, of course, the main ones paid for at the time out of local rates, should have been made the respon- sibility of parish councils in 1894. Reference was also made to the fact that Leatherhead, a place of somewhat similar size (population, 4,694 in 1901) had obtained urban powers, and it was felt that there was no reason why Windlesham should not follow suit. A committee was appointed to take the necessary action, and arrangements were made for a poll to be taken by means of postcards, 660 of which were sent out to parishioners inviting them to say whether they were in favour of urban powers or not. Of the 424 which were returned, 395 were in favour, 26 against, with three spoilt papers. A petition was made to Surrey County Council in January 1903, and on 21 September a Public Inquiry was held by a sub-committee appointed by the county council.[2]

The Clerk of the Parish Council (Mr. A. J. Smithers) presented their case, and a number of other people spoke in favour. Mr. Smithers pointed out the large increase in the total rateable value of the parish, which had risen from about £15,000 10 years ago to about £23,000 at the present time. He also mentioned the recent growth of the population, which at the 1901 census was 3,415 but was now considered to be in the region of four thousand. The chairman of the Inquiry expressed surprise at an increase of nearly 600 over such a short period, and then 'caused a smile round the room by asking, innocently enough, which was the most important part, Bagshot or Windlesham?' On being informed that Windlesham was the residential portion and Bagshot the business portion, he enquired why it was the name 'Windlesham' that was put forward for the urban district. It was necessary to explain that this was the name of the civil parish, which suggests that the chairman had not been too well briefed from Kingston, and adds point to another speaker's description of the parish as being 'in the far north west of the county'.[4]

No one spoke against the granting of urban powers and it seems to have been assumed that this would naturally follow. However, in March 1904 a parish meeting was told that although the Inquiry had found that Windlesham had a good case, a neighbouring parish having made a similar application on weak grounds, the county council felt it could not grant one application and not the other within the same rural district.[5] In July 1906 another petition from ratepayers in Bagshot (there were no signatories from Windlesham) urged the parish council to renew the application for urban powers, but it was decided to postpone action until after the Inquiry which was to be held in connection with the proposed detachment of Horsell from the Chertsey District for amalgamation with Woking. A renewed application was made in May 1907, and a parish meeting held the following December gave unanimous support to a motion that 'it was desirable for the welfare of the parish' that urban powers be granted. (The chairman had just informed the meeting that the parish was paying *to* district funds more than £200 per annum in excess of the expenditure on the parish made *from* district funds![3]) After a further Inquiry held at the Bagshot Institute on 16 January 1908 by Surrey County Council, a Provisional Order was issued constituting Windlesham an urban district. Chertsey Rural District Council, which had become apprehensive about the burden which would fall on the rest of the district for upkeep of staff if Windlesham was detached, made a last minute attempt to stop this taking place. In November 1908 the district council passed a resolution (the two Windlesham councillors present of course voting against) asking the Local Government Board to stay its hand on confirmation of the Order, with a view to the parish remaining part of the rural district. The reply received, however, was to the effect that as no petition against the Order had been made within the time fixed, the Local Government Board had no option but to confirm it.[6]

The first elections for Windlesham Urban District Council held in April 1909 aroused quite a bit of interest, as often happens on such occasions. There were 20 candidates for the nine seats, Mr. H. H. Longman of Lavershot Hall coming top of the poll with 371 votes, followed by Mr. W. R. Oldham with 265 votes.[7] Mr. Oldham became Chairman of the Council, an office which he held until 1914, when he was succeeded by Mr. S. W. Evans. Mr. Frank Waterer was chairman 1916–18, but did not stand again for the council after 1919. There was one year (1918–19) with a lady chairman, Mrs. Sarah Boyce.

Mr. Edwyn Close, solicitor, was appointed the first Clerk of the Council at a salary of £60 per annum, narrowly defeating the other applicant, Mr. H. O. Poulter, by five votes to four. Dr. H. Hanslow Brind was appointed Medical Officer of Health. Mr. Owen Stanley became Surveyor and Inspector of Nuisances, and Mr. A. J. Smithers Collector of Rates.[7] The Council at first met at the old council office in the Guildford road, but in April 1912 it was agreed to rent 'Hart Dene South' from Mr. Poulter for seven years at £32 10s. 0d. per annum.[8]

Parish Charities

A booklet called 'Account of the Parish Charities', by John Cree, was printed for Windlesham Parish Council in 1898 for sale at 2d. a copy. Recent charities were now included. These consisted of two gifts (£833 6s. 8d. each)—one for the poor and one for the National school—made in 1857 by the Duchess of Gloucester, a sum (£48 16s. 8d.) given by Ambrosia Hughes in 1859 for repair of gravestones of relatives, any surplus to go to poor widows, and a gift (£75) made by the Rev. E. Birch in 1862 for repair of the almshouses. A scheme for the administration of the income of all the parish charities was established by order of the Charity Commissioners dated 8 August 1899. All sums were to be invested in the name of 'The Official Trustees of Charitable Funds', and a body of trustees, consisting of one *ex-officio* member (the rector for the time being) and four representative trustees, was to be appointed by the parish, later the urban district, council. The yearly income of the charities was to be applied by the trustees in accordance with the existing trusts. (Further revisions were subsequently made to the scheme, and in 1957 10 charities were combined into Windlesham United Charities.)

Poor's Allotments Charity

The allotments (31 acres on East Common and 189 acres on West Common), which had been made in 1814 to poor parishioners not occupying houses of more than £6 yearly value, for cutting turf and furze for fuel, were managed by trustees appointed under the Enclosure Act. With the availability of coal, the allotments had long ceased to be used for their original purpose. They were too remote from the villages to be cultivated in small plots, and the land on East Common at Ribsden had been sold in 1870, the proceeds being invested and the income expended in coal for the poor. The land on West Common had been rented out to various people, but the Charity Commissioners pointed out in 1899 that this practice was illegal. According to Mr. F. B. P. Lory, several families living on the Poor's Allotment in rough wooden shacks were evicted, not without some trouble, early this century. In 1912 the trustees advised that the funds now held amounted to nearly £1,290 and produced about £34 a year. The present equivalent of the yearly house value stipulated at the enclosure (£6) was about £12, but they suggested that as many poor people had to pay rents out of proportion to their wages owing to the scarcity of houses to let at low rents, a value of £14 would be more appropriate. A scheme on this basis was

approved by the Charity Commissioners in 1913.[8] (No further
revisions of the scheme seem to have taken place before 1965,
when a change was made in the way in which benefits could
be distributed.)

Water Supply

It will be remembered that part of Bagshot had its own
supply of piped water from reservoirs on Waterers' nurseries,
while Windlesham continued to depend on wells. When the
South West Suburban Water Company (which had been given
powers to supply Windlesham by an Act of 1877[9]) first
proposed to bring water to the area in the late 1890s, the idea
did not find favour. In October 1898 a parish meeting was
called at Windlesham Board School to discuss the question
and about 85 people attended. Rev. J. M. Freshfield (district
councillor) pointed out the growing danger of contamination
of wells as the population grew and houses were built nearer
to each other. Mr. G. Fear suggested that a water supply would
'stave off' a sewerage scheme. A resolution was, however,
carried that a water supply was not needed, and it is obvious
that the objections were once again financial. When Windlesham Parish Council held a special meeting in April 1900 to
discuss the matter, the main complaint was that although the
South West Suburban Water Company had a monopoly of
powers to supply the parish, it was not prepared to do so unless
it received a guarantee of return on expenditure at an exorbi-
tant rate. Such a guarantee would, of course, have to be met
from parish rates in the (very likely) event that not enough
residents agreed to take a supply. The supply of water to
Windlesham was now felt by the parish council to be 'a bare
act of justice'.[2]

Negotiations between the water company and Chertsey
Rural District Council, which was actually responsible for
water supply, dragged on and on, though mains seems to have
been laid through Sunningdale as far as the *Windmill* inn, and
the real problem was to get them extended to Updown Hill
and the rest of Windlesham village. In November 1905 a parish
meeting was requisitioned by a number of people to protest
against the arrangement then under consideration by the
district council, which involved *inter alia* giving the water

company a guarantee of 10 per cent. on the outlay as was laid down in the Act. Mr. Fear explained that a new problem had arisen in that the Bagshot supply had been found on analysis to be contaminated and unfit for drinking. Contamination took place in the gathering ground in the nurseries and proper filtration was needed, which would probably cost between £1,000 and £2,000, land having to be purchased for filter beds. He thought it was possible that the South West Suburban Water Company could stop Bagshot people from using the present supply if it chose. If the mains were extended by means of a guarantee every ratepayer would naturally bear his contribution, although it would not be compulsory for every house to take a supply. A motion was carried asking the district council to reject the scheme as being unnecessary and leading to an increase in the rates.[3, 10, 11] Nothing seems to have been settled; in January 1908 the district council was considering the question of support to Surrey County Council, which was to oppose the Bill to raise fresh capital then being brought before Parliament by the South West Suburban Water Company, and ask for better terms throughout Surrey and particularly in Windlesham. However, the threat of opposition led to the offer of terms which were finally accepted.[6] The fifth schedule to the Act obtained by the water company in August 1908 consisted of an agreement between the company and Chertsey Rural District Council, by which the latter withdrew its opposition in return for a reduction in water rates.[12] Details of where mains were required to be laid in Windlesham were supplied by the district council, and by the beginning of 1909 the work had been started. Householders who had an adequate supply of water from wells did not necessarily connect up to the pipes.

Waterers now gave notice to discontinue the public water supply to Bagshot as from the following September, in view of the fact that the water had been condemned by the Medical Officer of Health on more than one occasion. The two parish meetings which were held in January 1909 to discuss the situation, had finally to accept that the special supply of water which had been enjoyed by a good part of Bagshot on the cheap for many years was now coming to an end. A last attempt was made to avert this by asking the district council if the present or any other 'local' supply could be adapted for the use of the whole of Bagshot, but the reply came that arrangements were to be made with the water company. A supply would be needed for 266 houses, not counting the Lightwater area. An agreement was sealed by Windlesham Urban District Council in August 1909, and posters were put up informing Bagshot residents that they must connect to the new water mains by 29 September. Some of the residents were so reluctant that there was still a long list of houses not connected in December![3, 7]

Having at last got the water laid on, over the next three or four years Windlesham Urban District Council, in common with other councils whose areas were supplied by the same water company, was constantly complaining about the unsatisfactory nature of samples analysed for it. In March 1912, following on a conference of the councils concerned at which it was recommended that each council should publicly pass a resolution condemning the water, the Windlesham Council in its resolution considered the quality '. . . to be so bad as to be a menace to the health of the consumers . . .'. However, the water was eventually found to be reasonably satisfactory.[7, 8]

Already in May 1910 some of the residents of Lightwater had petitioned for an extension of the water main the rest of the way down the Guildford road. A circular letter sent to house-owners found, however, very few in favour, while the water company complained of increasing costs and argued about the size of main required. It was not until September 1915 that an agreement was finally signed for a four-inch main, which was considered ample for the district to be served for many years to come.[7, 13] Further extensions took place after the war as the district developed.

Scavenging and Sewage

From the early 1890s, as we have seen, the parish had had a regular scavenging system whereby cesspools and closet tubs were emptied and dry house refuse was removed, although the latter service was less important at this period. In 1895 the contractor was receiving £135 a year. Complaints of neglect made against the contractor in 1898 led to a different contractor being engaged, but parishioners were still not satisfied with the service in November 1899.[14, 2] In September

1900, instead of contracting out the job by the week or the year, the district council entered into a contract for hire of horses and drivers by the hour, the rates being as follows:

> One horse, one man per hour   1s. by day, 1s. 3d. by night.
> Two horses, one man per hour   1s. 9d. by day, 2s. by night.

A year later, on the recommendation of a special committee which had been appointed to look into scavenging, it was decided to undertake this directly without a contractor, and £200 was allowed for purchase of horses, carts, etc. Rent was now paid for the scavenging depot, and contracts for supply of oats, hay, straw, etc., and for shoeing the horses, were made in 1903.[10]

Meanwhile complaints continued to be received, particularly from the Thames Conservators, about the pollution of the Bourn at Bagshot. In November 1899, a public meeting was called in order to obtain the views of the parish on the question of a sewerage scheme. It was explained that the probable cost would be £6,000. This would mean at least an 18d. rate, which would be levied on a special drainage area and not on the whole parish. The proposed area was the whole of Bagshot village between 'Ralph's Cottages' (on Jenkins Hill) and the railway bridge near the *Cricketers* (taking in College Ride), and down the Guildford road as far as 'Lightwater new cottages'. The Rev. J. M. Freshfield (district councillor) expressed the view, however, that so long as other parishes bordering on the Bourn were not compelled to take effective measures to prevent pollution, it would be a 'sheer act of tyranny' to force Bagshot to do so. A resolution was carried to the effect that those who polluted the stream should be compelled to stop. The resolution protested against any new arrangement for sanitation, on the grounds that the present system of scavenging was sufficient, if only it was properly carried out, which it was felt was not the case at present. On receipt of this resolution Chertsey Rural District Council appointed a committee to look into the whole question of disposal of sewage in Bagshot and in July 1900 a report was requested from Dr. G. V. Poore of Wimpole Street. Action on the report was, however, again confined to notices to houseowners to cut off drains leading into the stream and to clean offensive ditches.[2, 10]

Lack of proper supervision of the sanitary arrangements from Chertsey was one of the two main reasons advanced in

the application for urban powers made by the parish council
in 1903. The population was rising very rapidly and at the
Inquiry held in September of that year, it was stated that £721
had been spent on scavenging in the parish during 1902. Two
hundred and twenty-five tubs in Bagshot and 51 tubs in Windlesham were being emptied twice a week.[4] In 1907 Chertsey
Rural District Council purchased four acres of land in Swift
Lane for a new scavenging depot and built its own stables.
The estimate for scavenging for the half year from April to
September 1908 was £513, of which over half was labour costs.
In the September of that year a scavenging committee (com-
posed of the Windlesham representatives on the district council)
reported that scavenging was 'assuming large proportions'
and advised that the cost could be reduced by better management.[6] The actual cost of scavenging for the first year of
operation by Windlesham Urban District Council (1909–10)
was £806, so closer supervision does seem to have resulted in
some savings, but by 1914 the cost had already risen again to
£1,190.[15] Disposal of the increasing amount of sewage was
arranged by renting land for tips in various parts of the
district.

During the war years difficulties were experienced in keeping
the scavenging going properly. In October 1915 the council
surveyor reported that he was having trouble getting horses
shod and carts repaired. A circular letter was distributed to
householders asking them to help by reducing the work
required. In the following May, because of the difficulty in
replacing scavenging men called up for military service, the
Surveyor was authorised to apply to the local tribunal for
exemption for such men, and to employ women for sweeping
the roads. A further circular urged householders to economise,
suggesting possible ways.[16, 17]

Street Lighting

In 1895 there were 21 gas lamps in Bagshot. The parish
council deliberated from time to time about adding to their
number. In 1898, for instance, it was decided to have an extra
lamp between Webbs the butchers (near the *King's Arms*) and
the *Hero of Inkerman,* and another lamp opposite the council
room in the Guildford road. A new lamp having been erected

in Bagshot Square in 1897 to commemorate the Jubilee of Queen Victoria, the old lamp and fountain, which were thought to be 'highly dangerous to traffic' in their present position, were removed. The normal period for which the lamps were lit was for the six months from 1 October to 31 March from one hour after sunset until 10.30 p.m., at a cost of £2 to £2 2s. 0d. per lamp. The expense involved in an extra month's lighting or in keeping the lamps at the *Hero of Inkerman* and Bagshot Square alight all night received very careful consideration. Arrangements for lighting continued to be made with Mr. R. Kemp, owner of the Bagshot gasworks, but the works presumably went out of use after his death about 1900.[1, 2] In September that year the Ascot Gas Company, which had, in fact, had powers to supply gas in the area since 1882,[18] and was now laying mains in the district, was asked to tender. During the early 1900s the parish council tried to get the company to extend the gas mains along the Guildford road as far as Stone Hill. The company, however, said (October 1907 and again a year later) that the income from public lamps would not be enough and that insufficient response had so far been received from residents in the road.[3]

In 1909 Windlesham Urban District Council was lighting 28 flat flame burner gas lamps and five oil lamps.[15] In September 1915 the Ascot Gas Company having advised that the rate would now be £2 5s. per lamp, it was decided to reduce the number of lamps to eight, as a measure of war-time economy. One lamp was specified at each of the following places: Bagshot Bridge, The Square, opposite the *Hero of Inkerman,* at the corner of School Lane, near Mr. Ward's at Jenkins Hill, and at the corner of New Road. Two lamps were to be lit on the main road near the station. In the end, however, lighting was limited to three lamps only: near station approach, in the Square and near the *Inkerman.*[13]

There was no street lighting at this time in the village of Windlesham, which had turned down a suggestion of gas lamps in 1898. At a parish meeting held in January that year the chairman explained that the idea was for about 10 lamps to be erected at the dangerous corners, which would probably mean a 2d. rate. No one spoke in favour and when it was put to the meeting it was resolved that 'lamps at the present time are not necessary or desirable'.[1]

Fire Brigade

Since the 1830s the parish had possessed a manual fire engine—it had wooden handles each side and worked 'something like a blacksmith's bellows'[19]—and this was kept in part of the old workhouse building. In November 1896, having had the fire engine overhauled, the parish council decided to hold a public meeting to test the view of parishioners on the question of forming a fire brigade. A brigade was apparently formed, for in March 1897 30s. was allowed for instruction of the Windlesham Volunteer Fire Brigade, but the brigade then seems to have been more or less forgotten for a couple of years. In February 1899 Mr. Frank Waterer, who had taken on the job of captain, was asked for a report on the state of the fire engine and the brigade, but he replied that after the council refused to grant uniforms to the firemen he had resigned. Engine and gear had been put away in good order and he knew nothing more about the matter. After some discussion the parish council decided that owing to the scarcity of water which could be made available in many parts of the parish in case of fire, it would be useless to form a fire brigade! A form was received from the Local Government Board two months later asking for particulars of the fire brigade, but 'there being none, not much information could be given'.[1, 2] If any serious fire did occur in the parish the help of the nearest fire brigade was presumably sought. The *Aldershot News* of 5 March 1904 reported an outbreak of fire at 'Glenhurst' (Windlesham) early one morning. The occupier went to Camberley in his motor car, but there was some delay before the Camberley fire brigade could actually be called out because no one lived on the premises where the engine was kept. Once the alarm was raised it was only 40 minutes before the steam fire engine with a full muster of men arrived at the scene of the fire four miles away. The engine would have been horse drawn, and the captain of the fire brigade was very satisfied with the performance, but the occupier had meantime got the fire under control with other assistance.

In 1912, water being now available from hydrants at various points, Windlesham Urban District Council decided to obtain fire hoses and hand carts for use at Bagshot. Similar purchases were later made for Windlesham, where arrangements were made for them to be stored in a lock-up shed built onto the

Institute premises. In February 1913 a member of the council pointed out that when two fires occurred recently in Bagshot no one knew what to do, and so on 22 March Major Bunting and members of the Camberley fire brigade gave an exhibition at Bagshot for men enrolled as a 'First Aid Fire Detachment'.[8] It had been intended to provide a practical lesson as well, but a terrible thunderstorm put an end to operations. By June 1913 all the appliances had been received and men for working them obtained, Mr. J. Corbett being in charge of the Bagshot section and Mr. Edmunds of the Windlesham section. In July 1914 it was decided to purchase hose for the Sunningdale area, provided that Chobham residents would contribute £22 towards the cost. This was agreed by Mr. T. A. Roberts for the Ridgemount Company, and a shed to store the gear was later put up at the top of Ridgemount Road, but there is no mention of the formation of a brigade section for Sunningdale until early in 1917.[13, 20]

Meanwhile the question of fire protection at Lightwater was raised by Mr. W. Eustace, a retired C.I.D. inspector, who was a member of the council, and himself lived at Lightwater. In April 1916 he got together a force of 10 volunteers, consisting besides himself of Messrs. Fordham, Herring, Martin, Windybank, Hopkins, Church, Boid, Cooper, and Hardy. Owing to the war it was now very difficult to obtain fire hose, so it was decided to purchase two patent fire extinguishers with which to check fires while the other appliances were fetched from Bagshot. The extinguishers were to be kept inside the school room at the Lightwater Primitive Methodist church. Mr. Eustace and the Surveyor went together to a demonstration of the working of fire extinguishers at Merryweathers, probably the oldest manufacturers of fire-fighting equipment, and as a result it was agreed to buy three more extinguishers for Bagshot, Windlesham, and Sunningdale, at a cost of £2 5s. 0d. each. A brass helmet, so essential for entering burning buildings, had also been purchased by the Surveyor at Merryweathers, and the council decided to invest in three more helmets at £1 5s. 0d. each, so as to have one for each area.[17, 20]

12 Local Government 1919-1933

Windlesham Urban District Council: Extension of Activities

AFTER THE FIRST WORLD WAR the matters with which local government was concerned increased in number and complexity: this period saw, for instance, the general introduction for the first time of subsidised council housing for the working classes. The first post-war chairman of Windlesham Urban District Council was Mr. W. Eustace of Lightwater, who held the office from 1919 to 1921. Mr. W. R. Oldham of Fromows, was again chairman from February 1923 to October 1925. He then resigned the office owing to frequent absence from home on business, and in 1928 he retired from the council. Mr. Oldham, the most prominent personality in local affairs in the earlier part of this century, had, it was then pointed out, in 32 years of public service, held every possible position open to a citizen of his community: parish councillor, rural councillor, county councillor, school manager, guardian, and urban councillor since the formation of the urban district council 19 years previously.[1] Dr. H. A. Cruttwell was elected chairman in 1925 and remained in the office until the end of 1932.

Elections to the council do not seem to have often aroused a great deal of interest. In April 1925 there were six candidates for three seats, but according to the *Camberley News* of 24 April, 'the apathy shown . . . was the most pronounced ever known in the district', only some 25 per cent. of the electorate voting. In 1927 the newly-formed Lightwater Ratepayers' Association put forward as their nominee Mr. G. E. Barnett, a retired police inspector. The poll was the heaviest for many years and a record 58 per cent. voted in Lightwater, where the Ratepayers' Association went all out for their candidate. As a result he came top of the poll, unseating Mr. John Cree, who doubtless suffered because as usual Windlesham polled the smallest percentage of any of the voting districts.[2] In 1929 and again in 1930 the election was contested by two Labour candidates, Mr. J. Eastaugh and Mr. E. A. Lee, who were unsuccessful but all the same obtained a substantial number of votes.[3]

Mr. Owen Stanley, Surveyor and Inspector of Nuisances, did not return to resume his post (temporarily held by Mr. W. Bell during the war), and in 1919 a new Surveyor and Inspector was advertised for. Mr. J. E. Weeks was selected out of 47 applicants for the joint post, at a salary of £250 per annum.[4] When he resigned in March 1924 to take up an appointment as Engineer and Surveyor to Rugby Rural District Council, the news obviously came as an unwelcome shock at Windlesham, where the first connections to the new sewer were shortly expected, for Mr. Weeks had an intimate knowledge of the scheme. Windlesham Council wrote to Rugby, expressing regret at the loss of 'so capable an officer' and offering congratulations on obtaining his services. On this occasion there were 84 applications for the post, Mr. Cyril Gray (from Guildford) being chosen. The commencing salary was £320 per annum, and it was now stipulated that this was a full-time post, the Surveyor not being allowed to undertake any outside work. Allowance of £20 per annum for a motor cycle would be paid 'as in the past'.[5]

In the November of the same year it became necessary to provide assistance for the Surveyor and it was decided to have a separate Sanitary Inspector. The salary of Mr. A. Aldridge was to be up to £200 per annum, with £5 annual allowance for the upkeep of a bicycle. In May 1925 an assistant to the Surveyor was appointed on a temporary basis, but he had to provide his own bicycle. On 1 April 1927, following on the Rating and Valuation Act 1925, which made borough councils and urban and rural district councils the rating authorities (with the duty of preparing a new valuation list every five years), the post of Rating and Valuation Officer was created.[6] It replaced the old post of Rate Collector and was held by Mr. A. J. Smithers until 1930, when he retired after 33 years of service to the parish, beginning when he became Clerk to Windlesham Parish Council in 1897. In the following year the council lost another officer of long standing, when Dr. Hanslow Brind retired. He had been Medical Officer of Health in the district for 31 years, first to Chertsey Rural District Council and then to Windlesham Urban District Council also.[7]

Clerical staff were not engaged for the council officers until after the war. When the council moved to Hart Dene South in 1912, Mr. Edwyn Close (Clerk of the Council) gave up his private office elsewhere and the council allowed him the use of rooms for his private staff, in consideration of which no increase in salary was given to him for five years.[8] In January 1919 when the Clerk's salary was fixed at £200 per annum, it was specifically stated that it was to cover all clerical assistance in the discharge of his duties.[4] The council continued to allow him the use of rooms when the move to Laird House was made in 1921.

From December 1919 onwards clerical assistance was provided for the Surveyor—this was at first envisaged as temporary, but proved to be a permanent requirement. In May 1923 it was decided that Mr. Lee (then described as assistant to the Clerk and the Surveyor) should be dismissed because he had not become qualified in shorthand and typing. (Some councillors wondered what kept the unfortunate Mr. Lee at the office until 8 p.m.—he was probably struggling to keep up with the minutes, as in several books about this time the index gives out before halfway through!) A shorthand typist and accounts clerk was advertised for, but only three replies were received, and two of them were from girls, so it was decided to re-advertise more widely in the national newspapers. This brought 17 applications, and Mr. G. J. Read was engaged.[4, 9, 5] Two years later (May 1925), owing to an avalanche of work, the council resolved to engage another shorthand typist. This time they accepted a woman, Miss P. Mason, who received a commencing salary of 35s. per week. Miss Mason was to remain with the council as shorthand typist and later as costing clerk for almost seven years. In 1926 there were again such arrears of work, in spite of the devotion of the two clerks already employed who worked late in the evenings, that an additional clerk was approved, Mr. Read becoming committee and accounts clerk.[6] The clerical staff was again augmented later on. From 1925 the minutes of the council and of the various committees were printed and circulated to members.

The council continued to rent 'Hart Dene South' from Mr. Poulter until 1921, when a special committee appointed to consider office accommodation advised that new conditions regarding restoration of the property which Mr. Poulter wished to impose, made it inadvisable to renew the lease. It was recommended that the council offer to purchase 'Laird House', which was then up for sale. Agreement was finally reached with Mr. S. W. Evans to purchase for the sum of £1,260, the money to be spread over 25 years payable by annual instalments of principal and interest at six per cent.[10]

Scavenging

Not long after the end of the war a crisis arose in the scavenging department. It began in June 1919 with the scavenging men going on strike for two days and demanding an increase in wages. In February 1920 40 owners of property and residents at Bagshot sent a petition to the council asking for more speedy and hygienic emptying of cesspools, and careful disposal of sewage.[4] The new Surveyor, in a special report to the council, described the position as serious, saying that cesspools had had to be left full and overflowing for longer periods than ever before, especially in Bagshot. Contributory causes were the exceptionally wet weather, a shortage of horses, the dissatisfaction of the scavengers with their hours and rates of pay, and the consequent difficulty in replacing those who left, together with the lack of proper supervision owing to the work being done mainly at night. The scavengers worked two days and five nights a week for £2 6s. 0d., which was only six shillings more than roadmen, and was not sufficient to compensate for the unpleasant night work. The Surveyor estimated that the total cost of scavenging for the year ending March 1920 would be £2,840 (more than twice as much as in 1914), but to carry it out as it ought to be done, wages must be increased, and modern tanks and pumps provided so that the work of emptying cesspools could be done during the daytime. In Egham, for instance, the men got £2 10s. 0d. a week for daytime work with up-to-date plant.[11]

The Surveyor's report recommended the adoption of vacuum tanks. By this system a vacuum was created in a 300-gallon sealed cylindrical tank by means of a petrol-driven air-exhauster, which took from six to 10 minutes to exhaust the air. After this the valves were opened and the contents of a cesspool were drawn into the tank in three and a half minutes. There was no smell whatsoever, the whole of the apparatus was absolutely airtight, and the work was done in the daytime without the slightest inconvenience. At nearby Ascot the outfit had been working for two years without any trouble. To deal with cesspools in the Windlesham urban district four vacuum tanks would be needed (£740), together with two exhauster pumps (£325), and 40 lengths of suction hose, the total cost being just over £1,300.[12] By July 1921 all the new equipment had been purchased and was in use. Most of the work was now done by day, and the Surveyor suggested that the future working week should be six days and one night. On the instructions of the council, however, the men were given the option of six days and two nights work for their present pay (recently increased) or six days and one night for 2s. 6d. less wages. The men took the cut in pay.[11]

Reports made by the Surveyor from time to time build up a picture of scavenging when the work of emptying cesspools and tub closets was at its peak in the early 1920s. In 1922 the Surveyor complained that since the purchase of the new equipment, occupiers were making more frequent requests for cesspool emptying under the impression that the council was now able to carry out an unlimited amount of work. There were 360 cesspools in the district and on average 85 were cleaned each week. Thirty cesspools were emptied every week without notice, 49 every fortnight, 30 every three weeks, 43 every month, and 208 at intervals varying from one month to six months.[11] Early in 1925 as many as 23 rounds had to be made for the purpose of collecting tubs from closets,[13] the men commencing this at 5.30 a.m. and finishing at 8.30 a.m. As public sewers were laid in the district from 1925 onwards, scavenging of course progressively diminished, and the situation just described may be compared with that obtaining in the 1930s. There were only 106 cesspools early in 1931 and it was expected that the number would be reduced to 57 by the end of the year. Night soil was now collected from only 46 premises, and this number would soon be reduced to about a dozen.[14]

At one time the council owned 15 horses, but the first step towards mechanisation was taken in 1923, when the Surveyor reported difficulties with the collection of house refuse at Sunningdale by horse and cart owing to the distance between the houses. It was decided to purchase a Ford one-ton lorry for £170, and after a year's experience the Surveyor was able to report that the cost by lorry had been £291 for 678 loads, as compared with £364 for 598 loads by horse transport.[15] The number of horses required was reduced as the scavenging diminished. In April 1928 a new scheme involving the substitution of a petrol tractor for horses was put forward: one tractor would pull three tanks instead of two horses being needed for pulling one tank. A Fordson tractor was bought for £370, together with two trailers, the latter to be used for house refuse presumably. Finally in September 1930 the Surveyor recommended that the one horse which was still kept should be sold, together with the remaining carts, as it was cheaper to hire a horse than to keep one! So the stables built in 1907 finally went out of use.[13]

Sewerage

After 1900 the subject of a sewerage system was hardly mentioned for 20 years, although private sewers were laid down about 1907 in the new Ridgemount estate at Sunningdale, with a sewage farm off Charters Road. In 1920, owing to the enormous increase which was being experienced in the cost of scavenging, a preliminary report on main drainage was commissioned from Mr. T. J. Moss Flower. His report made in March 1921 estimated the total expenditure at just under £46,000, of which nearly £27,000 would be required for Bagshot and Lightwater, but this included the Air Compressor Station and Sewage Disposal Works. Sewers for the greater part of the village of Windlesham would cost well over £16,000, while to serve a part of the western portion of the village would involve getting on for £3,000 more.[10]

Windlesham Urban District Council resolved to take no action for the time being. In July 1922, however, encouraged by advice that the central Unemployment Grants Committee was now taking a wider view of objects suitable for grants, in order to provide work both directly and indirectly for the mounting number of unemployed, it was decided to apply for a grant. Sanction was given by the Ministry of Health (which had taken over from the Local Government Board in 1919) to borrow the necessary money, and arrangements were finally made in March 1923 to obtain a loan from the Public Works Commissioners of the following sums, to be repaid with interest at 5 per cent. by instalments of principal and interest combined:

> £1,946 for sewage disposal works, in 15 years.
> £42,704 for sewerage and sewage disposal works, in 30 years.
> £850 for purchase of land, in 30 years.

Major Moss Flower was appointed Engineer to carry out the scheme. In April a tender for £50,704 14s. 0d. from Geo. Stow & Co., Ltd., of Newport was accepted. This was, in fact, the lowest of 14 tenders, although two others were very close. Work was commenced on 16 April 1923. Sanction to borrow a further £11,120 for additional works was obtained in December 1923. Land had meantime been purchased in December 1922 for the sewage disposal works off Blackstroud Lane. The site had been cleared by a separate contractor, for one of the two stipulations made in connection with the grant was that work must be actively commenced by 31 December 1922. The other condition was that 75 per cent. of the labour required must be drawn from the Aldershot urban district, but in the event it seems that only 25 per cent. of the men were so engaged, local men accounting for the balance.[9]

By March 1925, almost exactly 50 years after Mr. R. Birch had advised Chertsey Rural Sanitary Authority (in December 1875) to pursue a policy of delay with regard to sewers in Windlesham, the first house in the district was linked up to the new sewer, the distinction actually falling to a house in Ambleside Road, Lightwater, owned by a Mr. Hamblin.[16] Every householder within 100 feet of a main sewer had to connect up, but as the cost fell on the individual connections were slow. Applications to delay connection were considered on their merits by the sanitary committee, for as the chairman of the council remarked, the district was progressing from a rural to an urban system and they could not expect to bring it to a modern standard 'at one jump'.[17] It was nearly a year before cesspool emptying on the line of the sewers in Lightwater and Bagshot could be stopped on 1 January 1926. Connections to the sewer were even slower in Windlesham, only 56 having been made after it had been available for six months, but scavenging was finally discontinued there in July 1926.[13]

In the years before 1933, extensions both large and small were made to the system, many being carried out with the help of further grants from the Unemployment Grants Committee, without which some at least might not have then been undertaken. In November 1929 the Surveyor suggested to the council that 'there would never be better grants than at present'. Sewer extensions were laid in Chertsey, Lightwater, Bracknell, and Windermere Roads in 1929-30, and also in Jenkins Hill and in School Road, Windlesham. The major scheme undertaken was for drainage of the whole Sunningdale area, which involved a new pumping station there as well as new sewers. A report was obtained from a firm of civil engineers in Birmingham, Messrs. Willcox & Raikes; the scheme, the total estimated cost of which was £23,000, was approved by the council in July 1929. A tender from W. G. Tarrant, Ltd., of Byfleet, to carry out the main works for £19,475 was accepted in June 1930.[7, 13] The work was immediately put in hand so as to qualify for a grant, and all scavenging ceased at properties along the line of the sewer at the end of 1931.[18] Some 95 per cent. of the district was now sewered, a considerable achievement in eight years, after a rather late start.[14]

Housing

Before the First World War relatively few local authorities were themselves involved directly in building houses. The majority were concerned only to see that new houses conformed with the requirements of the Public Health Acts regarding water supplies, drains, ashpits and privies, and with any building byelaws which they made in the interests of safety, light and air. From the late 1890s the minutes of Chertsey Rural District Council and Windlesham Urban District Council record an increasing number of applications to have plans passed for new buildings. During 1913 the *Camberley News* featured a whole series of articles on cheap housing for the working classes, and when Thomas Church, builder, applied to Windlesham Council for permission to build at Junction Road (Lightwater), the opinion was expressed that 'considering the discussions taking place in different districts regarding the housing of the working classes, the Council ought not to throw any obstacles in the way'.[19] In May 1914, in connection with a return of house inspections carried out under the Housing and Town Planning Act 1909, the Surveyor reported that the number of cottages in the district in which there was over-crowding, that is more than two persons to a 'room', was only eight. It was recommended that the answer made to the question on further houses needed should be that 'no further accommodation for working classes working and residing in the district is required'.[20]

After the war the general shortage of decent cheap houses was acute. The Housing of the Working Classes Act 1890 had merely provided that Part III, which dealt with the erection of such houses, could be adopted by certain specified local authorities. The Housing and Town Planning Act which was passed in 1919 stated for the first time that it was the duty of all such authorities to consider the housing needs of their area, and within three months to submit a housing scheme to the Local Government Board. Building costs and interest rates were abnormally high at the time, and the Treasury undertook to bear all losses incurred by local authorities in building houses in excess of a penny rate. Up to March 1927 rents, though they would take into account the superior amenities and the ability of tenants to pay, were to be fixed without regard to costs. It was apparently expected that the gap between economic rents of new houses, and rents which working class people could afford, would be only a temporary one, and that the economic rents of houses built from 1927 onwards would be within reach of most. It was intended that rents of the subsidised houses would then be fixed at the same level wherever possible.[21]

It had been suggested at a meeting of the sanitary committee of Windlesham Urban District Council in November 1918 that people working in other districts were attracted into Windle-sham by the lower rents, and that if there was any shortage of cottages the position would be eased when visitors who had come on account of air raids returned home again.[12] However, at a special meeting held in January 1919—six months before the Housing Act received royal assent—the council recognised the need for building houses in the district. It was estimated that 43 houses were required altogether, 35 to meet the unsatisfied demand owing to the growth of the population and overcrowding, and eight to replace unfit or sub-standard houses. As it was anticipated that 20 houses would be built during the next three years by other agencies, the council decided to build 24 houses. A special housing committee was set up, and seven acres of land in Guildford Road, Bagshot, had already been purchased by July 1919.[4, 22]

The council had made a rapid start but difficulties soon began to be encountered. The architect's layout proposed to erect 24 cottages on half the land (that is approximately seven to the acre), and the houses were to have earth closets. The minimum number of houses to the acre which the Housing Commissioner would sanction was 10, and he insisted on water closets, drainage to be treated on the septic tank system. The council maintained that, the district being still of a rural nature, the maximum number of houses which should be erected on the whole of the area in question was 48, and insisted that W.C.s were impracticable. The Commissioner was to be informed (September 1919) that 'the Council feels so strongly on the matter they are not prepared to proceed with any other scheme . . . so certain are they of the soundness and practicability of their views that they would welcome a personal visit from the Housing Commissioner and they feel confident that he would then be of the same way of thinking'. The Commissioner gave way and pressed the council to proceed on its chosen basis.[4, 22]

Meanwhile, however, another problem had arisen. The cost of brick houses alone (without roads, fences, etc.) was expected to be over £20,000. The council was so appalled at this figure that the housing committee even went to inspect huts at the Staff College, Camberley, which were being converted into dwellings for married officers, but did not find them suitable for dwellings for the working classes. A scheme for eight pairs of semi-detached houses and eight bungalows was finally approved by the Ministry of Health in July 1920.[4, 23] Tenders were advertised for, but when they were examined, it was found that the cost overall would, in fact, be more than £35,000. The council was not at all happy about the position, as the rateable value of the urban district was only £29,000, and although the present Government had laid it down that the cost to the rates was not to exceed a penny rate, 'the Council had no security for the future'. Under present instructions it must endeavour to let the houses at an economic rent after

seven years. It was estimated that an economic rent to pay
the interest on the money which would have to be borrowed,
and the rates (without allowing for repairs, cost of collection,
and repayment of capital), would have to be over £100 per
annum per house. It was resolved to inform the Housing Commissioner that the liability was too large for the district to
undertake. After further consultations a substitute scheme for
five pairs of bundalows only, to be built along the frontage
of the land without roads or drainage scheme, was approved
in April 1921. A tender was received from Jonathan Corbett,
the Bagshot builder, for £1,790 per pair.[10] However, in the
July of the same year the Government, which was finding the
subsidy too expensive, limited the number of houses to be
built under it to roughly those for which contracts had already
been signed.[21] Windlesham Urban District Council—thank-
fully perhaps—abandoned its first housing project. The back
half of the site was used for allotments, and sanction was
obtained to sell the front half for building plots, though it is
not clear how many sales took place.[9, 23]

New subsidies to encourage house-building were given under
Chamberlain's Housing Act of 1923. The Treasury was to pay
£6 per house per annum for 20 years in respect of any house,
built by either private enterprise or local authorities, which
could satisfy certain conditions as to size and amenities. Houses
could be let at any rent or sold at any price, but the subsidy
was only to be available for those built by 1 October 1925,
it being thought that by then the housing shortage would be
practically over. A year later, under the first Labour Government, Wheatley's Housing (Financial Provisions) Act 1924
made the Chamberlain subsidy available for houses completed
before 1 October 1939. This act also introduced, however, a
new and substantially larger subsidy (£9 per annum for 40
years in urban parishes, £12 10s. 0d. in rural parishes) for
houses built by local authorities and public utility societies
for letting only. For this subsidy restrictions were placed on
the average rent which could be charged by local authorities.[24]

Windlesham Urban District Council resolved in December
1923 that the Chamberlain subsidy should be given for
privately-built houses, together with an additional grant of £3
per annum at the council's discretion. It was stipulated that the
house must be for owner occupation and on the line of a main

Scheme No.	Period (approx.)	Location	Number of houses or flats	Number of bedrooms	Price per house or flat (to nearest £)
1	Sept. 1925–Mar. 1926	The Avenue	10	3	470
	May 1926–Feb. 1927	Thorndown Lane	10	3	463
2*	Jan. 1927–Sept. 1927	The Avenue	20	2	379
3*	Nov. 1927–Apr. 1928	The Avenue	6	2	353
4?		The Avenue	2	3?	
5*	June 1928–Dec. 1928	The Avenue	8	2	312
		Thorndown Lane	6	3	377
6	Apr. 1930–Dec. 1930	Stone Hill Road	26	2 (22 h.) 3 (4 h.)	320**
7	Aug. 1931–Jan. 1932	Guildford Road	12	2	331
		The Avenue	16 (4 blocks of flats)		229 and 234

*Built with aid of Chamberlain subsidy.   **Average

Fig. 14.—Houses built by Windlesham Urban District Council 1925–32

sewer. The council advised the Ministry of Health at that time that it did not intend to erect council houses, no speculative building was taking place, and private persons who wished to build could not afford to do so without a subsidy. By December 1926 subsidies had been approved by the ministry for 100 houses to be built by private individuals, and 93 such subsidies had been granted by the council, mostly to nursery workers and gardeners.[22] It may be that after its earlier experience, the council was not keen to undertake the building of houses, but it is also true that up to the end of 1924, officials were heavily committed with the main drainage scheme, the new Surveyor being obviously overworked until a separate Sanitary Inspector was appointed.

Between 1925 and early 1932 the council built 100 houses and 16 flats, rather more than a quarter of the total number of new houses built over the whole period from 1919. All of this building, apart from 16 houses at Thorndown Lane (Windlesham), was on the outskirts of the district at Lightwater, where land was cheaper (see Fig. 14). In November 1924 the Medical Officer of Health estimated that at least 30 families needed rehousing owing to houses which were overcrowded or unfit, and the council resolved unanimously to embark on a housing scheme for 40 houses. It was originally intended that 10 houses should be built for sale to owner-occupiers, but this was not carried out.[6] The acute shortage of rented accommodation is underlined by the *Camberley News* of 9 January 1925:

> Residents of Bagshot were astonished during last weekend to see a dwelling house in the Lightwater-road with the now very unusual notice 'To be Let' exhibited in the window, and the question was being asked 'Is it a joke?'

The council did not use any part of the abandoned housing site which it still owned, but in the first half of 1925 purchased land on both sides of the road to the new cemetery at Lightwater, later named The Avenue. Tenders were accepted from Jonathan Corbett for two pairs, and from Geo. Church & Co. for three pairs, of non-parlour type, three-bedroom houses. Work was commenced in September 1925 and the houses were completed in the spring of 1926, the rent being 14s. 6d. a week, inclusive of rates. When councillors disagreed about the size of bath to be installed, a bath was obtained from Bowditch & Green (ironmongers in the high street) and placed in the council chamber. The chairman and one of the council assistants then sat in the bath—not presumably at the same time —and pronounced that there was quite enough room for a person to take a bath! Five acres of land were also bought at Thorndown Lane, Windlesham, but there was some delay over building because tenders were too high. A tender was finally accepted from A. W. Viner in March 1926 for five pairs of houses, and these were occupied early in 1927. There is no record of any grant under the Housing Acts being applied for in respect of these first 20 houses, and in April 1926 a decision was taken to sell off the spare land at both sites. This decision was partially rescinded in the November, when it was resolved to erect five pairs of houses of a smaller two-bedroom type on the south side of The Avenue opposite the existing houses, and to apply for a grant under the 1923 (Chamberlain)

Act. It was apparently suggested at an interview at the Ministry of Health that the council should build instead with the 1924 (Wheatley) subsidy, but it was unanimously resolved in December 1926 not to build these houses under the latter Act, presumably because the rent restrictions were not found acceptable. The number of houses was increased to 20, a tender from Corbett being accepted. All the houses were completed by September 1927, the rent being fixed at 12s. a week.[6]

After the tenants for these first two housing schemes had been selected—it was specified in connection with the second scheme that only people living or working in the area should be eligible—there was still a list of 42 applicants. The council, however, in July 1927 'considered it inexpedient to build further houses at the present time'.[6] This may have been due to the fact that the Chamberlain subsidy had been reduced to £4 on houses completed after 30 September 1927.[24] Nevertheless in October 1927, three pairs of houses at The Avenue similar to the last ones were authorised, the builders this time being Geo. Church & Co. In the following May (1928) it was agreed that four more pairs on the north side of The Avenue and three more pairs at Thorndown Lane should be built by W. J. Drowley.[6,7] Altogether 40 houses were built with the aid of the Chamberlain subsidy before this was abolished for all houses not completed by 30 September 1929.[24] Over the period 1920-9 the local authority contribution to the total of 296 houses built in the urban district was 62 houses, 234 being supplied by private enterprise.[14]

There was now a pause in the council's house-building programme until in January 1930 it was found that at least 22 applicants still wanted houses and five other houses would be required owing to closing orders. It was decided to build 26 houses, mainly of the smaller type, in a new road to be opened off The Avenue, which was named Stone Hill Road. A tender from W. G. Tarrant for £8,313 for 26 houses and sheds was accepted. When these houses were finished in January 1931 there were about 40 applicants waiting. Land was bought in the Guildford road at the end of The Avenue, and six pairs of three-bedroom houses were erected there by G. Holt. Four blocks of flats of two different types were also built at the bottom of The Avenue by W. Denton. The rent of these houses was fixed at 11s. 6d. a week, and that of the flats at 8s., all the houses and flats being ready for occupation in January 1932.[7] It will be noted (Fig. 14) that the prices of the council houses had reduced pretty steadily in common with house prices generally.

Roads

With the increase in traffic from the early 20th century, the roads once again became important. Already in 1913 over 100,000 private cars were licensed; by 1922 there were over 300,000, and commercial vehicles, too, were growing rapidly in numbers. The Road Board was created in 1909 with power to subsidise special improvements, but it largely confined itself to improvements to main road surfaces by means of macadam and the new tarring process, and it was not until after the First World War that larger schemes for road widening and new road construction came to fruition under the Ministry of Transport set up in 1919.

One of the chief complaints which had been made by the residents of Windlesham against Chertsey Rural District Council was, as we have already seen, that the upkeep of the roads in the parish was neglected. The great west road was maintained directly by the County Surveyor, but its condition, too, was pretty poor! Lengths of this road were tarred about 1908, though when this was first requested by the parish council, Surrey County Council said that half the cost must be borne by the rural district council or be subscribed locally.[25] Additional expenditure to be made on this road by the county council for the year 1909-10, was estimated at £2,450, but this, of course, included road in Egham, Chertsey, and Frimley districts as well. The County Surveyor's explanation of this large sum was that 'very little progress has hitherto been made in changing this from a gravel to a granite surface'. The road was now much used as a through motor route and it was desirable that it be brought up to the standard of other main roads in the county with which at the time it compared 'very unfavourably'.[26] The highways committee set up by Windlesham Urban District Council in 1909 applied itself to the maintenance of the other roads and to minor widening and straightening. New Road, which was in a very bad condition, was almost entirely rebuilt during the First World War.[27] The increase in military traffic owing to War Office lands in the area led to further wear on road surfaces. In 1920 the Surveyor recommended extension of the tar-spraying area in the district, because owing to the lack of metalling in recent years the roads were 'very lean' and spraying was urgently needed to hold together what remained of the surfaces.[28]

In 1921 roads were classified as Class I, Class II, and other roads, according to their relative importance, and grants were made by the Ministry of Transport varying with the category of road and the urgency of the work. Class I roads in the district (in addition to the main road) were Devenish Road, Guildford Road and Mariners Lane, while Broomhall and Bracknell Roads, the Maultway, and the road through Windlesham (School Road, Updown Hill, Chertsey Road) were Class II. In 1922 the Surveyor submitted a scheme for a major widening of Guildford Road, which would increase the width of a narrow stretch near Stone Hill House by about 10 feet to 32 feet. The scheme was similar in most respects to one proposed by the urban district council in 1912, which had not been carried through because Surrey County Council was not then prepared to bear a substantial part of the cost. The total cost was estimated in 1922 at £420; the Ministry of Transport agreed to pay half the total and the county council a quarter of the remainder. The increase in motor bus traffic was already worrying the Surveyor in 1922, particularly when unclassified roads, whose maintenance fell largely on the urban district, were to be used.[11] In October 1924 a notice was put up in the buses which Messrs. Fox had just started to run through Windlesham that they would shortly be withdrawn owing to the condition of the roads.[5]

Bagshot By-pass

The most important improvement of the 1920s was the construction of a by-pass round Bagshot. It is only in quite recent times that small settlements have begun to press for the removal of through traffic on account of the nuisance and danger which it causes, and in the past the primary reason for making a by-pass was the obstruction presented to traffic by narrow town streets. It was on this score that already in 1913 the County Surveyor had in mind the possibility of by-passing Bagshot. The narrow, winding approaches to Bagshot

Bridge from Bagshot Park were dangerous and caused trouble with the increased traffic. Eighty years before, Egham and Bagshot Turnpike Trust had prepared plans to improve and straighten this same piece of road, but the work was never carried out owing to the advent of the railways. The County Surveyor now suggested either widening the highway and the bridge, or building a by-pass from the station to the *Fighting Cocks.* The second scheme would cost nearly twice as much as the first, but Windlesham Urban District Council supported it because, taking into consideration the major contributions expected from the Road Board and Surrey County Council, this scheme would give the least expense to the district. When the news reached Bagshot, however, 41 ratepayers protested against the by-pass proposal and asked for a public meeting. The first signature on the memorial was that of Mr. G. W. Green, a butcher in the high street, and it is possible that traders feared loss of custom. The council promptly changed its mind and appointed a sub-committee to go into the question of widening the road. Nothing was, however, actually done before the war.[29, 27]

In the early 1920s the purchase of land for improving this stretch of road was again under discussion by the urban district council and the county council. In March 1922 the county council (highways and bridges committee) received letters from several residents in West Surrey (including the Coroner) and from the Royal Automobile Club, about the dangerous state of the bridge and its approaches.[30] Estimates drawn up by the County Surveyor of the comparative cost of by-passing the village or widening the bridge were referred in January 1923 to the Ministry of Transport and the urban district council. The latter unanimously opposed the new road, being of the opinion that another road coming out at the war memorial would merely transfer the existing danger, as four roads would then converge at this spot. The Ministry of Transport, on the other hand, preferred the by-pass scheme, of which it could be expected to bear half the cost.[31] This scheme was therefore sanctioned by Surrey County Council in March 1923 at an estimated cost of £12,000, almost double that of 1913. The work was commenced in July 1924 and the road was opened to the public on 1 September 1925.[32] It was one of the very first by-pass roads actually to be completed in Surrey.

This was no doubt due to the fact that it was on a comparatively small scale, larger projects like the Kingston by-pass
taking longer to carry out. The approach to Bagshot Bridge
was widened subsequently, and the old brick bridge was
replaced by the present concrete structure.

Street Lighting

It will be remembered that only three lamps were being
lit in Bagshot during the war years. In the winter of 1918
the lamp near the corner of New Road was added to those
to be lit, and for the lighting season which began in October
1919 the number of street lamps was increased to ten. It was
not, however, until October 1922 that the lamps in use were
restored to their pre-war number of thirty-three. Ascot Gas
Company had meantime pointed out that, owing to the cost
of labour, it was relatively cheaper to light more lamps, quoting
£3 15s. 0d. per lamp for the six months, providing 33 were lit,
as compared with £5 18s. 0d. per lamp for the reduced number.
On the advice of the gas company, the existing lanterns were
converted to two-light inverted burners with reflector, in order
to obtain better distribution of light over the ground. There
was now for the first time to be some street lighting in Windlesham and Lightwater as well as Bagshot, it being decided to
arrange the street lamps so as to provide light in the most
dangerous positions on the roads in all three places, although
the total number of lights was not increased. A distribution
totalling 30 lamps was mentioned: 14 in Bagshot, 10 in Windlesham, and six in Lightwater.[11, 28]

Thereafter there was a steady increase year by year in the
street lamps, due partly to a policy of extending the lighting
to lesser roads and also to the development of the area itself.
By 1932 it was recommended that 74 lamps be lit from
14 September to 15 April. From 1924 the lamp in Bagshot
Square was lit all night, and from 1928 both this lamp and
the one at the corner by the shop of Morris Bros. were kept
alight all year round as well. Two lamps of a special new
type in the by-pass road were kept alight all night all the year
round. In 1929 two additional lamps in Bracknell Road were
to be electric lights, and these seem to have been the first not
lit by gas or oil.[33, 6, 7]

Fire Brigade

The arrangements made just before and during the war for fighting fires seem to have lapsed subsequently. In July 1921. in a report made to a special committee, the Surveyor said that it had taken considerable trouble including interviews with the South West Suburban Water Company before the hydrants could even be located! Of the 31 hydrants which he now listed, 14 were without identification plates, and he considered that five additional hydrants were needed. For the whole district there were at the various depots 26 lengths of hose and five extinguishers. The organisation was almost non-existent except at Windlesham, where Mr. Boyce had had occasional drills and could be depended on to keep a body of volunteers together. At Sunningdale, Mr. Baker, who had been captain of a small brigade, was now the only one left, while at Bagshot no one was responsible. Even Mr. Eustace's volunteers at Lightwater had failed to respond in recent heath fires, and it had been necessary to obtain the help of boy scouts. The Surveyor suggested that one man should be made responsible for the whole district.[11]

The council agreed to have the five extra fire hydrants fixed, and allocated £100 to be spent on additional fire appliances, 10 more extinguishers to be purchased immediately. After a deputation from the council had visited Egham to see the equipment of the Egham fire brigade, arrangements were made to call upon their fire engine in case of need, and the Egham brigade commenced regular visits to the district to check the hydrants and the supply of water. Mr. Eustace, whose advice had been sought about the raising of a volunteer brigade, suggested that there should again be four sections (each with six to 10 volunteers), the leaders selecting one of their number to be the representative of the brigade in dealings with the council. Volunteers seem to have been found fairly quickly for Bagshot and Lightwater, but it is not clear that a section was actually formed at Sunningdale.[28, 10, 9] The arrangement with Egham was maintained until 1929, a suggested arrangement with Frimley Urban District Council, to cover fires at the Bagshot and Lightwater end by their motor fire engine, coming to nothing because Frimley wanted too much money for checking the hydrants.[5, 6] The system of volunteer firemen as the first resort seems to have functioned reasonably well:

on at least one occasion when there was an outbreak of fire at the South Western Stores at Bagshot the volunteers put out the fire without the need to call a fire engine.[34] It is unlikely that Mr. Eustace's plan for one overall leader was, however, put into practice.

In the late 1920s the number of heath fires in the Lightwater area gave great cause for concern. On Easter Sunday 1929 there was a most extensive fire on the heath, to which the O.C. at Blackdown barracks sent soldiers and a fire engine. A special meeting of the highways committee held to consider the whole question of fire protection felt that the fire-fighting appliances of the council were inadequate, and the council called for a report from the Surveyor, as a result of which it was decided to purchase a fire engine.[33] A special fire brigade committee was set up in June 1929 to consider the make of engine, the construction of a fire engine house, and the formation of a proper brigade. It was decided to purchase an engine from Dennis Bros. of Guildford for £750, and a tender was accepted from Messrs. G. Church for £1,283 to build an engine-house on land near the old council room at Bagshot Green. There was some difficulty at first over the brigade itself, because of the natural desire of the volunteer firemen, especially those from Lightwater, who felt that they had borne the brunt of the heath fires in the past, to be chosen for the fire engine crew. The full strength of the brigade seems to have been nominally 30 men (chief officer, six sub-officers, 23 other ranks), from whom 12 engine crew could be selected, but in practice it was soon reduced to a permanent brigade of 12 men.[35, 7]

The chief engineer of the Windlesham fire brigade, Mr. T. Woodham, one of the council's drivers, lived in a flat over the fire station (for which he paid rent) and received £5 a year retaining fee. The telephone had to be manned continuously, and with Mr. Woodham away at work, this duty naturally fell to Mrs. Woodham who, in fact, continued to answer the calls and summon the brigade for the next 10 years! The firemen were at first alerted by a siren installed at the station, call boys being also used for a time.[7] In April 1932, however, on the occasion of a fire at the motor garage of Mr. A. J. Osman on Jenkins Hill, the siren failed to go off owing to an electrical failure caused by the fire itself. The garage was completely

destroyed, only the 'heroic efforts' of the brigade preventing
the 30 foot high flames spreading to the Methodist church and
houses nearby.[36] The council decided on the immediate installa-
tion of fire bells in firemen's houses, and the brigade was thereafter summoned by pulling down a lever at the fire station
which sounded a bell in every house.[7]

Windlesham Urban District Council was very proud of its
fire brigade, the creation of which was really its final achievement, and complimented the Chief Officer (Mr. W. Eustace)
on the smart turnout, in uniforms bought by private subscription, at the opening of the new fire station in June 1930. Mr.
Eustace for his own part was pleased with his fire engine, which
he considered to be the most efficient one within a 10-mile
radius.[7] At the first annual dinner held at the *Cricketers* in
January 1931 the Chairman of the Council expressed the hope
that the idea then mooted of a 'county brigade' might never
come about.[37]

Reorganisation: Setting Up of Bagshot Rural District Council

As we have already recorded, some notable old friends had
vanished from the council chamber and offices by 1931. A
greater change was already on the way, by which Windlesham
Urban District Council itself was to disappear. The Local
Government Act 1929 provided for a review—the first to be
made—by all county councils, in conference with the district
councils concerned, to decide whether it was desirable to effect
any changes in the areas within counties. It must be appreciated
that, outside the towns, the local government districts were
still the result of the areas defined for the boards of guardians
in 1835. From these areas, which consisted of a market town
and a number of parishes within a convenient 10-mile radius,
had subsequently been detached for local government purposes
a number of urban sanitary areas or (later) urban districts. Each
new urban district was the result of a separate decision made
within the existing framework, and the portions left behind
continued more or less automatically to constitute the rural
district.

Throughout the period during which the Windlesham urban
district was in existence, its population was never more than
five to six thousand. Statistics of districts in Surrey, which

were appended to the report of the special committee set up by Surrey County Council in January 1930, show Windlesham to have the lowest density of population per acre of all the urban districts (1.05). It had the second smallest rateable value, the produce of a penny rate being only £200, and the third smallest population.[38] If there were to be changes, Windlesham urban district was most likely to be effected. Local authorities were invited to give their views, and in February 1930 Windlesham Urban District Council put forward proposals which were shrewdly aimed at enlarging its own area.[7] At the same time Chertsey Rural District Council, which now covered only Bisley, Byfleet, Chobham, and Pyrford, made counter proposals involving the re-absorption of Windlesham. This provoked a letter to the *Camberley News* from the chairman of Windlesham Council, in which he referred to the 'long and strenuous fight' Windlesham had previously waged in order to get away from the Chertsey rural district.[39]

In view of the change which has just recently taken place, it is interesting to see that the county council committee at one time considered the union of Frimley and Camberley with Windlesham, but found certain difficulties in the way. The proposals finally made by this committee involved joining Bisley and Chobham to Windlesham and were substantially the same as those made by Windlesham itself. The urban district council was well pleased, though the de-urbanisation of the area, which was recommended in order that the new district might be assisted in the maintenance of its roads, cannot have been entirely welcome.[40] The new name 'Bagshot Rural District Council' met with some opposition from the Windlesham members of the existing council, though Bagshot was clearly the best centre.[7] The report made by the special committee was adopted by Surrey County Council on 26 May 1931 and submitted to the Ministry of Health. Under the Order made on 31 January 1933, Windlesham Urban District Council ceased to exist on 31 March 1933.[8] Since its inception nearly a quarter of a century before, the council had steered the district through a period of rapid growth and great change, in which it had, in the proud boast of the chairman, provided itself 'with every public service which a country residential urban district can require'.[39]

Notes

Chapter 1. The Framework

1. L. V. Grinsell, 'Analysis and list of Surrey barrows', *Surrey Arch. Coll.*, Vol. 42 (1934), pp. 29, 36, 39, 40.

2. O.S. map *Southern Britain in the Iron Age* (1962), Index, p. 36.

3. *V.C.H., Berks*, Vol. 1 (1906), p. 206.

4. I. D. Margary, *Roman Roads in Britain*, Vol. 1, South (1955), pp. 78–79; *Surrey Arch. Soc. Bulletin*, June 1973.

5. T. B. Handasyd, 'Account of antiquities discovered in neighbourhood of Bagshot July 1783', *Archaeologia*, Vol. 7 (1785), pp. 199 *sqq.*

6. Col. P. L. McDougall, 'The Roman Road between Silchester and Staines', *Surrey Arch. Coll.*, Vol. 1 (1857), p. 64.

7. O. F. E. Charleton, *Surrey Arch. Soc. Bulletin*, July 1972, and private information.

8. *Place-Names of Surrey* (E.P.N.S., 1934), p. 152; E. Ekwall, *Oxf. Dict. Eng. Place-Names*, 3rd edn. (1947), p. 498.

9. *P.N. Surrey*, p. 153; Ekwall, pp. 21, 22.

10. *Chronicon Monasterii de Abingdon*, ed. by Rev. J. Stevenson (1858), Vol. 2, pp. 7, 132.

11. *Rotuli Litterarum Clausarum*, ed. by T. D. Hardy (Record Commissioners), Vol. 2 (1844), p. 56.

12. For old roads in this area, see C. Cochrane, *Lost Roads of Wessex* (Pan 1972), pp. 70–72.

13. *V.C.H., Surrey*, Vol. 1 (1902), p. 358.

14. *V.C.H., Surrey*, Vol. 3 (1911), p. 377.

15. St. John's College, Cambridge, Muniments drawer 16, No. 7 (TS. Cal.).

16. Greater London Record Office (London), ARC/DW/PA/5/1604.

17. Surrey Record Office (abbreviated hereafter to S.R.O.), Surrey Quarter Sessions Rolls 1687–91 (TS. Cal.), Roll cxv, m. 95.

18. Cochrane, *Lost Roads*, pp. 73–74.

19. *Chertsey Abbey Cartularies* (Surrey Rec. Soc., Vol. 12, pt. 1 (1915–33), p. 128.

20. S.R.O., Windlesham vestry minutes, 1878–94.

21. *V.C.H., Surrey*, Vol. 2 (1905), pp. 563 *sqq.*

22. *Cal. Charter Rolls*, 1226–57, p. 70.

23. *V.C.H., Berks*, Vol. 2 (1907), p. 80.

24. *Cal. Patent Rolls*, 1377–81, p. 455.

25. Guildford Muniment Room (abbreviated hereafter to G.M.R.), 1081/19.

26. *Cal. State Papers Domestic*, 1638–9, p. 305.

27. F. B. P. Lory, *Reminiscences of Bagshot, 1874–1949*(priv. print., n.d.), p. 1; O. Manning & W. Bray, *History and Antiquities of the County of Surrey* (referred to hereafter as Manning & Bray), Vol. 3 (1814), p. lxxx.

28. St. John's College, parcel labelled 'Court rolls 1512–43'.

29. Manning & Bray, Vol. 3, p. 82.

30. E. W. Brayley, *Topographical History of Surrey* (1841–8), Vol. 1, pt. 2, p. 460.

31. St. John's College, Court rolls 1328–30.

32. St. John's College, Drawer 14, Nos. 158, 161 (TS. Cal.).

33. *Letters and Papers Hen. VIII*, Vol. 3, pt. 2, p. 1113.

34. P.R O., C 142/37, No. 132.

35. St. John's College, Drawer 16, No. 15.

36. St. John's College, Court rolls 1666–1749.

37. St. John's College, Court book 1813–1937.

38. St. John's College, Map 210.

39. P.R.O., L.R. 2/190, f. 160.

40. Manning & Bray, Vol. 3, p. 196.

41. G.M.R., 99, m.1.

42. G.M.R., 97/8/2, 97/8/3(3).

43. *Red Bk. Exchequer*, ed. by H. Hall (Rolls Series, 1897), Vol. 1, p. 561.

44. *Cal. Inquisitions post mortem*, Vol. 1, p. 88.

45. P.R.O., L.R. 2/190, ff. 158, 159.

46. P.R.O., L.R. 2/226.

47. Manning & Bray, Vol. 3, p. 85.

48. 21 Geo. II, c. *9* (Priv. Act.).

49. *Cal. Close Rolls*, 1441–7, p. 131.

50. *Cal. Close*, 1461–8, p. 393.

51. Manning & Bray, Vol. 3, pp. clxi, clxii.

52. *Surrey Fines, 1509–1558* (Surrey Rec. Soc., Vol. 19, 1946), p.1.

53. G.M.R., 1660/14/1, 5.

54. S.R.O., 278/1/28.

55. J. Cree, *Notes on Windlesham Parish Church* (1927), p. 29.

56. *Surrey Fines, 1509–1558*, p. 77.

57. P.R.O., C.P. 25(2)/225/3 Eliz. East., No. 426.

58. *Cal. Pat.*, 1558-60, p. 313.

59. P.R.O., C 142/594, No. 41.

60. Minet Libr., Cal. Deeds, No. 2988.

61. P.R.O., C.P. 25(2)/1067/5 Geo. I Mich.

62. S.R.O., Acc. 587/1/40-140, claim No. 71.

63. Canon J. N. Dalton, *MSS. St. George's Chapel, Windsor Castle* (1957), p. xxvii.

64. *Cal. Pat.*, 1467-77. p. 484.

65. *MSS. St. George's Chapel*, pp. 318–19, 348, 349.

66. Records of Dean and Canons of Windsor (abbreviated hereafter to W.R.), XV.3.16.

67. W.R., XV.21.100, XV.21.101.

68. W.R., IV.B.5, ff. 70-71.

69. W.R., XI.M.1.

70. W.R., XV.38.78.

71. W.R., XV.38.100.

72. W.R., IV.A.3.

73. *MSS. St. George's Chapel,* p. 294.
74. W.R., XV.38.101.
75. S.R.O., 278/2/1-5.
76. S.R.O., 278/2/6-9, 10-11.
77. Church Commissioners, file No. 41470.
78. G.M.R., 97/8/2.

Chapter 2. The Main Features

1. J. Aubrey, *Natural History and Antiquities of Surrey* (1718-19), Vol. 3, pp. 211-13.
2. J. Cree, *Notes on Windlesham Parish Church* (1927), referred to hereafter as Cree; *Surrey Arch. Coll.,* Vol. 37 (1927), pp. 249-50.
3. *V.C.H., Surrey,* Vol. 3 (1911), p. 378.
4. *Registrum Johannis de Pontissara* (Surrey Rec. Soc., Vols. 1 and 6, 1913-16), p. 607.
5. *Rotuli Litterarum Clausarum,* ed. by T. D. Hardy (Record Commissioners), Vol. 2 (1844), p. 145.
6. Hants. Record Office, Reg. Waynflete, Vol. 1, f. 83v.
7. *Fines relating to County of Surrey* (Surrey Arch. Soc., 1894), pp. 162-3.
8. Hants. R.O., Reg. Waynflete, Vol, 1, f. 2.
9. Cree, pp. 38-9.
10. *V.C.H., Surrey,* Vol. 3, pp. 416-17.
11. Hants. R.O., Reg. Morley, Vol. 2, ff. 143-7.
12. C. T. Cracklow, *Lithographic Views of all Surrey churches* (1823).
13. Cree, pp. 47, 51.
14. Compton return. Information kindly supplied by Librarian, William Salt Library, Stafford.
15. Canon J. N. Dalton, *MSS. St. George's Chapel, Windsor Castle* (1957), p. 348.
16. Hants. R.O., Reg. Courtney, f. 39.
17. Greater London Record Office (London), abbreviated hereafter to G.L.R.O.(L), ARC/DW/PA/7/2, f. 105.
18. G.L.R.O.(L), ARC/DW/PA/7/4, f. 166.
19. Cree, pp. 68-74.
20. E. W. Brayley, *Topographical History of Surrey* (1841-8), Vol. 1, pt. 2, p. 467; Surrey Record Office, Acc. 924/1/I.
21. Cree, pp. 52-53.
22. E. W. Brayley, *Topographical History of Surrey,* revised by E. Walford (1878-81), Vol. 1, p. 235.
23. Cree, pp. 63-64.
24. Cree, pp. 59-61.
25. Cree, pp. 57-58, 61-62, 64-67, 26-35.
26. *Taxatio Ecclesiastica,* ed. by Rev. S. Ayscough and J. Caley (Record Commissioners, 1802), p. 208.
27. *Valor Ecclesiasticus,* ed. by J. Caley and Rev. J. Hunter (Record Commissioners, 1810-34), Vol. 2, pp. 32, 33.

28. P.R.O., L.R. 2/190, f. 160.

29. Cree, pp. 29–30.

30. P.R.O., Prob. 11/151, f. 17.

31. Hants. R.O., B/2/A–1.

32. Cree, pp. 80–84.

33. Surrey Record Office, Acc. 587/1/40–140, claim No. 29.

34. *Rep. Charity Commissioners*, H.C. 433, pp. 704–5 (1824), xiv.

35. Cree, p. 85.

36. *Surrey Hearth Tax 1664* (Surrey Rec. Soc., Vol. 17, 1940), p. 122.

37. Surrey R.O., Acc. 587/1/2.

38. Cree, p. 86.

39. Minet Libr., S.P. 115/188; B.L., N.L. Crach Tab 1 b 1, O. Manning and W. Bray, *History and Antiquities of the County of Surrey* (referred to hereafter as Manning and Bray), grangerised by R. Percival (1847), Vol.17, between pp. 88 and 89.

40. Brayley, *History of Surrey* (1878–81), Vol. 1, p. 236.

41. *Cal. Patent Rolls*, 1476–85, p. 204.

42. Manning and Bray, Vol. 3 (1814), pp. 87, 110.

43. *Reg. Woodlock* (Cant. and York Soc., Vol. 44, 1934–40), p. 895.

44. P.R.O., E 301, Vol. 2, f. 277.

45. *Regs. Gardiner and Poynet* (Cant. and York Soc., Vol. 37, 1930), p. 171, n.2.

46. *Regs. Gardiner and Poynet*, p. 185.

47. Guildford Muniment Room, 1660/14/1, 3c.

48. T. Craib, 'Surrey Chantries', *Surrey Arch. Coll.*, Vol. 25 (1912), p. 28.

49. Manning and Bray, Vol. 3 (1814), p. 85.

50. G.L.R.O.(L), DW/VB/1, ff. 51, 57, 67, 69, 72.

51. Hants. R.O.

52. Manning and Bray, Vol. 3 (1814), p. clxii.

53. Manning and Bray, Vol. 3, p. 82.

54. *Cal. Pat.*, 1494–1509, p. 215.

55. P.R.O., L.R. 2/190, f. 159.

56. B.L., Harl. MS. 3749, Table XV.

57. P.R.O., S.P. 14/53, f.11; B.L., Add. MS. 5755, f. 243.

58. J. Summerson, *Architecture in Britain 1530–1830*, 4th edn. (Pelican History of Art, 1963), p. 75.

59. *Cal. State Papers Domestic*, 1660–1, p. 56.

60. *Dictionary National Biography*, Vol. 11, p. 1277.

61. *Cal. S.P. Dom.*, 1655–6, p. 150; 1660–1, p. 286.

62. P.R.O., E 317 Surrey 5.

63. *Surrey Hearth Tax 1664*, p. 111.

64. *Surrey Quarter Sessions Records*, 1663–6 (Surrey Rec. Soc., Vol. 16, 1938), p. 51.

65. *Cal. Treasury Bks.*, 1681–5, pp. 655, 713.

66. P.R.O., T 54/11, ff. 192–3.

67. *Diary of John Evelyn*, ed. by E. S. de Beer (1959), pp. 822, 830.

68. Manning and Bray, Vol. 3, p. 84.

69. Surrey Arch. Soc. Lbr., PDA/2/30, 39; PDB/BAG/1.

70. G. M. Hughes, *History of Windsor Forest* (1890), pp. 336–7.

71. D. M. Stuart, *Daughters of George III* (1939), pp. 240–3; *History of the King's Works*, ed. by H. M. Colvin, Vol. 6 (1973), p. 258.

72. *Guide to great encampment at Chobham in 1853*, pp. 20–21. Surrey Arch. Libr., bound with C. MacFarlane, *Camp of 1853* (1853).

73. G. E. and K. R. Fussell, *The English Countryman 1500–1900* (1955), p. 138.

74. Lt.-Col. G. C. E. Crew, *Short guide to Bagshot Park* (priv. print. Royal Army Chaplains' Dept., 1969).

75. D.N.B., 1941–50, p. 18.

76. *Surrey Taxation Returns* (Surrey Rec. Soc., Vol. 11, 1922, 1932), p. 47.

77. St. John's College, Cambridge, Court rolls 1328–30; muniments drawer 14, No. 158 (TS. Cal).

78. Records of Dean and Canons of Windsor, IV.A.3, XV.38.100.

79. *Surrey Musters* (Surrey Rec. Soc., Vol. 3, 1914–19), pp. 275–6.

80. *Surrey Wills*, 1484–9 (Surrey Rec. Soc., Vol. 5, 1922), p. 74.

81. St. John's College, Drawer 13, No. 79 (TS. Cal.).

Chapter 3.   Twin Occupations

1. *Surrey Musters* (Surrey Rec. Soc., Vol. 3, 1914–19), pp. 275–6.

2. *Universal British Directory*, Vol. 2 (1791), p. 292.

3. Greater London Record Office (London), abbreviated hereafter to G.L.R.O.(L), ARC/DW/PA/5/1570.

4. G.L.R.O.(L), ARC/DW/PA/5/1604.

5. Records of Deans and Canons of Windsor, IV.A.3.

6. Canon J. N. Dalton, *MSS. St. George's Chapel, Windsor Castle* (1957), p. 295; Surrey Record Office (abbreviated hereafter to S.R.O.), 278/2/1–11b.

7. O. Manning and W. Bray, *History and Antiquities of the County of Surrey*, Vol. 3 (1814), p. 81.

8. P. A. L. Vine, *London's lost route to Basingstoke* (1968), p. 136.

9. S.R.O., Q.S.6/8/10.

10. Vine, *Lost route to Basingstoke*, pp. 78–79.

11. A. G. Parton, '1801 Crop Returns for Surrey', *Surrey Arch. Coll.*, Vol. 64 (1967), p. 122.

12. G.L.R.O.(L), ARC/DW/PA/5/1555, 1587.

13. J. Aubrey, *Natural History and Antiquities of Surrey* (1718–19), Vol. 3, p. 213.

14. W. James and J. Malcolm, *General View of Agriculture of Surrey* (1794), p. 23.

15. W. Stevenson, *General View of Agriculture of Surrey* (1813), pp. 519–21.

16. James and Malcolm, *Agriculture of Surrey*, p. 72–73.

17. James and Malcolm, p. 71.

18. S.R.O., Acc. 587/1/2; Acc. 587/1/40–140.

19. Stevenson, *Agriculture of Surrey*, pp. 84–85.

20. Guildford Muniment Room, Fosters court book, 97/8/2.
21. Guildford Muniment Room, 99, m.1.
22. St. John's College, Cambridge, parcel labelled 'court rolls 1512-43'.
23. G.L.R.O.(L), ARC/DW/PA/7/4, f. 166.
24. P.R.O., L.R., 2/190, f.160.
25. St. John's College, Court rolls 1666-1749.
26. Guildford Muniment Room, 97/8/3/5.
27. S.R.O., Surrey Quarter Sessions Rolls 1687-91 (TS. Cal.), Roll cxv m.95.
28. St. John's College, Muniments drawer 14, No. 81.
29. S.R.O., Acc. 924/4/5.
30. S.R.O., 278/1/28.
31. B.L., Harl. MS. 3749, Table XV.
32. H. C. Darby, ed., *Historical Geography of England before 1800* (1969), p. 342, fig. 64.
33. Geo. C. B. Poulter, *Golden Farmer, The Inn and the Highwayman* (1969); see also Poulter, *The History of Camberley* (1969), pp. 12-14.
34. Celia Fiennes, *Through England on a side-saddle in the time of William and Mary*, ed. by E. W. Griffiths (1888), pp. 21, 47, 234.
35. D. Defoe, *Tour through Gt. Britain* (Penguin 1971), p. 156.
36. *Correspondence of Alexander Pope*, ed. by Geo Sherburn (1956), Vol. 1, p. 519.
37. *Surrey Quarter Sessions Records*, 1663-6 (Surrey Rec. Soc., Vol. 16, 1938), p. 141.
38. *Surrey Q.S. Records*, 1663-6, p. 210.
39. S.R.O., Surrey Quarter Sessions Rolls 1678-82 (TS. Cal.), Roll lxxix, m.90.
40. 1 Geo. II sess. 2 c.6; 10 Geo. II c.12.
41. *Gentleman's Magazine* Aug. 1754, p. 349.
42. 26 Geo. II c.66; 26 Geo. II c.60; 26 Geo. II c.69; 26 Geo. II c.74.
43. 29 Geo. II c.54; 27 Geo. II c.32; 28 Geo. II c.44; 29 Geo. II c.46; 30 Geo. II c.61; 2 Geo. III c.66.
44. Greater London Record Office (Middlesex), Tp.BED/1, minute book 1728-57.
45. 3 Geo. III c.47.
46. G.L.R.O.(M), Tp.BED/4, minute book (Western) 1763-1804.
47. *New Guide to Stage Coaches* (Lowndes, 1788, 1798).
48. E. Vale, *Mail Coach Men of late 18th century* (1960), p. 230.
49. B.L., N.L. Crach Tab 1 b 1, Manning and Bray's *History of Surrey*, grangerised by R. Percival (1847), Vol. 29, between pp. xxxviii and xxxix.
50. S. and B. Webb, *English Local Govt.: Statutory Authorities for Special Purposes* (1922), pp. 282-5; Carl Moritz, *Travels in England*, reprint Eng. trans. of 1795 (1924), p. 29.
51. *Cal. Patent Rolls*, 1416-22, p. 102.
52. *Cal. Pat.*,1494-1509, p. 215.
53. P.R.O., L.R. 2/190, f. 158.
54. P.R.O., L.R. 2/226, f. 1.
55. St. John's College, Drawer 14, No. 158.
56. *Cal. State Papers Domestic*, 1603-10, p. 390.

57. *Surrey Arch. Coll.*, Vol. 12 (1895), p. 88.

58. *V.C.H., Surrey*, Vol. 3 (1911), p. 343.

59. *Cal. Pat.*, 1548-9, p. 414.

60. Domestic Buildings Research Group (Surrey), report dated Sept. 1973.

61. *Surrey Wills*, 1595-1608 (Surrey Rec. Soc., Vol. 4, 1915-20), p. 45.

62. *Surrey Arch. Coll.*, Vol. 19 (1906), p. 196.

63. P.R.O., L.R. 2/226, f. 10.

64. P.R.O., E 146/1/6.

65. Guildhall Libr., Hand-in-Hand policy No. 87961. I am indebted for this information, and also for that in notes 74 and 75, to Mr. Rowland G. M. Baker.

66. Manning and Bray, *History of Surrey*, Vol. 3 (1814), p. clxii.

67. Geo. C. B. Poulter, 'Bagshot's ancient taverns' (TS., Camberley Mus.).

68. *Surrey Hearth Tax 1664* (Surrey Rec. Soc., Vol. 17, 1940), p. 91 (Kinsington), p. 109 (Mower).

69. A. R. Bax, 'Suspected persons in Surrey during the Commonwealth', *Surrey Arch. Coll.*, Vol. 14 (1899), p. 188.

70. *Surrey Quarter Sessions Records*, 1661-3 (Surrey Rec. Soc., Vol. 14, 1935), p. 25.

71. J. L. and N. L. Wetton, 'Surrey 17th cent. traders' tokens', *Surrey Arch. Coll.*, Vol. 56 (1959), p. 30.

72. G.L.R.O.(M), Tp.BED/4; E. W. Brayley, *Topographical History of Surrey*, revised by E. Walford (1878-81), Vol. 1, p. 237.

73. Camberley Mus., presumably the copy of coloured print of Rowlandson drawing in Christmas number of the *Graphic* about 1890 (not found), described by Mr. F. B. P. Lory in *Reminiscences of Bagshot 1874-1949* (priv. print., n.d.), p. 4; B.L., Print Room, Rowlandson 1787 (not caricatures) and see also J. Grego, *Rowlandson the caricaturist*, Vol. 1, p. 222.

74. Guildhall Libr., Hand-in-Hand policy No. 81086.

75. Guildhall Libr., Hand-in-Hand policy No. 78500.

Chapter 4. The People of the Parish

1. T. Craib, 'Surrey Chantries', *Surrey Arch. Coll.*, Vol. 25 (1912), p. 28.

2. B.L., Harl. MS. 595, f. 245.

3. Information kindly supplied by Librarian, William Salt Library, Stafford.

4. *V.C.H., Leics.*, Vol. 3 (1955), p. 142.

5. *Surrey Musters* (Surrey Rec. Soc., Vol. 3, 1914-19), pp. 275-6.

6. P.R.O., L.R. 2/226, ff. 5, 6, 7, 8, 9.

7. *Surrey Hearth Tax 1664* (Surrey Rec. Soc., Vol. 17, 1940), Intro. p. cxxix.

8. Guildford Muniment Room, 97/8/3/3.

9. J. Cree, *Notes on Windlesham Parish Church* (1927), pp. 96 *sqq.*

10. Hants. R.O., B/2/A-2.

11. W. U. S. Glanville-Richards, *Registers of Windlesham 1677–1783* (priv. print. 1881).

12. Domestic Buildings Research Group (Surrey), Report No. 619 (1974).

13. 31 Eliz. c.7: *Surrey Quarter Sessions Records*, 1666–8 (Surrey C.C., 1951), p. 197.

14. *Surrey Quarter Sessions Records*, 1661–3 (Surrey Rec. Soc., Vol. 14, 1935), p. 209.

15. M. Lightbody, *A History of Erl Wood*, 2nd edn. (priv. publ. Lilly Research Centre, Windlesham), pp. 12–13.

16. Church Commissioners, file No. 41905.

17. Surrey Heath Borough Council, Capt. Cooper's papers, envelope No. 9.

18. *Universal British Directory*, Vol. 2 (1791), p. 292.

19. O. Manning and W. Bray, *History and Antiquities of the County of Surrey*, Vol. 3 (1814), p. clxii.

20. Information kindly supplied by Mr. David Graham, Headmaster, Hall Grove School.

21. *Correspondence of Alexander Pope*, ed. by Geo. Sherburn (1956), Vol. 3, p. 223.

22. *Corres. Alexander Pope*, Vol. 4, pp. 161, 203.

23. B.L., N.L. Crach Tab 1 b 1, Manning and Bray's *History of Surrey*, grangerised by R. Percival (1847), Vol. 17, opposite p. 82, and between pp. 82 and 83.

24. J. Senex, map of Surrey (1729).

25. *Country Life*, 27 Oct. 1960, p. 986. I am indebted for this information to Mr. B. F. J. Pardoe.

26. Surrey Record Office (abbreviated hereafter to S.R.O.), 278/1/2, 6, 7, 8, 9.

27. B.L., N.L. Crach Tab. 1 b 1, Manning and Bray (Percival), Vol. 17, between pp. 88 and 89.

28. Greater London Record Office (London), abbreviated hereafter to G.L.R.O.(L), ARC/DW/PA/5/1550.

29. P.R.O., L.R. 2/190, f. 160.

30. G.E. and K. R. Fussell, *The English Countryman 1500–1900* (1955), p. 23.

31. P.R.O., C.P. 25(2)/225/3 Eliz. East. No. 426.

32. Cree, *Windlesham Church*, p. 29.

33. G.L.R.O.(L), ARC/DW/PA/5/1587.

34. *Surrey Arch. Coll.*, Vol. 19 (1906), p. 70.

35. P.R.O., Prob. 11/151, f. 17.

36. J. Aubrey, *Natural History and Antiquities of Surrey* (1718–19), Vol. 3, p. 212.

37. *Wills proved in P.C.C., 1653–56* (Index Libr., Vol. 7), p. 20.

38. J. Foster, *Alumni Oxonienses*, early series, Vol. 2 (1891), p. 489.

39. *Surrey Wills*, 1595–1608 (Surrey Rec. Soc., Vol. 4, 1915–20), p. 247.

40. Guildford Muniment Room, 97/8/2.

41. G.L.R.O.(L), ARC/DW/PA/5/1592.

42. G.L.R.O.(L), ARC/DW/PA/5/1604.

43. G.L.R.O.(L), ARC/DW/PA/5/1684.

44. G.L.R.O.(L), ARC/DW/PA/7/8, f. 212.

45. D. L. Powell, *Surrey Parish Records Civil and Ecclesiastical* (Surrey C.C., 1927), pp. 124-5.

46. S.R.O., Quarter Sessions Order Book 1727-30.

47. *Reports Sel. Cttees. on Poor Laws*, 1775-7, and 1787, H.C. Ser. 1, Vol. ix, p. 470.

48. E. W. Brayley, *Topographical History of Surrey* (1841-8), Vol. 1, pt. 2, p. 470.

49. *Report Charity Commissioners*, H.C. 433, pp. 704-5 (1824). xiv.

50. Surrey Heath B.C., Windlesham church rate assessments 1765-81.

51. Cree, *Windlesham Church*, p. 73, n.4.

52. *Reports Sel. Cttees. on Poor Laws*, 1775-7 and1787, H.C. Ser. 1, Vol. ix, p. 680.

53. *Abstract Returns Maintenance Poor*, H.C., 175, p. 508 (1803-4), demi. fol. xiii.

54. S.R.O., Acc. 587/2/3a.

55. S.R.O., Acc. 587/1/1.

56. H. C. Malden, 'Answers to Visitation Articles of Dr. Willis 1724-5', *Surrey Arch. Coll.*, Vol. 39 (1931), p. 102.

57. S.R.O., Acc. 587/1/2.

58. Hants. R.O., B/2/A-1.

Chapter 5. A Period of Expansion

1. *Universal British Directory*, Vol. 2 (1791), p. 292.

2. Greater London Record Office (London), Bishop's transcripts, DW/T/9058-70.

3. Surrey Record Office (abbreviated hereafter to S.R.O.), Acc. 587/1/2.

4. Surrey Heath Borough Council, Windlesham overseers' accounts 1804-35.

5. S.R.O., Acc. 587/1/40-140, claims Nos. 111, 112.

6. Surrey Heath B.C., Windlesham poor rate books, 1800-36.

7. Windlesham parish church, Register of baptisms, 1813-39, of burials, 1813-38; G.L.R.O.(L), Bishop's transcripts DW/T/9071, 9072.

8. P.R.O., Prob. 11/1581, f. 303.

9. G.L.R.O.(L), Muniment books DW/OB, 1807/23.

10. D. L. Powell, *Surrey Parish Records Civil and Ecclesiastical* (1927), pp. 124-5.

11. *Paterson's Roads*, remodelled by E. Mogg (1826), p. 701.

12. S.R.O., Acc. 587/6.

13. J. Woodforde, *The Truth about Cottages* (1969), p. 121.

14. W. Howitt, *Rural Life of England*, 2nd edn. (1840), p. 404.

15. *Pigot's Directory of . . . Surrey . . .* (Sept. 1839).

16. M. Lightbody, *A History of Erl Wood*, 2nd edn. (priv. publ., Lilly Research Centre, Windlesham), p. 8.

17. E. W. Brayley, *Topographical History of Surrey* (1841-8), Vol. 1, pt. 2, p. 470.

18. *Report Charity Commissioners*, H.C. 433, p. 706 (1824), xiv.

19. *V.C.H., Surrey*, Vol. 2 (1905), p. 241.

20. Information kindly supplied by Records Officer, National Society.

21. *Abstract Returns Education*, H.C. 62, p. 956 (1835), xliii.

22. C. T. Cracklow, *Lithographic views of all Surrey Churches* (1823).

23. Brayley, *History of Surrey*, Vol. 1, pt. 2, p. 467.

24. Surrey Heath B.C., Windlesham highway surveyors' accounts, 1836.

25. F. B. P. Lory, *Reminiscences of Bagshot 1874-1949* (priv. print., n.d.), p. 2.

Chapter 6. Economic Factors

1. 52 Geo. III c. clxvi.

2. Surrey Record Office (abbreviated hereafter to S.R.O.), Acc. 587/1/40-140.

3. D. L. Powell, *Surrey Parish Records Civil and Ecclesiastical* (1927), pp. 124-5.

4. W. James and J. Malcolm, *General View of Agriculture of Surrey* (1794), p. 23.

5. Guildford Muniment Room, 97/8/7/3, 5.

6. W. Stevenson, *General View of Agriculture of Surrey* (1813), p. 459.

7. S.R.O., Acc. 587/1/6.

8. S.R.O., Acc. 587/1/1.

9. S.R.O., Acc. 587/1/7.

10. S.R.O., Acc. 924/5/2.

11. S.R.O., Acc. 587/1/11.

12. S.R.O., Acc. 587/1/40-140, claim No. 112.

13. *Rep. Charity Commissioners*, H.C. 433, p. 704 (1824), xiv.

14. *Rep. Royal Com. on Poor Law*, H.C. 44, App. A, p. 576a (1934), xxviii 1.

15. *Rep. Sel. Cttee. on Labouring Poor*, H.C. 402, p. iii (1843), vii.

16. J. Cree, *Notes on Windlesham Parish Church* (1927), p. 91.

17. S.R.O., Acc. 587/1/40-140, claim No. 82.

18. E. W. Brayley, *Topographical History of Surrey* (1841-8), Vol. 2, pt. 1, p. 27.

19. S.R.O., Acc. 587/1/192.

20. Brayley, *History of Surrey*, Vol. 1, pt. 2, p. 471.

21. *New Guide to Stage Coaches* (Lowndes or Critchett Woods, 1808, 1818. 1829).

22. *Pigot's London and Provincial Directory for 1826-7*.

23. *Pigot's London and Provincial Directory for 1832-3-4*.

24. E. Vale, *Mail Coach Men of the late 18th century* (1960), p. 230.

25. Brayley, *History of Surrey*, Vol. 1, pt. 2, p. 464.

26. E. W. Bovill, *English Country Life 1780-1830* (1962), p. 152.

27. *New Guide to Stage Coaches* (1798, 1828).

28. *New Guide to Stage Coaches* (Kelly, 1838).

29. S.R.O., Acc. 587/4.

30. Greater London Record Office (Middlesex), Tp.BED/4.

31. G.L.R.O.(M), Tp. BED/5.

32. 56 Geo. III c. xviii.

33. G.L.R.O.(M), Tp. BED/6.

34. G.L.R.O.(M), Tp. BED/7.

35. 3 and 4 Will. IV c. xxxviii; S.R.O., Q.S.6/8/147.

36. Robson's *Commercial Directory of the Seven Counties of . . . Surrey . . . for 1839* (re-issue of part vol. dated 1838).

37. Geo. C. B. Poulter, 'Bagshot's ancient taverns' (TS., Camberley Mus.).

38. J. Hillier, *Old Surrey Water Mills* (1951), pp. 152-3; K. G. Farries and M. T. Mason, *Windmills of Surrey* . . . (1966), p. 268.

39. Geo. C. B. Poulter, *The History of Camberley* (1969), p. 18.

40. *Rep. Sel. Cttee. on Poor Rate Returns*, H.C. 420, App. D 1, p. 11 (1824), vi.

41. *Abstract Returns Maintenance Poor 1813-15*, H.C. 82, p. 448 (1818), demi. fol. xix.

42. *Rep. Sel. Cttee. on Poor Rate Returns*, H.C. 748, p. 7 (1821), iv; H.C. 556, p. 172 (1822), v.

43. 59 Geo. III c.12.

44. Surrey Heath Borough Council, Windlesham weekly relief to poor 1827-35.

45. Surrey Heath B.C., Windlesham overseers' accounts 1804-35.

46. *Rep. Sel. Cttee. on Poor Rate Returns*, H.C. 334, p. 210 (1825), iv.

47. *Money expended relief of poor every place Eng. and Wales for 1825-9*, H.C. 83, p. 199 (1830-1), xi; *for 1830-4*, H.C. 444, p. 194 (1835), xlvii.

48. S.R.O., Acc. 734, vestry order book 1812-26, overseers' accounts 1834-47.

49. A. Wilson Fox, 'Agricultural wages in England and Wales during the last half century', *Essays in Agrarian History*, ed. by W. E. Minchinton (1968), Vol. 2, p. 128.

50. *Rep. Royal Com. on Poor Law*, H.C. 44, App. A, p. 545a (1834), xxviii, l.

51. G. H. Sumner, 'Life of Charles Richard Sumner', quoted in G. M. Hughes, *History of Windsor Forest* (1890), p. 337.

52. R. J. White, *Life in Regency England* (1963), pp. 1-4.

53. M. Quinlan, *Victorian Prelude* (1941).

54. W. Howitt, *Rural Life of England*, 2nd edn. (1840), pp. 526-9.

Chapter 7. A Temporary Depression

1. Quoted in S. E. Ayling, *The Georgian Century 1714-1837* (1966), p. 489.

2. R. A. Williams, *London and South Western Railway, Vol. 1. The Formative Years* (1968), pp. 11 *sqq*.

3. 10 and 11 Vic. c. lviii.

4. Surrey Record Office (abbreviated hereafter to S.R.O.), deposited plan No. 389.

5. 16 and 17 Vic. c. lxxxv.

6. W. T. Jackman, *Development of Transportation in Modern England*, 2nd edn. (1962), pp. 616 *sqq.*

7. *New Guide to Stage Coaches* (Critchett Woods, 1836, Kelly 1838).

8. *Robson's Commercial Directory of the Seven Counties of . . . Surrey . . . for 1839.*

9. Williams, *L.S.W.R., Vol. 1*, p. 34.

10. Stella Margetson, *Journey by Stages* (1967), p. 211.

11. *Pigot's Directory of . . . Surrey . . .* (Sept. 1839).

12. *Kelly's Directory of the Six Home Counties . . . Surrey* (1845); *Kelly's Directory of Surrey* (1855).

13. S.R.O., Q.S.6/3, accounts 1837–50.

14. Greater London Record Office (Middlesex), Tp. BED/7.

15. S.R.O., Acc. 1262, Windlesham vestry minutes 1840–56.

16. Records of Dean and Canons of Windsor, XVII.52.7.

17. G.L.R.O.(M), Acc. 809/Tp. BED/145, 146, 147, 148, 149.

18. G.L.R.O.(M), Acc. 809/Tp.BED/187, 266, 269.

19. E. W. Brayley, *Topographical History of Surrey* (1841–8), Vol. 1, pt. 2, p. 464.

20. J. Copeland, *Roads and their traffic 1750–1850* (1968), p. 191.

21. S.R.O., Sale notice with enclosure award.

22. Brayley, *History of Surrey* (1841–8), Vol. 1, pt. 2, p. 471.

23. Brayley (1841–8), Vol. 1, pt. 2, p. 465; Brayley, revised by E. Walford (1878–81), Vol. 1, p. 233.

24. Brayley (1841–8), Vol. 2, pt. 1, p. 27.

25. *Gardener's Chronicle*, 16 Nov. 1844.

26. *Gardener's Chronicle*, 27 May 1848.

27. *Gardener's Chronicle*, 15 Feb. 1845.

28. M. Hadfield, *History of British Gardening* (1969), pp. 329–30.

29. *Guide to great encampment at Chobham in 1853*, p. 22. Surrey Arch. Libr., bound with C. Macfarlane, *Camp of 1853* (1853).

30. Geo. C. B. Poulter, *The History of Camberley* (1969), p. 15.

31. O. Manning and W. Bray, *History and Antiquities of the County of Surrey*, Vol. 3 (1814), p. 81.

32. Poulter, *Camberley*, p. 18.

33. S.R.O., B.G. 1/11/5.

34. *Abstract Returns Maintenance Poor*, H.C. 175, p. 508 (1803–4) demi. fol. xiii.

35. S.R.O., B.G. 1/11/2.

36. S.R.O., Acc. 587/7.

37. M. Lightbody, *A History of Erl Wood*, 2nd edn. (priv. publ., Lilly Research Centre, Windlesham), pp. 15–16: quotes unpublished material.

Chapter 8. Renewed Growth

1. *Murray's Handbook for Travellers in Surrey*, 1st edn. (1865), p. 125; 5th edn. (1898), pp. 301, 304.

2. R. A. Williams, *London and South Western Railway, Vol. 2.Growth and consolidation* (1973), p. 68.

3. H. F. Howard, *An Account of finances of College of St. John . . . Cambridge 1511-1926* (1935), p. 234.

4. House of Lords Record Office, Sunningdale and Cambridge Town Railway, Schedule of replies with deposited plan, H.C., 1863; Minutes of Evidence, H.C., 1864, Vol. 62; H.C., 1865, vol. 59.

5. Surrey Record Office (abbreviated hereafter to S.R.O.), deposited plan No. 634.

6. 27 and 28 Vic. c. ccvii.

7. S.R.O., deposited plan No. 675.

8. 28 and 29 Vic. c. cxcvii.

9. *Surrey Advertiser*, 24 Feb., 8 Mar. 1866. (Surrey Arch. Soc. Libr.).

10. 36 and 37 Vic. c. lxxi.

11. S.R.O., Acc. 924/5/1, Report to shareholders 1872.

12. Williams, *L.S.W.R. Vol. 2*, pp. 72-73.

13. *Bradshaw's Monthly Railway Guide for August 1887* (David and Charles, 1968), p. 65.

14. Surrey IX.SE, X.NW, X.SW, XV.NE, XVI,NW, 1st edn. (1869-72); 2nd edn. (1897-8).

15. Geo. C. B. Poulter, 'Bagshot's ancient taverns' (TS., Camberley Mus.).

16. F. B. P. Lory, *Reminiscences of Bagshot 1874-1949* (priv. print., n.d.), p. 3.

17. E. W. Brayley, *Topographical History of Surrey*, revised by E. Walford (1878-81), Vol. 1, p. 236.

18. *Surrey Advertiser*, 1864-66 (Surrey Arch. Soc. Libr.).

19. W. Howitt, *Rural Life of England*, 2nd edn. (1840), p. 491.

20. *Surrey Advertiser*, 11 Mar. 1865.

21. *Surrey Advertiser*, 5 July 1884.

22. P.R.O., H.O. 129/38-3-3.

23. *Kelly's Directory of Surrey* (1895).

24. Brayley, *History of Surrey* (1841-8), Vol. 1, pt. 2, pp. 464-5.

25. *Return Nonconf. Churches*, H.C. 401, p. 87 (1882), 1.

26. Information kindly supplied by Supt. Minister, Camberley circuit.

27. S.R.O., Windlesham School Board minute books 1872-3.

28. P.R.O., Parish agricultural abstracts, M.A.F. 68/261, 432, 717, 1002, 1287, 1572, 1857.

29. H. Evershed, 'On the farming of Surrey', *Jnl. Royal Agric. Soc.*, Vol. 14 (1853), pp. 399-400.

30. S.R .O., Acc. 225.

31. *Surrey Advertiser*, 23 Dec., 11 Nov. 1865.

32. Howard, *Finances of College of St. John*, p. 229.

33. *Gardener's Chronicle*, 3 Jan. 1857.

34. S.R.O., Acc. 225, O.S. parish area book; O.S. map 25-inch. 1st edn. Surrey X, 6, 9, 10, 13, 14.

35. P.R.O., M.A.F. 68/432, 717, 1002, 1287, 1572.

36. Information kindly supplied by the late Mr. A. S. Fromow.

37. *Surrey Advertiser*, 9 Dec. 1893.

Chapter 9. The Beginnings of Public Services

1. P.R.O., B.T. 31/945/1247c.

2. Greater London Record Office (Middlesex), Acc. 809/Tp. BED/187, Minute Bk. 1850-78.

3. 3 and 4 Will. IV c. 90.

4. Surrey Record Office (abbreviated hereafter to S.R.O.), Acc. 1262, Windlesham vestry minutes 1857-78.

5. S.R.O., Acc. 1244, vestry minutes 1878-94.

6. S.R.O., Q.S.2/1/91.

7. G.L.R.O.(M), Acc. 809/Tp.BED/294, 310.

8. S.R.O., Acc. 1262, vestry minutes 1840-56.

9. Runnymede District Council, Chertsey Rural Sanitary Authority (abbreviated hereafter to R.S.A.) minutes 1872-7.

10. G. M. Hughes, *History of Windsor Forest* (1890), p. 14.

11. Runnymede D.C., R.S.A. minutes 1877-81.

12. Runnymede D.C., R.S.A. minutes 1881-5.

13. Runnymede D.C., R.S.A. minutes 1885-9.

14. S.R.O., Acc. 1262, R.S.A. minutes 1889-92.

15. *Surrey Advertiser*, 2 and 9 Aug. 1884.

16. *Surrey Advertiser*, 27 Sept. 1884.

17. S..R.O., Acc. 1262, R.S.A. minutes 1892-4.

18. Information kindly supplied by Records Officer, National Society.

19. S.R.O., Windlesham National school cttee. minutes 1864-72.

20. *Kelly's Directory of Surrey* (1855).

21. *Account of the Parish Charities* (priv. print. Windlesham Parish Council 1898), p. 18.

22. S.R.O., Bagshot St. Anne's school cttee. minutes 1870-2.

23. S.R.O., Windlesham School Board minutes 1872-3.

24. *Kelly's Directory of Surrey* (1895).

25. S.R.O., School Board minutes 1873-89.

26. S.R.O., School Board minutes 1900-3.

27. S.R.O., School Board minutes 1889-1900; *Aldershot News*, 30 Nov. 1901.

28. *Aldershot News*, 30 Nov., 7 Dec., 21 Dec. 1901.

Chapter 10. A Residential District

1. *Aldershot News*, 14 Nov. 1903; Surrey Record Office (abbreviated hereafter to S.R.O.), Acc. 1244, Windlesham Parish Council minutes, Nov. 1903, Windlesham Urban District Council (abbreviated hereafter to U.D.C.) minutes Dec. 1912, U.D.C. Sanitary cttee. minutes, Nov. 1918.

2. S.R.O., Acc. 1244, U.D.C. Sanitary Cttee. minutes, Dec. 1931.

3. 6 Edw. VII c. cxlvi.

4. Church Commissioners, file No. 21475, pt. 1.

5. Surrey sheets IX.SE, X.NW, X.SW, XV.NE, XVI.NW, 2nd edn. (1897-8), 3rd edn. (1920), revised edn. (1934).

6. *Kelly's Directory of Surrey* (1895, 1907, 1911, 1915, 1918, 1924, 1927, 1938).

7. Church Commissioners, file No. 21471, pt. 1.

8. Church Commissioners, file No. 80988.

9. Information kindly supplied by Supt., Camberley Methodist circuit.

10. S.R.O., Acc. 1244, Parish Council minutes 1898–1905.

11. S.R.O., Acc. 1244, Parish Council minutes 1905–9.

12. Surrey Arch. Soc. Libr., 140/3 (WIN).

13. S.R.O., Acc. 1244, U.D.C. Highways cttee. minutes 1912–18.

14. J. Aubrey, *Natural History and Antiquities of Surrey* (1718–19), Vol. 3, p. 212.

15. Church Commissioners, files Nos. 41470, pt. 5, 41905.

16. *Camberley News*, 17 May, 13 Sept. 1913.

17. S.R.O., Acc. 1262, U.D.C. Special Housing Cttee. minutes 1919–21.

18. *V.C.H., Surrey*, Vol. 3 (1911), p. 376.

19. S.R.O., Acc. 1244, Chertsey Rural District Council minutes 1903–6.

20. H. F. Howard, *An account of the finances of the College of St. John, Cambridge 1511-1926* (1935), pp. 234–5.

21. *Kelly's Directory* (1927).

22. *Bradshaw's Monthly Railway Guide for April 1910* (David and Charles, 1968), p. 148.

23. *Bradshaw's Guide for July 1938* (David and Charles, 1969), p. 191.

24. S.R.O., Acc. 1244, Parish Council minutes 1898–1905; *Aldershot News*, 14 Nov. 1903.

25. Church Commissioners, file No. 81619.

26. *Woking News and Mail*, 29 Jan. 1904, 21 July, and 3 Nov. 1905, 25 May 1906 (editorial), 31 Aug. 1906.

27. *Woking News and Mail*, 23 and 30 Mar., 4 and 25 May 1906.

28. S.R.O., Acc. 1262, U.D.C. Surveyor's report book 1909–22.

29. S.R.O., Acc. 1244, U.D.C. Highways cttee. minutes 1924–33.

30. *Aldershot News*, 26 Sept. 1903.

31. Information kindly supplied by Mr. G. H. Pinckney.

32. Information kindly supplied by the late Mr. A. S. Fromow.

33. S.R.O., Acc. 1244, U.D.C. minutes 1920–1.

34. *Camberley News*, 13 Nov. 1931.

35. S.R.O., Acc. 1244, U.D.C. minutes 1928–32.

36. *Camberley News*, 1925–31.

37. *Kelly's Directory* (1907).

38. J. Creé, *Notes on Windlesham parish church* (1927), p. 106.

Chapter 11. Local Government 1895–1918

1. Surrey Record Office (abbreviated hereafter to S.R.O.), Acc. 1244, Windlesham vestry and Parish Council minutes 1878–98.

2. S.R.O., Acc. 1244, Parish Council minutes 1898–1905.

3. S.R.O., Acc. 1244, Parish Council minutes 1905–9.

4. *Aldershot News*, 26 Sept. 1903.

5. *Aldershot News*, 12 Mar. 1904.

6. S.R.O., Acc. 1244, Chertsey Rural District Council minutes 1906–8.

7. S.R.O., Acc. 1244, Windlesham Urban District Council (abbreviated hereafter to U.D.C.) minutes 1909-11.

8. S.R.O., Acc. 1244, U.D.C. minutes 1911-13.

9. 40 and 41 Vic. c. clxii.

10. S.R.O., Acc. 1244, Chertsey R.D.C. minutes 1899-1903.

11. S.R.O., Acc. 1244, Chertsey R.D.C. minutes 1903-6.

12. 8 Edw. VII c. xciv.

13. S.R.O., Acc. 1244, U.D.C. minutes 1913-16.

14. S.R.O., Acc. 1244, Chertsey R.D.C. minutes 1895-9.

15. S.R.O., Acc. 1262, U.D.C. Surveyor's report book 1909-22.

16. S.R.O., Acc. 1244, U.D.C. Sanitary cttee. minutes 1912-16.

17. S.R.O., Acc. 1244, U.D.C. minutes 1916-18.

18. 45 and 46 Vic. c. cli.

19. *Camberley News*, 16 Jan. 1931.

20. S.R.O., Acc. 1244, U.D.C. Highways cttee. minutes 1912-18.

Chapter 12. Local Government 1919-1933

1. *Camberley News*, 13 Apr. 1928.

2. *Camberley News*, 18 Mar., 8 Apr. 1927.

3. *Camberley News*, 29 Mar. 1929, 11 Apr. 1930.

4. Surrey Record Office (abbreviated hereafter to S.R.O.), Acc. 1244, Windlesham Urban District Council (abbreviated hereafter to U.D.C.) minutes 1918-20.

5. S.R.O., Acc. 1244, U.D.C. minutes 1923-4.

6. S.R.O., Acc. 1244, U.D.C. minutes 1924-8.

7. S.R.O., Acc. 1244, U.D.C. minutes 1928-32.

8. S.R.O., Acc. 1244, U.D.C. minutes Feb. 1933.

9. S.R.O., Acc. 1244, U.D.C. minutes 1921-3.

10. S.R.O., Acc. 1244, U.D.C. minutes 1920-1.

11. S.R.O., Acc. 1262, U.D.C. Surveyor's report book 1909-22.

12. S.R.O., Acc. 1244, U.D.C. Sanitary cttee. minutes 1916-21.

13. S.R.O., Acc. 1244, U.D.C. Sanitary cttee. minutes 1924-30.

14. S.R.O., Acc. 1233/3, return to Surrey County Council questionnaire, 2 May 1931.

15. S.R.O., Acc. 1244, U.D.C. Sanitary cttee. minutes 1921-4.

16. *Camberley News*, 20 Mar. 1925.

17. *Camberley News*, 10 Apr. 1925.

18. S.R.O., Acc. 1244, U.D.C. Sanitary cttee. minutes 1930-3.

19. *Camberley News*, 15 Feb. 1913.

20. S.R.O., Acc. 1244, U.D.C. Sanitary cttee. minutes 1912-16.

21. See Marian Bowley, *Housing and the State 1919-44* (1945), pp. 17-22.

22. P.R.O., H.L.G. 48/280/file No. 701/1.

23. S.R.O., Acc. 1262, U.D.C. Housing cttee. minutes 1919-21.

24. See Bowley, *Housing and the State*, pp. 36-45.

25. S.R.O., Acc. 1244, Windlesham Parish Council minutes 1905-9.

26. S.R.O., *Surrey County Council Yellow Book* (reports of cttees.) for 1909, p. 571.

27. S.R.O., Acc. 1244, U.D.C. Highways cttee. minutes 1912–18.

28. S.R.O., Acc. 1244, U.D.C. Highways cttee. minutes 1918–24.

29. S.R.O., Acc. 1244, U.D.C. minutes 1913–16.

30. S.R.O., *Surrey C.C. Yellow Book* for 1922, p. 245.

31. *Surrey Advertiser*, 6 Jan. 1923; *Surrey C.C. Yellow Book* for 1923, p. 235.

32. S.R.O., *Surrey C.C. Yellow Book* for 1925, pp. 9, 1211.

33. S.R.O., Acc. 1244, U.D.C. Highways cttee. minutes 1924–33.

34. *Camberley News*, 27 Mar. 1925.

35. S.R.O., Acc. 1262, U.D.C. Fire Brigade cttee. minutes 1929.

36. *Camberley News*, 15 Apr. 1932.

37. *Camberley News*, 16 Jan. 1931.

38. S.R.O., Acc. 1233/1, *Report of special Surrey C.C. cttee. to review districts*, 26 May 1931, p. 12.

39. *Camberley News*, 21 Mar. 1930.

40. S.R.O., Acc. 1233/2, notes of meetings of special cttee., Sept. and Nov. 1930.

Bibliography (Principal Sources)

PRIMARY MANUSCRIPT SOURCES

Surrey Record Office

Surrey Quarter Sessions records 1669-72 (MS. Cal.), 1673-91 (TS. Cal.).

Land Tax returns 1780-1831.

Papers of Clerk to Enclosure Commissioners 1801-57.

Enclosure Award (and map) 1814.

Tithe Award (and map) 1843.

Egham and Bagshot/Bedfont and Bagshot Turnpike Trust accounts 1822-77.

National school, Windlesham, managers' minutes 1864-72.

National school, Bagshot, managers' minutes 1870-72.

Windlesham School Board minutes 1872-1903 (4 vols.).

Windlesham vestry minutes 1840-94 (3 vols.).

Chertsey Rural Sanitary Authority minutes 1889-94 (2 vols.).

Windlesham Parish Council minutes 1894-1909 (3 vols.).

Chertsey Rural District Council minutes 1895-1908 (4 vols.).

Windlesham Urban District Council minutes 1909-33 (11 vols.).

    Sanitary and Highways cttees. minutes 1909-12.

    Sanitary cttee. minutes 1912-33 (5 vols.).

    Highways cttee. minutes 1912-33 (3 vols.).

    Surveyor's report book 1909-22.

    Housing cttee. minutes 1919-21.

    Fire brigade cttee. minutes 1929.

Guildford Muniment Room

Manor of Fosters:

    Court book 1683-1871.

    Separate rent rolls and misc. papers 18th and 19th cent.

Hampshire Record Office

Diocese of Winchester:

    Bishop's registers.

    Visitation returns 18th cent.

Greater London Record Office (London)
Commissary Court of Bishop of Winchester and Court of Archdeacon of Surrey:
> Registered wills, original wills, probate act books, etc. 16th–19th cent.

Bishop's transcripts of parish registers 1800–13.
Greater London Record Office (Middlesex)
Bedfont and Bagshot Turnpike Trust:
> Minute books 1728–56, 1850–77.
> Minute books western district 1763–1850.
> Misc. papers 19th cent.

Dean and Canons of Windsor
> **The Aerary, St. George's Chapel, Windsor**

Manor of Windlesham:
> Deeds, court rolls, leases, terriers 15th–18th cent.
> Parliamentary survey 1649.
> Misc. papers 19th cent.

St. John's College, Cambridge:
Manors of Windlesham and Broomhall:
> Court rolls 1328–30, 1512–47, 1666–1749.
> Court books 1666–1937 (5 vols.).
> Rent rolls 1588, 1606.
> Deeds, etc., 13th–15th cent. (TS. Cal.).
> Maps and misc. papers 19th cent.

Parish church, Windlesham
Registers:
> Burials 1783–1838 (2 vols.).
> Baptisms 1783–1839 (2 vols.).

Surrey Heath Borough Council Offices
> **Bagshot Manor, Guildford Road, Bagshot**

Parish of Windlesham:
> Churchwardens' rates and accounts 1765–81.
> Poor rate books 1800–36 (4 vols.).
> Overseers' accounts 1804–35.
> Weekly relief to poor 1827–35 (3 vols.).
> Highway surveyors' accounts 1828–40.

Runnymede District Council Offices
> **Station Road, Addlestone**

Chertsey Rural Sanitary Authority minutes 1872–89 (4 vols.).

PRIMARY PRINTED SOURCES

Texts and Calendars:

Registrum Johannis de Pontissara, Surrey Rec. Soc., Vols. 1 and 6 (1913-16).

Registra Stephani Gardiner et Johannis Poynet, Cant. and York Soc., Vol. 37 (1930).

Registrum Henrici Woodlock, Cant. and York Soc., Vol. 44 (1934-40).

Surrey Musters, Surrey Rec. Soc., Vol. 3 (1914-19).

Surrey Wills, 1595-1608, Surrey Rec. Soc., Vol. 4 (1915-20).

Surrey Wills, 1484-9, Surrey Rec. Soc., Vol. 5 (1922).

Surrey Taxation Returns, Surrey Rec. Soc., Vol. 11 (1922, 1932).

Surrey Quarter Sessions Records, 1659-66, Surrey Rec. Soc., Vols. 13, 14, 16 (1934, 1935, 1938).

Surrey Quarter Sessions Records, 1666-8, Surrey County Council (1951).

Surrey Hearth Tax 1664, Surrey Rec. Soc., Vol. 17 (1940).

Surrey Fines 1509-58, Surrey Rec. Soc., Vol. 19 (1946).

Windlesham Parish Registers, 1677-1783, priv. print. (1881).

The MSS. of St. George's Chapel, Windsor Castle (1957).

Contemporary publications:

J. Aubrey, *Natural History and Antiquities of the County of Surrey,* Vol. 3 (1718-19).

W. Cobbett, *Rural Rides* (1830).

A. D. Hall and E. J. Russell, *Agriculture and Soils of Kent, Surrey and Sussex,* (Bd. of Agric. 1911).

W. Howitt, *Rural Life of England,* 2nd edn. (1840).

W. James and J. Malcolm, *General View of the Agriculture of the County of Surrey* (1794).

W. Stevenson, *General View of the Agriculture of the County of Surrey* (1813).

New Guide to Stage Coaches (Lowndes, Crichett Woods or Kelly, 1782-1838).

Universal British Directory of Trade and Commerce, Vol. 2 (Wilkes, 1791).

Pigot & Co.'s Directories of Surrey (1826-39).

Kelly's Post Office Directories (1845-1938).

Census reports (H.M.S.O., 1801-1931).

MAPS

J. Senex, Surrey, one inch to one mile 1729.

J. Rocque, Surrey two inches to one mile 1768–70.

A. Bryant, Surrey, one and a half inches to one mile 1823.

O.S. six inches to one mile 1869–72, 1897–8, 1920, 1934.

Geological survey of Surrey 1910–11 (Libr. Inst. Geological Sciences).

BOOKS (Secondary Sources)

Local:

E. W. Brayley and others, *A Topographical History of Surrey* (R. B. Ede, Dorking, 1841–8; G. Lewis, London, 1850; revised by E. Walford, Virtue, London, 1878–81).

R. H. Clark, *A Southern Region Chronology and Record 1803–1965* (Oakwood Press, 1964).

C. Cochrane, *The Lost Roads of Wessex* (Pan, 1972).

J. Cree, *Notes on Windlesham Parish Church* (Hickmott & Co., Camberley, 1927).

Lt.-Col. G. C. E. Crew, *Short guide to Bagshot Park* (priv. print., Royal Army Chaplains' Dept., 1969).

G. M. Hughes, *History of Windsor Forest* (Ballantyne & Co., 1890).

M. Lightbody, *A History of Erl Wood,* 2nd edn. (priv. publ., Lilly Research Centre, Windlesham).

F. B. P. Lory, *Reminiscences of Bagshot 1874–1949* (priv. print., n.d.).

O. Manning and W. Bray, *History and Antiquities of the County of Surrey,* Vol. 3 (White Cochrane, 1814).

Geo. C. B. Poulter, *The History of Camberley* (Frimley and Camberley Urban District Council, 1969).

D. L. Powell, *Surrey Parish Records Civil and Ecclesiastical* (Surrey County Council, 1927).

Victoria County History of Berkshire, Vol. 2 (1907).

Victoria County History of Surrey, Vol. 3 (1911).

P.A.L. Vine, *London's Lost Route to Basingstoke* (David & Charles, 1968).

R. A. Williams, *London & South Western Railway, Vol. 1, The Formative Years; Vol. 2, Growth and Consolidation* (David & Charles, 1968, 1973).

General:

W. Albert, *The Turnpike Road System in England 1663–1840* (C.U.P., 1972).

G. Best, *Mid-Victorian Britain 1851-75* (Weidenfeld & Nicolson, 1971).

E. H. Bovill, *English Country Life 1780-1830* (O.U.P., 1962).

M. Bowley, *Housing and the State 1919-44* (Allen & Unwin, 1945).

M. Campbell, *The English Yeoman under Elizabeth and the Early Stuarts* (Yale U.P., 1942).

J. D. Chambers and G. E. Mingay, *The Agricultural Revolution 1750-1880* (Batsford, 1966).

A Clifton-Taylor, *The Pattern of English Building* (Batsford, 1962).

J. Copeland, *Roads and their traffic 1750-1850* (David & Charles, 1968).

Lord Ernle, *English Farming Past and Present,* 6th edn. revised (Heineman, 1961).

G. E. Fussell, *The English Rural Labourer* (Batchworth Press, 1949).

G. E. and K. R. Fussell, *The English Countryman 1500-1900* (Andrew Melrose, 1955).

W. T. Jackman, *The Development of Transportation in Modern England,* 2nd edn. revised (Frank Cass, 1962).

J. F. C. Harrison, *The Early Victorians 1832-51* (Panther, 1973).

R. T. Mason, *Framed Buildings of England* (Coach Publishing House, Horsham, 1973).

H. Perkin, *The Age of the Railway* (Panther, 1970).

W. Plowden, *The Motor Car and Politics 1896-1970* (Bodley Head, 1971).

K. Smellie, *A History of Local Government,* 4th edn. (Allen & Unwin, 1968).

B. and S. Webb, *The Story of the King's Highway* (Frank Cass, 1963).

B. and S. Webb, *English Local Govt.: Statutory Authorities for Special Purposes* (Longmans Green, 1922).

J. Woodforde, *The Truth about Cottages* (Routledge & Kegan Paul, 1969).

Periodicals and Newspapers: *Surrey Archaeological Collections,* Vols. 1-68 (1857-1971); *Surrey Advertiser* (1864-93); *Aldershot News* (1894-1904); *Camberley News* (1905-32); *Woking News and Mail* (1904-7).

Index

Abel, Mr.: 172

Acts, Local: *see* Ascot Gas and Electricity Co.; Bedfont and Bagshot Turnpike Trust; London and South Western Railway; South West Suburban Water Co.; Staines, Wokingham and Woking Junction Railway; Sunningdale and Cambridge Town Railway; Windlesham Enclosure; Windsor, Staines and South Western Railway

Acts, Public: Education (1870), 157; Education (1876 and 1880), 161; General Turnpike (1766), 59; Highways (1835), 146; Highways (1862), 147; Highways and Locomotive (1878), 147; Housing of the Working Classes (1890), 214; Housing and Town Planning (1909), 214; Housing and Town Planning (1919), 214; Housing, etc. (1923), 216; Housing (Financial Provisions) (1924), 216; Lighting and Watching (1833), 146; Local Government (1894), 5, 192; Local Government (1929), 226; Local Government (1972), 5; Motor Car (1903), 169; Nuisance Removal (1846), 149; Public Health (1848), 148; Public Health (1872 and 1875), 149; Rating and Valuation (1925), 207; Road Traffic (1930), 169, 182; Select Vestry (1819), 113

agriculture: medieval, 39-43; 16th-18th cent., 44-7; 19th cent., 110, 124, 139-141; 20th cent., 184; See also Windlesham Enclosure Act

Albert, Prince: 38, 141

Aldershot: Camp, 125; Traction Company, 181-2; urban district, 212

Aldershot News: 163, 168, 180, 187-8, 204

Aldridge, A.: 207

allotments (spade): 101

All Saints, Lightwater: 173, 179

almshouses (poor house): 82, 197

Alsford, W. J.: 173

Ambleside Road (Ambleside Hill): 172, 212

Anabaptists: 85

Anne, Queen: 37

arable land: 41-2, 44-6, 139-140

Arrow, Richard and Sons: 138

Ascot: 132, 181, 210; Gas (Gas and Electricity) Co., 165, 203, 223; races, 123, 136, 168, 176

Ash: 115

ashpits: 150, 155

Ashton, William: 158

Astagehill Farm: 18, 49, 51, 172, 185; house, 70, 72

Attfield: family, 76-8; James, 22, 52, 71, 77-8; John (1561), 21; John (1588), 21; John (1592), 78; John (1593), 77; John (1596), 77; John (1628), 30, 77, 80; John of Broadways (1637, 1655), 77; John, churchwarden (1665), 14; John, churchwarden (1680), 27, 78; John (1683), 22; John (1838), 112; Mrs., 115; Nicholas, 76-7, 80

Attride, Thomas: 122, 145

Aubrey, John: 25-8, 34, 47, 63, 77, 170

Avenue, The: 173-4, 218-9

Bacon, William: 193